KNOWLEDGE AND CURRICULUM PLANNING

A.V. Kelly is Dean of the School of Education, Goldsmiths' College. He has written and edited numerous books on education and the curriculum, including *The Curriculum, theory and practice*, *The Primary Curriculum* and *The Primary Curriculum in Action* (both with Geva Blenkin), *Micro-computers in the Curriculum*, and *Theory and Practice of Education*, with Meriel Downey

KNOWLEDGE AND CURRICULUM PLANNING

A.V. KELLY

Harper & Row, Publishers
London

Cambridge Mexico City
New York Philadelphia
San Francisco São Paulo
Singapore Sydney

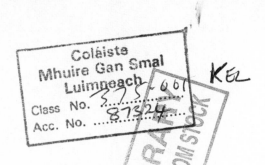

First published 1986

Harper & Row Ltd
28 Tavistock Street
London WC2E 7PN

British Library Cataloguing in Publication Data

Kelly, A.V.
  Knowledge and curriculum planning
  1.Curriculum planning
  I.Title
  375′.001   LB1570
  ISBN 0-06-318348-X

Typeset by Gedset Ltd, Cheltenham
Printed and bound by Butler & Tanner Ltd, Frome and London

CONTENTS

vii

It is hard to criticise the theories of one's friends but truth is more important than friendship (Aristotle)

FOREWORD

This book is the product of almost two decades of growing dissatisfaction over the main thrust of 'philosophy of education' towards a content-based view of the curriculum, and the encouragement it has consequently offered to behaviourist psychology and positivist forms of sociology. That concern has during the last decade been aggravated by the adoption of similar assumptions and attitudes in both the pronouncements and the practices of recent and current political interventionism in the curriculum. The book's concern is to identify the serious weaknesses of these approaches to educational planning, especially their conflict with certain major educational ideals, and to reassert the viability of other more attractive alternatives. If it does no more than encourage a raising of the tone and level of the curriculum debate to include consideration of the underlying principles of curriculum planning, it will have achieved most of what it sets out to do.

My thanks are due to Ivor Goodson, Keith Kimberley and Keith Thompson for their detailed and constructive criticisms of the first draft. They must take a great deal of the credit for any improvement in the quality of this final draft although not, of course, responsibility for the sentiments expressed. I must also thank Jill Thorn who again has helped me enormously with many aspects of the logistics of producing the final text.

INTRODUCTION

Knowledge is conceptually integral to education, since whatever else is involved in the process of education there must be some form of engagement with knowledge. Values too are central in the same way since, on most definitions, education must involve the exposure of pupils to what is believed to be worthwhile, or what someone decides, for whatever reasons, they ought to be exposed to. Thus, while there are many facets to discussions of education and of curriculum, those which centre on the nature of knowledge and the problem of values must be central.

It is, therefore, surprising to note how inadequate the educational debate has been in this area. Quite often this kind of issue is completely ignored. All those attempts at the 'scientific' study of education, for example, conducted mainly by psychologists, have been fundamentally and methodologically quite incapable of encompassing issues of this kind and thus have ignored them either implicitly or explicitly. They have made assumptions, tacit or open, concerning knowledge and values — what kinds of knowledge are valuable, for example, and thus ought to be included in any curricular provision — and concerning the relation of knowledge to education — that education is no more than the transmission of knowledge — assumptions which themselves should be part of the debate and which cannot and certainly should not be made so casually nor so readily in an area which is so highly problematic. Throughout the period when psychology dominated the scene in educational theory this was the picture. The concentration inevitably was on *means:* the ends were not debated, not only because they are beyond the scope of the discipline, but also because they were not seen as problematic. Sometimes they were discussed as 'principles', but in a manner usually lacking the kind of rigour, and even the kind of understanding, such discussion requires.

It was the inadequacy of this kind of approach to the study of education which prompted the emphasis on 'philosophy of education' which was a feature of the 1960s both in the UK and the USA. For it was felt, quite rightly, that a philosophical perspective was needed if issues of this kind were to be properly faced and tackled, and that the kind of rigour which was required could only come from the discipline of the philosopher.

In the event, however, this development has proved equally unsatisfactory. Indeed, it may be true to say that it has led to the emergence of a more unsatisfactory situation, since it is probably better not to have a job done at all than to have it done badly. And badly this job has been done for several reasons. The most important of these is that what should have been a detached objective analysis of the fundamental epistemological questions raised by education quickly became in most cases (although not, one must stress, in all) a form of prescriptivism — probably out of a laudable desire to contribute something positive to the debate. Thus, instead of drawing attention to the problematic nature of this area, to the many questions which we need to ask and to continue to ask, this movement devoted itself to the production of answers, particularly those which would offer justification of the *status quo*. Its style was Platonic rather than Socratic; and it was thus totally out of phase with developments in philosophy generally — certainly British philosophy — during the present century.

Yet its claim was that it was applying the techniques of these developments to the issues of education. 'Conceptual analysis' was the watchword. However, probably because most of its exponents were educationists dabbling in philosophy rather than philosophers applying their skills to education, there was not that breadth of philosophical understanding there to recognize that conceptual analysis can only lead to prescriptions when it has gone wrong, or when one has gone beyond what it permits, and that the fundamental role of philosophy in education theory is to apply its skills, its techniques, its understandings to questions of the status of knowledge, the meaning of truth and the justification of values, not to find answers to such questions but to reveal the many dimensions of their complex nature.

Thus the effect of 'philosophy of education' was to compound the assumptions about knowledge and values which had impaired the educational debates and much of the research of the past and to promote similar muddle in the debates and research which were to come.

For these debates and a good deal of the research have continued to take place within a context of assumptions about knowledge, truth and values which should themselves be part of the debate or subject to educational research, so that 'philosophy of education' has become, as Herbert Feigl once said of philosophy itself, 'the disease of which it should have been the cure'. Worse, it has not only failed to focus on issues it should have been attempting to clarify for us, it has confused matters by concealing those issues from us. For by suggesting that knowledge and values are non-problematic it has discouraged us from questioning the assumptions made about them, or by claiming that they are susceptible to objective verification, it has encouraged us to ask the wrong kinds of question.

Furthermore, where views of education have derived from different epistemological traditions and thus have been built on different epistemological assumptions, the existence of these different traditions and assumptions has not been recognized, so that the debate has been conducted in a false context. Thus, for example, many of the critics of 'progressive' theories of education, and some who have professed to be researchers in this field, have failed to recognize the distinctive and particular form of epistemology upon which such theories are based, or even that there is a different epistemology, and have attacked or attempted to research them from their own, quite different, perspective — a procedure analogous to criticizing poetry by the rules of prose.

Traditionally the exploration of educational 'principles' had been undertaken through an examination of the work of the 'Great Educators' and this kind of approach is characterized in most works of this nature by a superficial consideration of their views on education with little or no concern to analyse the epistemological base upon which these views had been built. The new wave of 'philosophy of education', although claiming to replace this approach with something far more rigorous, merely offered what was substantially the same at a higher level of sophistication and thus in an ostensibly more compelling form.

Instead of recognizing that the techniques of conceptual analysis represent a revolution in philosophy and thus an attempt by mainstream philosophers to replace traditional essentialist and metaphysical approaches with something far more tentative, they have too often seen them, and attempted to use them, merely as a new device for obtaining the same kinds of eternal truth. In short, the attempt to be prescriptive has led most 'philosophers of education' to accept — often uncritically and always too readily — a *rationalist* epistemology and to offer this to the rest of the world as largely non-problematic. This has not only confused the educational debate; it has also seriously and severely limited it. It must be to the lasting disgrace of this movement that it was left to the sociologists to do this job, to highlight the problems of many of its assumptions about knowledge and about values, and, worse, that its own reaction to this development within sociology, to these 'new directions', was to close ranks and attempt to fight it off.

This same failure to recognize or acknowledge the problematic nature of both knowledge and values can also be seen to permeate the thinking of politicians and educational administrators. In most official pronouncements on educational policy and curricular provision, and, indeed, in most of the many prescriptions with which teachers are currently being bombarded in these areas, the same assumptions about knowledge and values are to be seen. There is no suggestion that these assumptions represent one particular view or ideology, nor that other views of and approaches to education are not only possible but also equally legitimate. One particular ideology is being pressed upon us and that is the ideology of rationalism. Thus, leaving aside the economically utilitarian dimensions of the current curriculum debate as it is conducted at the political level (since this dimension is outside the scope of any discussion of the nature of knowledge, being concerned not with that nature as such but with its consequences, the economic usefulness rather than the intellectual or educational value of certain kinds of knowledge), the emphasis is again on traditional subjects, on academic standards and values, and the basic assumption is that there can be no other legitimate definition of knowledge, of education or of curriculum. Again, therefore, the major weakness of this approach, and its major source of intellectual danger, is its failure to recognize its own ideology, the existence and legitimacy of competing ideologies and the deeper level at which the educational debate must be conducted if it is to evince any real intellectual honesty.

If I had to state the aim and purpose of this book in a sentence, then, I would say that it has been written to discourage such educational dogmatism. Its concern is to suggest that education theory, and especially that branch of it calling itself 'philosophy of education', has been badly misdirected, and has gone seriously wrong by seeking educational prescriptions, by treating and thus encouraging others to treat the study of education as if it were some kind of science, a search after knowledge, and by failing to recognize that all prescriptions represent ideological positions and that all claims to scientific exactitude in this sphere are spurious. A further concern is to demonstrate that these same mistakes are now being repeated and the same kinds of dogmatism reasserted at the level of practical prescription by current attempts at direct political intervention in the work of our schools.

Briefly, the case it sets out to parade is that, contrary to what appears to be the current popular belief, there is more than one theory of knowledge which can, with equal justification, be adopted, that this suggests that questions about the status of knowledge remain problematic, and that that in turn also implies that all educational prescriptions are ideological. It will further be argued that this is a lesson still to be learnt by many people, both within the education profession and outside it, so that much of the current debate about educational issues is bedevilled by assumptions which, although unwarranted, are too often allowed to go unquestioned. Pre-eminent among these assumptions is the assumption that there are educational truths to be found or, worse, that they already have been found and are in the proud possession of those currently conferring upon us the benefit of their knowledge and wisdom. One purpose of this book, then, is to argue that all such pronouncements reflect the values and ideologies of their authors, whether they be educational theorists or politicians, so that any claims to greater assurance or more widespread acceptance than that permits must be taken with a very large pinch of salt.

A second intention is to argue not only that the rationalist perspective on knowledge and on education must be seen for what it is, as only one kind of perspective which can be adopted, but, further, that it is a perspective which evinces several major weaknesses. The first of these is undoubtedly its own unwillingness, and, indeed, inability, to see itself as one of several ideologies. For its fundamental tenet is that its own prescriptions can be shown to be indisputable, that its own value positions can be demonstrated to represent eternal truths and thus that the theory of education which it has generated is not *a* theory but *the* theory, so that all other views are not merely different but positively mistaken. This is the source of that educational dogmatism which this book aims to discourage.

It is necessary to go further than this, however. For such dogmatism would seem to be directly opposed to any notion of education as concerned with the development of autonomy, of understanding, of critical awareness in the educand. There would seem to be a fundamental conceptual contradiction between a concern to develop such capacities and any form of dogmatism. If this is so, not only are there serious inconsistencies in those theories which attempt to argue for education as a process by which such qualities and capacities are developed and, at the same time, for a curriculum consisting of certain fixed, 'intrinsically worthwhile' bodies of knowledge, but also any theory of education which is built upon an epistemology which claims this kind of status for certain bodies of knowledge must itself fall short of providing an adequate account of education as a process of development towards autonomous thinking, valuing and behaving.

Thus, a further contention of this book is that a theory of education based on this kind of rationalist epistemology is inadequate as a theory of education in the full sense. While recognizing, therefore, that such a theory is only one of several theories we might adopt, we must also acknowledge that it is not by any means the most attractive on offer, not only because of its own many flaws but also because of its inability to provide us with an adequate theoretical base for the development of a view of education as a series of processes towards the achievement of intellectual, and, indeed, human, autonomy. If this is the view we take of education (and there is no attempt to deny that this in itself might be seen as a particular ideology — although its major principles are the acceptance of uncertainty, the avoidance of dogmatism and a concern to assist individuals to reach their own conclusions), then we will find that that rationalist epistemology advocated by most 'philosophers of education', and adopted uncritically by most of those wielding political power and influence in the current scene in the United Kingdom, is woefully inadequate as a base for the development of such a form of education and, indeed, that it is grossly inhibiting of such a development.

If we are influenced at all, then, by the claims of the 'new directions' in the sociology of education that to press such views upon schools, teachers and especially pupils is to use the distribution of knowledge as a form of social control rather than to use the education system as a device for intellectual liberation, and, if we are also impressed in any way by the work of those developmental psychologists who have attempted to steer us away from an obsession with the content of pupils' education towards a concern for the quality of the learning processes they experience, then we must look elsewhere for a theory of knowledge and of education which will support our view of the curriculum and provide us with an adequate base for our curriculum planning.

Thus the theme of this book is twofold. First, it is concerned to show there is more than one legitimate theory of knowledge and thus more than one acceptable and respectable theory of education. And, second, it argues that that rationalist theory which has dominated educational theory and practice for so long is by no means the most adequate theory of knowledge or of education, and that it does not fit easily, or even at all, with the views of education which are emerging from the different perspectives of the sociology of education and developmental psychology.

It is the intention to set out this case in two parts. First, an attempt will be made to summarize the epistemological debate in order to reveal the quite different elements within it and the fundamentally different stances which can, quite legitimately, be taken. Secondly, this analysis will be applied to a number of issues within the current educational debate in order to show not only that this kind of discussion must be a crucial part of those issues, but also that it is unreasonable and unhelpful to approach those issues as though the epistemological questions do not matter or are non-problematic. The intention will be to show, for example, that the 'progressive' or 'process' view of educational planning does derive from a different epistemological tradition and can only be properly debated in that context; that notions such as those of a common core curriculum and of 'curriculum balance' are far more problematic than their current usage suggests and that again what is crucial to any attempt to define such notions is that one must begin from the epistemological questions they raise; that one of the things which has held back the achievement of anything like equality of educational opportunity has been the assumptions which have been made about the knowledge-content of the curriculum, so that this debate too must start from a questioning of those assumptions; and that current attempts to establish more direct external control over the curriculum in the UK reflect a failure or an unwillingness to open up such debate.

In general, the intention is to argue that questions of knowledge are fundamental to questions of education, that, because the status of knowledge, the meaning of truth and the justification of values are highly problematic matters, the search for answers, for certainty in education is misdirected, and that consequently we must be far more tentative and less dogmatic in our assertions about education than most people — both inside and outside the profession — have usually been inclined to be. In short, the intention is to do the only job philosophy can honestly turn its hand to, to identify and delineate the questions, to show the inadequacies and difficulties of all the attempted and suggested answers, and to encourage a continuous questioning and exploration.

To these ends, Part One of the book will address itself to theories of knowledge. It will look first at early versions of both rationalist and empiricist theories in order to reveal the focus of the debate. It will then look at more developed forms of both views, and in particular at the difficulties of the rationalist's 'transcendental argument' which has been at the root of that acceptance of rationalism which in my view has bedevilled education theory for more than two decades. It will then explore pragmatism as a particular form of empiricism, in part to draw attention to its merits and attractions, but also, and mainly, to suggest that its fundamental difference be recognized and that it should no longer be evaluated within a rationalist perspective which is quite alien to it and thus completely inappropriate. Part One will also look at the recent development of a sociology of knowledge and will in particular attempt to explore those political implications which emerge very clearly from this perspective and which, it will be argued, are fundamental to the whole current curriculum debate. It will also draw attention to some of the claims made by the developmental psychologists, especially those emanating from recent work in that field, in order to reveal the support which is emerging there for a view of education which is fundamentally different from the subject-based view to which a rationalist epistemology leads.

Against that backcloth, Part Two will then focus on some educational issues, such as those mentioned above, to which this debate about knowledge is particularly relevant. Each will be discussed in full and in its own right, but the prime intention will be to demonstrate that each represents a manifestation of the same fundamental epistemological problem and its associated political attitudes and that discussions of them will continue to be inadequate until that is recognized, until those discussions go beyond, and are permitted to go beyond, that superficial level at which they are so often now conducted and dig into the questions raised by their underlying assumptions. It will also emerge that this kind of exploration will lead to a recognition not only of the existence of an alternative view of knowledge but also of the superior attractions of the equally distinctive view of education this encourages us to take.

Thus Chapter 5 sets out to argue for an approach to curriculum planning based on the idea of education as a process of development, to show, further, that such a view is implicit not only in the rationalism of the philosophers but also in many of the assumptions of the politicians and to suggest that this marks a fundamental and crucial inconsistency in such views and assumptions. And Chapter 6 goes on to argue that a corollary of this view of education as process is that we must see it as an individual matter and not as something which can be planned in detail and implemented by remote control.

Chapter 7 attempts to argue that it is this kind of move towards not only central planning but also planning in subject terms, in terms of the content of the curriculum, and in particular in terms of a content defined by reference to traditional and rationalist notions of what constitutes academic values and standards, which has seriously hampered the development of a successful and effective form of universal education and thus of the achievement of anything approaching educational equality. It is claimed that this is particularly to be deplored in the kind of pluralist and multi-ethnic society for which current educational provision must be made. Again the proferred solution is the idea of education as a process of individual development and of the selection of content by reference to criteria which derive from that.

Chapter 8 tries to take the discussion beyond a consideration merely of forms of cognitive growth by suggesting that, once we see education as a process of individual development, we must also see it as concerned with development in dimensions other than that of the purely intellectual. It further argues that again the obsession of rationalism, and of the politicians who uncritically accept its premises, with the content of the curriculum makes it impossible to develop a theory of education or a pattern of curriculum development which can encompass these affective dimensions.

Finally, Chapter 9 turns its attention directly onto the major manifestations of the recent escalation of direct external political control of the curriculum in the United Kingdom, in order to show that, because these have invariably been based on rationalist premises, whether overt or assumed, they have had, and are having, the effect of inhibiting the development of that view of education as process which the earlier chapters have set out and that they are aggravating the difficulties those chapters have identified. Thus this chapter offers a summary of what has gone before in the specific context of current political initiatives.

In general, then, the aim of this book is to reveal that there are at least two views which can be held about knowledge; that they give quite different perspectives on education, especially in respect of their implications for the role of subject-content in the educational process and for the bases of curriculum planning; that the existence of these two views has seldom been fully recognized or acknowledged nor the significance of their existence properly appreciated; that it is the traditional, rationalist view which has dominated the educational debate and thus determined and directed the focus of much research, not only as these have been conducted by the theorists but also as they have been interpreted by the politicians, to the detriment of those attempts to base educational planning on the other view; that it is this other view, reinforced by the work of developmental psychology and of the 'new directions' in the sociology of education, which offers the more compelling and enabling approaches to educational planning; and that this alternative view must be recognized and asserted, not merely because of what some will claim are its superior attractions, but also, and primarily, to avoid the intellectual and political dishonesty of failing or refusing to acknowledge the existence of alternative theories, not least because to do so suggests a refusal to recognize one's own position and values as representing a particular ideology.

PART ONE
KNOWLEDGE

CHAPTER 1

EARLY THEORIES — IDENTIFYING THE ISSUES

> Myself when young did eagerly frequent
> Doctor and Saint, and heard great Argument
> About it and about: but evermore
> Came out by the same Door as in I went
> (Omar Khayyam, *The Rubaiyat*)

This chapter sets out to reveal what are the main features of the epistemological debate which it is being claimed is central to educational theory. Its concern is to identify the fundamental tenets of both the rationalist and the empiricist views of what knowledge is, in order to demonstrate not only what are the major differences between them, but also, and more importantly in view of the lack of understanding the Introduction described, to establish that there are differences, that these differences are irreconcilable and that these two viewpoints lead to quite different analyses of the role of knowledge in education.

In order to achieve these goals, an examination will be made of the views of early theorists in both of these schools of thought, since it is in its primitive form that one can best recognize the weaknesses of any theory. The work of Auguste Comte, for example, shows up the inadequacies of positivist approaches to the study of society in a way that subsequent, more sophisticated versions of it do not, since once the cracks begin to appear they can be papered over. So it is with epistemology, the weaknesses and difficulties of the rationalist perspective being more readily apparent in the work of early theorists such as Plato and, in the 'modern' era, Descartes, and the different but equally serious problems raised by empiricism in the work of men like John Locke, David Hume and Bishop George Berkeley.

The nature of epistemological enquiry and its importance in education theory

First, however, we must briefly set out what it is that epistemology directs its attention to. There is an important sense in which the term is virtually synonymous with philosophy. Certainly, some philosophers would accept that kind of definition of philosophy, seeing it as a study of knowledge in various fields. Thus all the many 'branches' of philosophy — moral philosophy, political philosophy, philosophy of science, philosophy of religion, aesthetics and so on — may be seen as the application of the same kind of study, the same skills and techniques to different areas of human experience. The concern in each area is not to extend human knowledge in that field — that is the task of the 'resident expert' — but to raise questions about the validity of the claims made by those 'resident experts'. Thus the questions epistemology addresses itself to are questions such as What is truth? What is knowledge? What bases exist for truth or knowledge claims? What grounds have we for claiming that any utterance is true? What might constitute such grounds? And in different fields, of course, the answers to these questions might be different. For example, if we pose these questions of our scientific utterances we will probably come up with quite different answers to them from those which are likely to emerge if we apply them to a field such as religion.

It will be quickly apparent too that there are likely to be some fields where answers to these questions are likely to be more difficult to come by and to be highly problematic even when they are produced. In particular, value utterances of all kinds — moral, aethestic, educational — are likely to fall into this category. Assertions concerning the rightness or wrongness of abortion, for example, or the literary merits of Hamlet, or the educational advantages and disadvantages of various curriculum subjects, are likely to be far less readily accepted than Boyle's Law or any basic mathematical computation. This is why all philosophers who have wished to establish a base for moral or aesthetic claims have recognized the need to begin with a critique of knowledge. Thus a major problem for epistemology is not only the nature and status of human knowledge, not only the meaning of truth, but the differences in that nature and status, the different meanings of truth, which might apply in different contexts. And, indeed, as we shall see, the study known as epistemology is also concerned to ask whether terms like 'knowledge' and 'truth' can legitimately and meaningfully be used in some of the contexts we have just referred to.

It will be clear, then, why it is being argued that such issues are fundamental to the educational debate. For education is essentially concerned with knowledge, with truth and with values. These come together in what are perhaps the most important questions we face when engaged in curriculum planning — What basis is there, if any, for claiming that there are qualitative differences between kinds of knowledge? And, a related question, what kind of justification is appropriate for decisions we make about the content of the curriculum? and so the answers epistemology offers to these questions are of crucial importance to the educator. So too is the fact that different schools of epistemology offer different answers. It is this that has gone for too long unappreciated by theorists of education.

For there are many current issues in education to which these questions about knowledge and about values are crucially relevant. These include all of those problems which divide the subject-based curriculum planner from the 'child-centred' theorist or practitioner (a division which goes far deeper than much of the debate has recognized) — the merits of enquiry-learning, the meaning of 'learning by discovery', the value of children's interests as a basis for educational provision, the rival claims of processes, products and content as the starting-point for curriculum design and so on. They include all of those questions which emerge from discussions of the relative advantages of some kind of centrally determined common core curriculum raising, as such discussions do, questions about the qualitative differences between various subjects (why, in *educational* terms, do some include science in that core but not, say, history?), about subject hierarchies and about the role subject studies should play in the education of teachers. And they include all of those problems which centre on the idea of equality of educational opportunity. How much of that could there be when a good education was equated with the study of the Classics? How much can there still be if we equate it with the study of the currently fashionable common core of academic subjects? How equal can the access to education be for members of different races and cultures if we define education in terms of some conception we may have of the 'common culture' of today's society? And so on again.

Yet these issues can be debated at two levels. The tendency is to discuss them at the level of shared assumptions about knowledge and values, without ever establishing whether those assumptions are shared or not — either because such assumptions are accepted uncritically or because their problematic nature is not recognized or understood. Many of the recent discussions of 'discovery-learning', of the 'common culture curriculum' and of 'multicultural education' have been bedevilled by this kind of approach, as have recent HMI/DES pronouncements on the content of teacher education and on the school curriculum generally. Yet these discussions are of a second-order kind and remain at a superficial level. There is a deeper level at which they must begin, where the assumptions are not taken uncritically as shared but are recognized as themselves part of the debate. There is little evidence of this level of debate, however, in recent literature.

When one gets to that deeper level it becomes apparent that there is more than one view which can reasonably be taken about knowledge and about values. In fact, there are two broad perspectives which can be and have been taken and each will lead to quite different conclusions both in general and in the specific context of educational planning. We must look at the major features of these two perspectives in some detail. Before we do so, however, it may be helpful to summarize briefly the major points of divergence between them.

The *rationalist* perspective, as the term implies, places the emphasis on rationality, on reason, on mind and sees the rational mind as in itself a source of valid knowledge. It thus opens up a whole world of metaphysics, a world which transcends — in every sense — that of experience and perception, since it accepts the validity of knowledge which is *a priori*, independent of any experience of the senses. Indeed, it regards such knowledge as superior to that which comes directly from the experience of the senses, arguing that, while the senses are notoriously deceptive, reason is not. Thus it offers a 'strong' view of 'truth', sees large areas of knowledge as being certain, or at least as potentially certain, regards knowledge for the most part as propositional, as 'knowledge *that*' and believes that justification can be found for assertions of value — moral, aesthetic and educational — in reason itself, in the concept of the rational mind.

Its resultant approach to education is one which is largely knowledge-based, which is hierarchical in that it finds no difficulty in accepting that some kinds of knowledge are intrinsically superior to others, and which sees few problems in establishing the validity of those value claims which form the roots of its educational prescriptions. It is this view that lies behind the notion of education as initiation into intrinsically worthwhile activities, or rather, to be quite specific, those versions of that view which see few difficulties in going on to tell us what these intrinsically worthwhile activities are, what 'educational knowledge' is. It is thus also associated with approaches to education which stress the academic or the intellectual, and it has some difficulty in accommodating views of education as development of a broader kind, and especially of education as a process which must embrace some form of emotional development as well as the intellectual. In fact, it must regard even the emotional reaction of pupils to what is presented to them as of little or no real significance. For this theory sees knowledge as having a status quite independent of the knower and reason tends to be seen as opposed to the emotions, so that rationalism, as we shall see, is a theory of what constitutes knowledge, especially in the area of values, for rational beings rather than for human beings.

It is the contention of this book that this kind of theory has underpinned much official and unofficial thinking about education in the Western world for a long time and that, in the interests of establishing a proper base for theoretical discussions of education, it must now be challenged.

The *empiricist* perspective is best seen as such a challenge to rationalism under all its main heads. (It is not, of course, as some assume, a rejection of rationality, of man's powers of reason, merely of the view of this as a source of eternal and timeless truths.) It cannot accept the idea that some knowledge comes *a priori* from the rational mind, independently of the experience of the senses. As the term implies, it can only accept the validity of knowledge which is either logically necessary or for which some kind of tangible evidence can or could be produced. Thus its view of 'truth' is a 'weak' one; it sees knowledge as uncertain and hypothetical; it sees it as largely procedural, as 'knowledge *how*', a means of coming to learn, to understand and to think; and it believes that no kind of ultimate justification of an objective kind can be found for any assertions of value, that values are relative, man-made, 'socially constructed'.

Its view of education, therefore, is a tentative one. It cannot make hard and fast assertions about the qualitative superiority of certain kinds of knowledge, so that it cannot take a knowledge-centred stance in relation to educational planning. It has to see the development of the individual as the central concern of education and the selection of knowledge content as subsidiary and subordinate to that. It is thus much more sympathetic to the possibility that children's interests, their 'commonsense knowledge', may have a justifiable right to be taken account of and thus may be a better starting-point for the process of their educational development than the 'educational knowledge' of curriculum planners. Its approach is thus an open approach, lending itself more readily to adaptation and development. There is also nothing within this view that makes it difficult to encompass the concept of emotional development as an important dimension of education, since it is not tied to the academic, or the intellectual or the rational. It is also a contention of this book that a further reason why such a view must be explored is because there are important ways in which it reflects many current developments not only in philosophy itself but also in our thinking about culture and society. For the notion of value pluralism has come not only from the work of philosophers but, perhaps more clearly and emphatically, from the work of people such as Richard Hoggart (1957), in the field of working-class culture and from others whose concern has been with the cultures of ethnic minorities. We must not, therefore, permit that traditional rationalist perspective to continue to hinder such exploration.

If these contentions are to be substantiated, the case for both approaches to the problems of knowledge and values must be made more fully. It is to this that we must now turn.

Early rationalist theories of knowledge

Rationalist theories begin from the belief that some kind of certainty in human knowledge must be possible and go on to assume that, since the evidence of the human senses is notoriously fallible, such certain knowledge must somehow originate with the rational mind. Thus their fundamental tenet is that there can be *a priori* knowledge, knowledge which is independent of the experience of the senses, and they argue for this either on the basis of some notion of innate ideas and knowledge or by reference to God as the source of such knowledge or by some more sophisticated form of argument. All of these are, however, versions of what is at root the same view, that certain knowledge is attainable by the intellect independently of the fallible and suspect senses. As a corollary of that first premise, such views also believe that the knowledge which derives from these rational sources is superior to that which comes from less certain origins. And thirdly, there follows some form of mind/body dualism, from the almost mystical elevation of the mind to a different metaphysical world which is a feature of Plato's philosophy, via the emphasis on man's spiritual nature which characterizes much of Christian theology and was the source of those dilemmas created for the early philosophers of the 'modern' era by the complete separation of mind and body, to that emphasis on the intellect at the expense of man's emotional life, that view of man's reason as always unfortunately having to contend with his 'passions', that conflict between rationality and humanity, to which reference was made earlier.

All of these features emerge very clearly in the earliest versions of this theory of knowledge where no attempt is made to protect it from the criticisms which were to be directed towards it rather later.

The first attempt to formulate any theory of knowledge is that of Plato and here we can see the essential thrust of rationalism. For that theory of knowledge is formulated quite explicitly in order to combat the relativism of much of the then current thinking, to inject some stability into an uncertain and fluctuating social situation, to resolve the problems of change, especially social change, by generating a theory of permanence, to impose order on shifting reality. Plato rightly recognized that the world of our experience, the world of *phenomena*, the world which we apprehend through our senses, is uncertain, shifting, ever-changing. For him such change was decay and could only be dealt with by some device which would arrest the process. This is perhaps another story, but is certainly one we should not lose sight of, since it is not totally absent from the minds and intentions of those who would press similar views today. At all events, the world of sense experience for Plato was uncertain, a matter of 'belief' or 'opinion' rather than of 'knowledge' in the full sense. Our senses deceive us; the world is in a constant state of flux, a state of 'becoming' rather than of 'being'; it is a world in which 'you cannot step into the same river twice', as Heracleitus had said; it is a world in which all things are relative, in which everything 'both is and is not'. Such a world cannot be the source or the object of knowledge. The view of Socrates had been that one must accept this uncertainty and see the search for knowledge as a process of constant questioning. Plato, however, set the world on a search for certainty, for answers.

For he saw, contrasted with this, the stability and certainty of that knowledge generated by the mind as it superimposes its rationality on this chaos. For the mind, says Plato, is capable of generating universal, objective knowledge. The objects of the mind's attention are not those particular, shifting, uncertain, changing *phenomena* of the world of the senses, but certain universal concepts, 'forms', what he calls *noumena*, the objects of intellectual rather than experiential apprehension or awareness. Thus, although in the physical world every line has thickness and every point an area, so that every triangle or circle is less than a perfect triangle or circle, nevertheless the mind can reach certain universal conclusions about the properties of triangles and circles, because it can consider them as ideal 'forms' rather than having to rely on the particular and imperfect manifestations of them. It can thus generate universal knowledge which is superior to that 'belief' or 'opinion' which is all that one can have of the imperfect manifestations themselves. Thus this kind of intellectual knowledge is superior; it is superior exactly because it is intellectual, abstract, independent of the imperfections of sense experience.

Thus too man's proper activity as a creature characterized primarily by the possession of intellect is to engage in those pursuits which exercise that intellect and which allow him to transcend the imperfections of a life of the senses. Man's essence is his rationality and from that we are to deduce that it is the function and purpose of his existence to extend that rationality. Education then is the development of those powers in man which are fully rational and intellectual. Man's passions, his desires are to be suppressed in the interests of this development. And the truly educated man is the man in whom these intellectual qualities have come to dominate, to control all other aspects of his personality. To use his own analogy, man's soul is tripartite, consisting of reason (that which is the essential characteristic of humanity), 'spirit' or self-assertiveness (likened to a lion in his imagery) and the appetites or passions (what he calls 'the beast with many heads'). The last must be tamed and placed firmly under the control of reason, with 'spirit', the lion, trained to assist in this process. This is the function and purpose of education.

Society too is to be seen in the same tripartite form and is to be developed in the same way with those intellectually superior — and thus morally superior — citizens educated in this manner to take charge of the others. The political implications of rationalism, although again seldom fully appreciated, emerge very clearly in this primitive and naive version of it and must be recognized as an essential feature of it in all of its forms and manifestations. We must return to this later, since it is mainly the political implications of this kind of theory in education that has prompted the most recent challenge to it — that of the 'new directions' in the sociology of education.

The last point which needs to be made, and emphasized, in looking at this early form of rationalism is that the certain knowledge we are being told the intellect, if properly developed by education, can attain is not confined to a 'scientific' knowledge of the world or to mathematical understanding. The same certainty, the same kind of objective truth can be attained in the same way by the intellect in the area of values — moral, aesthetic and political. For the peak of this knowledge which the intellect can attain with the aid of a proper education is what Plato calls the 'Form of Beauty, Truth and Goodness', the crowning pinnacle of knowledge, which is the origin and source of all knowledge and which welds all human knowledge into one complete whole, a total system of interlocking knowledge of which the Form of Beauty, Truth and Goodness is the keystone. It is thus being claimed that we can hope to achieve the same kind of certain truth in the realms of Beauty and Goodness as in that of mathematics. There is no doubt in Plato's mind that, although all examples of moral behaviour are context-bound, so that, while in one situation a certain kind of behaviour is right, in another context the same behaviour would not be right, this is again merely a manifestation of that shifting, imperfect character of the particular phenomena of the world of the senses which we noted above. It does not hinder the intellect from recognizing that there is a form of perfection which transcends these particular, imperfect phenomena, that there are universal moral and aesthetic truths which make beauty and morality not matters of individual taste or judgement but matters of certain, objective truth. It is this certainty over values that makes possible a highly prescriptive theory of education, not least in the area of its knowledge content, and, what is possibly more sinister, that highly prescriptive political theory which we referred to just now. For it gives meaning to the concept of the ideal or perfect society.

Thus, in this earliest version of rationalism, all of its major features shine through — its search for certain knowledge, its appeal in this search to the intellect, its distrust of sense-experience, its mind/body dualism, its inability to cope with the emotional dimension of human existence other than by a theory of suppression or repression, its certainty over questions of value, and its consequent ability to generate highly positive and directive theories both of education and of politics.

This view, or this kind of view, held sway in Western philosophy for many subsequent centuries. In part, this was because of the sheer weight of Plato as a philosopher and the volume of his published works. In part, it was because, fundamentally, this is a view that fits very well with Christian theology. For that too wishes for certainty of knowledge; that too has emphasized the mind/body distinction; that too has often wished to play down the sensual and emotional aspects of human existence; that too has operated on the basis of a fixed view of morality, a clear notion of universal moral values, and a firm concept of perfection in both man and society. In addition, it offered something that Plato's theory lacked, some kind of explanation of this mystical source of knowledge, the source of supreme concepts like that of 'Beauty, Truth and Goodness'. The absence of this is a serious weakness in Plato's theory. It was put right by the Neo-Platonists, such as Plotinus, by the addition of a deity. There was a clear role, therefore, for the Christian God, when Neo-Platonism and Christianity became fused, largely through the work of St. Augustine. The last piece had been added to the early rationalist jigsaw. Thus through the work of St. Augustine and, later, St. Thomas Aquinas, Platonism and Christian theology became fused, so that with the support of the early Christian church, rationalism could hardly go wrong. The source of all true knowledge continued to be the intellect. The manner by which such knowledge became available to man was through progressive stages of 'revelation' by God, so that knowledge came to be seen as, literally,

God-given. Thus the notion of 'revealed knowledge' was added to the basic philosophy of rationalism and in some ways seemed to make more sense than a theory, such as that of Plato, whose weakness was its lack of any clear explanation of the source of such knowledge. And human beings were seen, in Aquinas' term, as 'rational souls', the ideal life for whom was 'the intellectual love of God'. The intellect is all.

It is not surprising, therefore, in view of the complete dominance of this theory, that when philosophy attempted to reassert itself independently of theology in the seventeenth century, it did so in a clearly rationalist form. It was René Descartes who ushered in the 'modern' era in philosophy, and he did so by first attempting to establish a theory of knowledge. His method was to begin from a universal doubt and scepticism, rejecting any kind or category of belief which could on any grounds be seen as doubtful. Inevitably, this led him to doubt all the evidence of his senses, since the senses deceive us and there is no clear basis upon which we can distinguish between our dreams and our waking perceptions nor even to establish beyond doubt that we do not live in a continuous dream world, so that there seems to be no basis upon which we can distinguish between reality and delusion. It is even possible, he adds, that God may be perpetually deceiving us, providing us with sense experiences which bear no relation to any kind of reality. Thus there began again that debate over 'sense data' and that mind/body dualism which was to bedevil philosophy for further centuries.

Having thus defined the problem, Descartes then turned his attention towards seeking a solution. The solution which emerged is rationalist in a simple but fundamental way; in essence it is Plato's rationalism restated. For Descartes' first item of certain knowledge is the knowledge of his own existence. *Cogito, ergo sum.* I think, therefore I am. *Dubito,* 'I doubt', might have been better. For his argument is that if I am able to doubt the validity of my sense experience, I must exist to do this. Even if I am being perpetually deceived, whether by God or by my senses, I must exist so to be deceived. (The more you think about this, the more evident its truth becomes!) He then goes on to argue that it is the clarity and distinctness of this knowledge that make it knowledge in the full sense. These are the marks of truth. Furthermore, there are other perceptions which are characterized by the same kind of clarity and distinctness. It is not surprising to hear that these are those 'innate ideas' which derive not from sense experience, which is the source of those other ideas which are unclear and indistinct, but *a priori* from the mind itself. Nor is it surprising to discover that among these clear and distinct innate ideas is that of a Perfect Being, God, whose perfection does not permit of the concept of his perpetually deceiving us. Thus it is God who gives us those clear and distinct ideas which constitute the only true and certain knowledge we have. Furthermore, among these clear and distinct 'innate ideas' are certain 'practical' or moral principles whose validity is thus established by this same device.

Thus the major tenets of rationalism are reasserted for the benefit of the modern era. This time, however, they are to attract immediate criticism and it is from a criticism of this view of the supremacy of reason as a source of knowledge, and especially this notion of innate ideas, that a new form of epistemology is born, that of the empiricist.

Early empiricist theories

The early empiricist theories can be seen as attempts to provide a common-sense answer to this problem of the validity of knowledge (although we shall soon see how far-fetched some of these theories themselves became), and in particular to establish some kind of base for the validity of sense experience, not least in order to create a secure foundation for the development of the physical sciences, whose dependence on observable experience is total. Thus the fundamental tenet of empiricism is that there can be no knowledge which does not derive from empirical observation or logical necessity. In short, an assertion can only be true if it can be shown to reflect observable experience or to be logically entailed by some prior assertion.

This movement began in Britain and, if not completely confined to British philosophy, has been a major characteristic of it since the time of Sir Francis Bacon (1561-1626) and, especially, John Locke (1632-1704), who was its first major exponent.

Locke began from a total rejection of the notion of 'innate ideas'. It was this that prompted his famous assertion that the mind of man at birth is a *tabula rasa*, a clean slate. For, he argues, the major objection to the notion that everyone comes into the world ready armed with certain 'innate ideas' is the fact that so many people do not recognize them. 'For, first, it is evident that all children and idiots have not the least apprehension or thought of them . . . But to imprint anything on the mind, without the mind's perceiving it, seems to me hardly intelligible . . . If, therefore, children and idiots have souls, have minds, with those impressions upon them, they must unavoidably perceive them, and necessarily know and assent to these truths; which since they do not, it is evident that there are no such impressions' (*Essay*).

This is a claim which may of course be disputed. It is less easy to argue with him when he focuses directly on the practical or moral principles which are claimed to be innate. For whether what he says of the 'speculative' principles is true or not, the case is much stronger when applied to the practical, or moral, where it is not just a matter of failure to recognize these principles but of positive disagreement over them. 'I think it will be hard to instance any one moral rule which can pretend to so general and ready an assent as *What is, is* or to be so manifest a truth as this, that *It is impossible for the same thing to be and not to be*' (op.cit.). In short, moral principles are not characterized by any kind of logical necessity and it is a fundamental error in rationalism to claim that they are.

Having thus rejected the notion of innate ideas, Locke goes on to make the classical statement of the empiricist position: that no knowledge comes into the mind except through the gate of the senses. 'Let us then suppose the mind to be, as we say, white paper void of all characters, without any ideas. How comes it to be furnished? . . . To this I answer, in one word, from *experience;* in that all our knowledge is founded, and from that it ultimately derives itself' (op.cit.). 'I see no reason therefore to believe that the *soul thinks before the senses have furnished it with ideas* to think on' (II.I.a).

By rejecting this source of knowledge, hitherto regarded as the only source of real knowledge, and re-establishing not only the respectability but the primacy of sense experience, Locke has raised a whole series of questions for subsequent philosophers to occupy themselves with. He has also ensured that questions about human knowledge, its scope and limitations, would play a central role in modern philosophy. He has done this by challenging the existing agreed wisdom and this is why his *Essay* is so important a contribution to the debate about knowledge.

His own answers to the questions he has raised are less convincing, especially in the area of moral and value assertions, and thus less significant, although they reflect a more commonsense approach than was to be apparent in the work of his immediate successors. For, although stressing the primacy of sensative knowledge, his empiricist stance does not lead him to claim that this is the only source of knowledge. For not only is he quite happy to accept the validity of that *a priori* knowledge which consists of assertions to which the rational mind is led by *reflection* on these sensations, he also sees *introspection* as equally valid a source of knowledge as sense-perception, in fact as a possibly more reliable source, since he accepts that the senses often deceive us. This is not, therefore, a thoroughgoing empiricism, in that we have not yet reached the point where experience is regarded as the *only* source of knowledge.

Nor does Locke acknowledge the far-reaching consequences of his rejection of innate practical or moral ideas for the whole issue of values, moral, aesthetic and political. For, taken to its logical conclusion, this raises fundamental issues about the validity of general moral principles, those moral 'truths' which are of crucial importance to the rationalist, and of course to Christian theology. Locke's acceptance of the validity of reflection, of introspection and even of intuitive knowledge, combined with his allocation in his theory of a crucial role to God, not totally dissimilar from that given him by Descartes, assists him to avoid the consequences of this issue or at least to resolve its problems in a largely unsensational manner.

Thus, while Locke may be seen as the man who threw down the gauntlet to rationalism, it is clear that he did not himself appreciate fully the implications of his challenge. It was left to others to take things on and, in doing so, they showed that, far from representing a commonsense approach to knowledge, empiricism taken to its extreme was capable of generating theories every bit as fantastic as those of the rationalist. As Bertrand Russell said of David Hume's contribution to empiricism, 'by making it self-consistent [he] made it incredible' (1939, p.685).

For, first, Bishop George Berkeley (1685-1753), whose expressed concern it was to oppose 'sceptics and atheists', drew attention to the inevitable conclusion that, if all knowledge is experience and all experience is sensation, then there is no evidence for the existence of anything independently of our sensations of it. *Esse est percipi.* To be is to be perceived. If experience or perception is the only source of knowledge, there can be no evidence to support that knowledge other than the experience or perception itself. We cannot separate objects from our perceptions of them. Perception, however, provides no basis for any permanent form of knowledge. Experience cannot generate any knowledge which goes beyond the particular. The things I am observing at this moment I can claim to exist because I am observing them, but when I leave the room what evidence have I of their continuing existence? Berkeley's answer inevitably is 'God'. God is continuously perceiving everything and thus everything exists because it is the subject of this divine perception, a theory neatly summed up in the famous limerick of Ronald Knox:

There was a young man who said, 'God,
I find it exceedingly odd
That this tree which I see
Should continue to be
When there's no-one about in the Quad.'
Reply:
'Dear Sir,
Your astonishment's odd:

I am always about in the Quad.
And that's why the tree
Will continue to be
Since observed by,
    Yours faithfully,
        GOD.'

Thus a doctrine which set out to avoid the metaphysical claims of the rationalist and to accept the evidence of the material context of our existence has become a doctrine of immaterialism, and a doctrine which began from a commonsense view of knowledge as rooted in perception and the evidence of our senses as reliable has led to even more fantastic claims than the doctrine it set out to replace.

We can of course criticize Berkeley's theory, not least on the grounds that its major tenet, the existence of God, is not itself a matter of empirical or experiential knowledge and thus represents a major inconsistency in the doctrine. Unfortunately, while this may invalidate Berkeley's view, it does not solve the problem of empiricism, as David Hume (1711-1776) is about to show.

For Hume sets out to avoid the inconsistencies of both Locke and Berkeley and, in doing so, he highlights for us the problem of empiricism and the major dilemma of epistemology. His is a total version of empiricism. For him there can be no knowledge of any kind which is not attained through the senses. Thus he deprives himself not only of the assistance of a benevolent God to establish the truth and validity of our claims about the world, both physical and moral or spiritual, but also of that source of knowledge that Locke had found in reflection, in introspection, in the ability of the mind to work on the evidence presented to it by the senses and generate new knowledge from this evidence. For such knowledge is *a priori;* it is independent of experience and thus is not consistent with a view of knowledge which sees its only source as sense experience.

There are two major consequences of this. First, this view of knowledge makes it impossible to generate any body of organized, coherent knowledge, even in the sphere of the physical sciences. For, as Berkeley had shown, all experience is particular and offers no grounds in itself for any kind of general assertion. Those universals, those general assertions, for which the rationalist had sought justification in rationality, can be given no justification from sense experience, since we experience only the here and now and cannot claim to have any kind of general or universal experience.

Furthermore, our understanding of the world depends not only on our being able to develop some general conclusions about it, it depends also, and perhaps more crucially, on our being able to establish causal links between events within it — not only to identify general occurrences but to be able to explain them in causal terms and link them together in causal relationships. Yet these causal relationships, as Hume points out, are also not subject to any kind of empirical, experiential substantiation. If we claim that there is a causal link between two events, this is an assumption on our part; it is not part of our direct perception; it is what Locke had called reflection or introspection; it is an example of the mind going beyond the experience of the senses. If we do not accept this as legitimate, as Hume does not, then we cannot accept the validity of that kind of knowledge. Furthermore, it can be added that often we make mistakes in assuming causal links between events, as in the case of the young child experimenting with a frog, who, having given it the command 'Sautez!', concludes and records, as it jumps, that 'all frogs understand French'. As Hume puts it, contiguity and succession do not guarantee causality. Or, in the classic case of the fallacy hunters, although it is true that 'Milton married; he wrote *Paradise Lost;* he lost his wife; he wrote *Paradise Regained*', there is no empirical basis for claiming any causal connections between this sequence of events.

Thus no kind of coherent knowledge can be developed at all. 'If we believe that fire warms, or water refreshes, 'tis only because it costs us too much pains to think otherwise.' In steering us away from that certain knowledge of the rationalist because of doubts — very serious doubts — about the validity of its base, he has succeeded in depriving us of all coherent knowledge and of any base for the generation of such. To repeat the comment of Russell quoted above, 'by making [empiricism] self-consistent, [he] made it incredible' (1939, p.685).

The second consequence of this inevitably takes us into the realm of values, as it is clear Hume has all along intended it to do, since for him 'morality is a subject that interests us above all others' (*Treatise*). For, as Locke had shown in discussing the theory of 'innate ideas', if a theory of knowledge has difficulty in establishing a base for speculative or scientific knowledge, it is likely to have much more difficulty in the practical or moral sphere. In some ways, Hume does not himself recognize the full import of his theory for morals (this is quite understandable in an age when Christian morality was dominant), and it was left to later philosophers, especially in the twentieth century, to draw out fully its implications. The elements of the problem, however, are there, as are the basic elements of some of those later theories.

For he offers us a view of morality, a moral philosophy, which is essentially descriptive, emotive and social or sociological. It is descriptive because it can find no basis for offering prescriptions. It thus concentrates on the observable phenomena of human morality not on any search for 'moral truths'. It is emotive because, in viewing these phenomena, it recognizes that the principles on which we act are the result of beliefs and feelings rather than based on reason. Men do reason about practical or moral affairs but this reasoning is based on beliefs and feelings which are not themselves the result of reason. Moral principles arise not from reason but from feeling; and reason has the secondary role of translating those feelings into actions. 'Reason is, and ought to be, the slave of the passions, and can never pretend to any other office than to serve and obey them' (op.cit.). The fundamental springs of human action are desire and aversion, not reason. Man is a creature of feeling as well as a rational being, and here we have an attempt to develop a moral philosophy which acknowledges that. However, what holds Hume back from stepping from this point to a complete relativism is the sociological dimension of his view. For in his view there are general moral sentiments which are common to all men, moral principles 'which nature has made universal in the whole species' (op.cit.). It is here, of course, that he can be seen to have abandoned his basic tenet, so that it might be kind to leave him at this point.

   In doing so, however, we should note that what this approach has introduced into discussions of values is, first, the idea that reason cannot generate universal truths in this area; second, that no acceptable theory of values can be developed which does not take full cognizance of the role that human emotions play in such matters (an argument which we noted as significantly missing from, and, in fact, deliberately rejected by, the rationalist views we considered earlier); and, thirdly, the beginnings of a consequential notion of value and cultural pluralism, that there are different codes of value to be found among different groups of people and that each must be understood on its own terms. For there is the suggestion that those things that men have feelings of approbation towards, and thus call 'good' or 'right', are those things that are either pleasant or useful, either to the individual or his society, and, although Hume himself slips quickly into attempting to establish universals here, much of what he says leads one towards some form of pluralism. For example, 'The sense of justice and injustice is not derived from nature, but arises artificially though necessarily, from education and human convention' (*Treatise*). Self-interest drives men into society and self-interest gives rise to the 'natural obligation' of justice. 'Thus self-interest is the original motive to the establishment of justice: but a sympathy with public interest is the source of the moral approbation which attends that virtue' (op.cit.). It is not difficult for us to see the seeds of pluralism in this doctrine, even though Hume did not see them himself. We must also note the implied rejection of the reified concepts of 'good' and 'bad', 'right' and 'wrong' and even of 'rationality' itself, which characterize the rationalist position.

Before we leave Hume completely, let us return to the point made earlier about his attempt to concentrate on description in the field of values and to avoid all forms of prescription for which he could find no base. For it was Hume who first drew our attention to what later came to be called the 'Naturalistic Fallacy', that illicit progression from 'is' to 'ought' which still characterizes so much of our 'reasoning' especially in the field of values and is not too notably absent from discussions of the kinds of issue in education this book is attempting to shed some light on. Let us listen to Hume himself on this, since his words are in themselves an important criticism of rationalism in ethics.

> In every system of morality, which I have hitherto met with, I have always remarked that the author proceeds for some time in the ordinary way of reasoning, and establishes the being of a God, or makes observations concerning human affairs: when of a sudden I am surprised to find that, instead of the usual copulations of propositions, 'is' and 'is not', I meet with no proposition that is not connected with an 'ought' or an 'ought not'. This change is imperceptible; but is, however, of the last consequence. For as this 'ought' or 'ought not' expresses some new relation or affirmation, it is necessary that it should be observed or explained; and at the same time that a reason should be given for what seems altogether inconceivable, how this new relation can be a deduction from others that are entirely different from it (*Treatise*).

There is a logical distinction here which cannot be transgressed without invalidating the argument. Yet so few discussions of morals, or of any other area of values, and even fewer discussions of education, have recognized this important logical distinction. Hume has here put his finger on what is the fundamental error of essentialism, and thus of rationalism, its assumption that from an analysis of essences, from definitions of rationality, of man, of society, or of anything else, prescriptions — aesthetic, moral, political or educational — can legitimately be deduced.

There are, of course, loopholes and inadequacies in this theory of knowledge and its consequential theory of morals. These will emerge later as we consider more sophisticated and developed versions of empiricism in both fields. There are, however, some crucial questions which it has raised in its challenge to rationalism, and, in its sheer simplicity, it highlights for us what are the central problems of knowledge and of values and the dilemma we face when we try to establish a certain base for human knowledge in any field, but especially in that of human values. It is this that makes it of relevance and importance still.

Summary and conclusions

What may seem like an antiquarian's trip into the history of philosophy has been undertaken in order to highlight in their stark simplicity the main features of a problem which it is being contended has bedevilled much discussion of educational issues. That problem is focused on questions about the nature and status of human knowledge and, in particular, of those value assertions which are integral to all discussions of education.

The chapter began, therefore, by attempting to define what are the central purposes of epistemological enquiry, showing that these are the search for some fundamental base for human knowledge, for some explanation of what might constitute true knowledge, for some source from which the validity of our assertions may be shown to derive, or for some answer to the question of whether these are sensible and legitimate quests. In particular, it was suggested that, while this is an important problem in all fields of human knowledge and endeavour, it is a particularly important, and a particularly intractable, problem in the field of values — moral, aesthetic, educational and political.

Two kinds of answer to these basic epistemological questions were then delineated. One was shown to be essentialist and rationalist, claiming reason as the only source of real knowledge and disparaging sense experience as beset by uncertainty and error. The other, in turn, we saw rejecting the metaphysical, even mystical, claims of rationalism concerning this source of knowledge which remains independent of experience, and arguing the exact converse, that the only source of knowledge is the experience of our senses and that there can be no way of demonstrating the validity of any assertion made on any other grounds. We also saw the first view, because of the great stress it placed on reason, experiencing difficulties in explaining man's emotional or affective existence, having in fact to repudiate it as an undesirable adjunct of a creature whose true essence was to be found in his rationality, while the second view had far less difficulty in coming to terms with the emotional side of humanity and was inclined, if anything, to regard it as of more importance, or at least as of more significance as an explanation of human behaviour, than reason itself. Thirdly, we noted that while rationalism offered us certainty in the realm of values, empiricism could only point to the existence of doubt, of scepticism, of difference, of pluralism in this realm.

These are the major polarities of these two kinds of view and they are crucial for the educational debate. For there the concern must be with questions of knowledge and truth, with the issue of human development in the emotional as well as the intellectual dimension and, most importantly, with values — moral values, aesthetic values, educational values and, indeed, social and political values.

CHAPTER 2

DEVELOPED THEORIES — TRANSCENDENTAL ARGUMENTS AND THEIR LIMITATIONS

He hoped, he said, to arrange and sum up all the knowledge of his time, symmetrically and synoptically, around a central idea. That is precisely what the Glass Bead Game does.

(Herman Hesse, *The Glass Bead Game*)

We saw in the last chapter how attempts to demonstrate that the intellect, man's power of reason, was a source of knowledge which is not only valid but also superior in its status and certainty to knowledge derived from other sources had generated theories which were highly mystical and which thus became increasingly theological rather than philosophical, or at least depended on the existence of God, and that a benign God, as both the ultimate source of such knowledge and the author and guarantor of its truth. We also saw that this provoked a challenge from philosophers who regarded this as an unsatisfactory line of argument, particularly unsatisfactory as a basis for the development of any sophisticated body of scientific knowledge, and who had, as a result, attempted to establish the validity of sense experience and to argue that the direct experience we have of the world in which we live is the only source of any knowledge which we can generate about it. We saw finally, however, that this approach itself in turn emerged in a number of versions which were equally unsatisfactory and that, in spite of being prompted and motivated by an attempt to return to a more commonsense and down to earth view, some of the theories propounded were perhaps even more bizarre than those they were intended to replace. Thus the mysticism of Plato's 'Forms' had given way to Berkeley's notion of all existence as explicable only in terms of the continuous perceptions of God. With both Locke and Berkeley, the ultimate appeal had again been to the benignity of a divine being. And, when Hume had rightly rejected this solution, he had found himself in a position only to say that certain knowledge is impossible, that there are no grounds upon which we can assert anything which goes beyond our perceptions of the here and now.

However, the battle has now been joined and what follows on both sides is a debate characterized by a good deal more sophistication than we have seen so far. For no rationalist theory could now be mounted which did not take full account of the empiricists' criticisms and, in turn, no empiricist theory could be proffered which did not allow for the developed arguments which the rationalists were about to produce. It is to this advanced version of the debate that this chapter will address itself.

The restatement of the rationalist view — the transcendental argument

It is not a simplification, nor an exaggeration, to say that the whole of the German Idealist movement which, through the work of men like Kant, Fichte, Schelling, Hegel and, in a somewhat different form, Marx, dominated philosophy in the Western world throughout the late eighteenth century and more or less the whole of the nineteenth century, was a response to the criticisms offered of earlier forms of rationalism, and particularly those of David Hume. For Immanuel Kant (1724—1804) had worked with Hume, had learned to respect his arguments (in fact, at an early stage he had himself been convinced by them and had regarded metaphysical speculation as a waste of time) and thus was well aware that any attempt to set up a new rationalism would have to take full account of them. He was also disturbed by the conclusions they appeared to lead to, especially in the field of morals and values generally, and was concerned that a theory of knowledge ought to offer more security and certainty than this.

Such a theory he set out himself to produce and, in doing so, he provided the classical statement of the rationalist theory of knowledge, the fundamentals of which have remained virtually unaltered to the present time. For this is the view of knowledge which underpins the claims more recently made by Richard Peters (1965, 1966) and others for the existence of intrinsically worthwhile knowledge. This is the 'transcendental argument', which he offers in justification of those claims. All that has changed is the language in which it is presented. In looking at Kant's philosophy, then, we are not engaged in dilettante historical enquiry; we are face to face with the central elements of current rationalist epistemology.

Kant's familiarity with British empiricism led him to recognize that all philosophical enquiry must commence with a critique of knowledge. It is of no use speculating about morals, about aesthetics, about politics, or even about education unless one is first clear about the status and validity of one's speculations. (It will be remembered that the criticism offered in the Introduction to this book of much 'philosophy of education' was that it has ignored this and has steamed into the educational debate without an adequate epistemological base.) For Kant a critique of knowledge is the only satisfactory base for any philosophical enquiry and for any philosophical conclusions. Thus, although it is one of his major concerns to demonstrate the validity of moral judgements and other judgements of value, he recognizes that, in order to do this, it is necessary first to reveal the source of the validity of claims which cannot be empirically demonstrated, as all judgements of value clearly cannot. His concern, then, is first to show that human knowledge can be, at least in part, *a priori*, that it can, although not in any mystical sense, transcend experience.

Unable now to seek a solution to the problem of knowledge in the benevolence of the deity or the notion of 'innate ideas' or in some mystical concept such as that of the 'Form of Beauty, Truth and Goodness', Kant seeks to establish that the source of *a priori* knowledge is to be found in reason itself, in the very concept of rationality. He starts, as most philosophers, both rationalist and empiricist, have, with the view that sense experience can never lead to certain knowledge, so that *a posteriori* knowledge, that which is dependent on experience, must always be of doubtful validity. However, whereas Hume, and other later philosophers, have claimed that this is the only kind of knowledge which is available to us, so that we must learn to live with and accept its uncertainties, Kant wishes to argue that one can go beyond this and make *a priori* assertions (i.e. assertions which are independent of direct sense experience) with full confidence and validity. For, while he recognizes that sense experience is the only source of data the mind of the rational being can look to, he argues that the mind can and does transcend that experience by bringing to bear on it certain rational concepts by which that experience is understood. Experience for Hume seemed to consist of a series of snapshots of the world and could of itself offer us no coherent, unified picture. This is true also for Kant, but he goes beyond this to claim that a coherent, unified picture becomes possible by the fact that the rational mind supplies certain concepts which have this unifying effect. Thus the general assertions which are made find their validity not in the observable evidence of the senses but in the rational concepts which the mind brings to bear on that evidence. To adapt a simile which Bertrand Russell uses to illustrate this point, just as if we wear blue spectacles we see the world as blue, so if, as Kant claims, we are perpetually wearing rational spectacles, then we will see the world as rational. This is a view that gains some empirical support from the more recent work of the Gestalt psychologists whose claim that we do in fact see the world in wholes rather than in isolated glimpses is borne out by a good deal of our day-to-day experiences (although to note that we do in fact behave in this way is not of course to establish in any sense the validity of such behaviour). It is also a view which, albeit in more sophisticated form, reminds us of Locke's notions of reflection and introspection.

Those concepts which the rational mind brings to bear on its perceptions are of course the concepts of rationality itself. They constitute what it means to be rational. Strictly speaking these are not concepts; they are forms of 'intuition' (the word Kant himself uses is *Anschauang* — 'views' or 'ways of looking at the world'). Put simply, the case is that the rational mind cannot avoid viewing the world in this rational way. It imposes on its perceptions certain standards of universality and of necessity. It thus makes assertions which, although *a priori*, are valid and objective in that they satisfy the criteria of rationality, they have the assent of all rational minds, they represent the only rational explanation of the phenomena in question. To deny them is to deny the nature of rationality itself; it is to be irrational.

This theory, then, offers a base for all of those assertions of universal 'truths' and of causal relationships which Hume's theory had appeared to make impossible and thus provides a theory of knowledge which does seem to make scientific exploration and the development of scientific knowledge possible. Kant proceeds to apply it to the realm of values, however, and in particular that of moral values, and it is here, as we shall see, that the plot thickens and its inadequacies begin to emerge.

In his search for an ethical doctrine, Kant will have nothing to do with any subjective, utilitarian explanation. In the scientific sphere, although our sense experiences may differ, we accept that there cannot be one truth for you and one for me, we accept that there can be only one rational explanation of phenomena. So it must be in the sphere of morals. There cannot be different sets of values for different individuals or groups. At least, if there are, they cannot all be valid. His search therefore is for the *a priori* element in morals, that element which is independent of individual experience. His concern is to discover the *a priori* principles according to which we make moral judgements, the rational, objective basis for such judgements, those universal principles which will be found not in the subjective standards of desire, inclination or custom, but in the rational being's capacity to determine his own conduct through the exercise of those rational faculties which he shares with all other rational beings. The ultimate basis of moral law is to be found not in human nature or life or society, but in reason itself. Thus the moral law will be the same for all men since 'the ultimate criterion of rightness is deducible from the concept of a rational being as such' (Broad 1930, p.116).

This is the logic of the application of his critique of knowledge to the sphere of values. If knowledge is a result of the constructions rationality enables us to place upon our observations of the phenomena of the world, then moral knowledge must also be the result of the similar application of rationality. To search for the bases of moral knowledge, therefore, is to search for those rational concepts which make this kind of *a priori* utterance possible, and moral philosophy for Kant is 'nothing more than the investigation and establishment of the supreme principle of morality' *(Groundwork of the Metaphysics of Morals)*.

The details of the moral theory this enquiry leads him to are perhaps more than is needed here. What is important is, first, that he sees moral philosophy as the search for 'the supreme principle of morality' and thus regards moral values as the subject of some kind of objective knowledge, as matters of truth and falsehood like all other forms of knowledge, and, second, that he sees, as the source of this supreme principle, rationality, reason itself, viewed independently of any specifically human conditions which may be seen to surround it.

The essential element in rationality for Kant is the universal, since it is only by formulating universal laws that knowledge can be developed and it is assertions of this general, universal kind that his whole critique of knowledge is designed to demonstrate the validity of. Thus the essential element in morality is the same kind of universal law. The concern, however, cannot be to develop particular laws relating to particular, human circumstances, since to do that would be to go beyond rationality, beyond the *a priori*, beyond the 'metaphysics of morals' which it is his concern to argue is the proper object of moral enquiry. It would be to become involved in those considerations of human desire, inclination or custom which we saw he regards as subjective matters and thus beyond the scope of his rationalism. Rather rationalism will offer us an objective criterion by which to evaluate our subjective moral principles in order to establish whether they are right or not. That criterion, then, is to be found not in any particular law or laws but in the concept of law as such. 'As I have deprived the will of every impulse which could arise to it from obedience to any particular law, there remains nothing but the universal conformity of its actions to law in general, which alone is to serve the will as a principle' *(Groundwork)*. He then goes on to delineate that principle in the first formulation of what he calls his 'categorical imperative' — 'I am never to act otherwise than so that I could also will that my maxim should become a universal law' (op.cit.). If the maxim, the principle upon which my intended action is based, can be universalized or generalized, then it has passed the test of rationality and thus is right. All our principles of conduct must satisfy this criterion of universality or universalizability if they are to be fully moral.

It is clear that Kant is of the opinion that in every case the application of this principle will lead to one answer only, that there can be only one right course of action in any given set of circumstances. For, unless he can assume that, there is little point to the case he is making. He is attempting to establish the kind of objective base for moral knowledge which, as we saw in Chapter 1, Hume's empiricism had seemed to make impossible. It is at this point, then, that we can begin to recognize a number of emergent difficulties inherent in this theory. These, however, must wait until later.

First, it is necessary to add that, in order to strengthen this claim, Kant goes on to give five different formulations of his categorical imperative, each intended to offer a different approach or a different analogy for what remains essentially the same fundamental moral principle. One of these formulations, however, is of particular importance and relevance for our main concern here. For him the will is a crucial element in moral behaviour — what makes an act right or wrong is not the act itself but the will or the intention of the person performing it. In order to be sure that the will is not prompted by some subjective desire or inclination or by some extrinsic kind of motivation (i.e. by anything other than the duty of doing right for its own sake), we need to find some objective 'end' which is assigned by reason itself and not by any kind of subjective consideration. Such an 'end' will be valid for all rational beings and will be above and beyond the subjective desires or inclinations of any individual. It will be an end in itself. 'Supposing, however, that there were something whose existence has in itself an absolute worth, something which, being an end in itself, could be a source of definite laws, then in this and this alone would lie the source of a possible categorical imperative, a practical law' *(Groundwork)*. He then goes on to claim that 'man and generally any rational being exists as an end in himself' (op.cit.), that it would be inconsistent with any fundamental rational principle for a rational being not to regard rationality, and thus any other rational being, as an end in itself. 'Accordingly the practical imperative will be as follows: So act as to treat humanity, whether in thine own person or in that of any other, in every case as an end withal, never as means only' (op.cit.). (We must use some people sometimes as a means, for example a barber as a means to getting a haircut, but we must never treat people *merely* as a means or as a means *only* — talk to him about the weather — and mean it!)

This, as was indicated above, is merely a different formulation of the same categorical imperative. What was morally right according to the previous formulation will be found to be morally right also according to this, and vice versa. Both after all are rational principles, so that they cannot be in conflict. What this new principle does, however, apart from offering us another route to the testing of our decisions concerning our behaviour, another kind of criterion to apply, is to strengthen the general rationalist case for an objective, rationally based morality by introducing the notion of respect for persons as a crucial criterion of moral action.

There are obvious attractions in this kind of theory. At one level it makes rational discourse and the advance of knowledge possible, after Hume had seemed to bring it all to a halt. At the moral level, it also has its appeal. For it claims to provide a basis for making objective moral judgements which are not a matter of subjective opinion and which turn out to be very much the kinds of judgement that most people would want to make — and probably would make if pressed to it — judgements that take as their basic principle 'respect for persons' and the attempt to be rational in one's behaviour.

A third attraction is that, if this basis for moral knowledge is accepted, it seems to make possible the generation of comparable knowledge in all areas of values — in aesthetics, in politics, in education as well as in morals. Some would wish to argue, of course, that this is Kant's theory of morals only and that he offers us elsewhere a theory of aesthetics. This is true, but his theory of aesthetics makes appeal to the same rationalist principles, and in all spheres of values he argues that we can legitimately seek for objective truth by the same method of relating our claims to the fundamental concepts and principles of rationality. Certainly, this is the thrust of current restatements of his position such as that offered in Richard Peters' 'transcendental argument'. For this takes the same view of all kinds of value assertion and claims that it is possible to demonstrate objectively that certain kinds of activity are superior to others, that they are in some sense more 'rational' and thus more worthy of the time and attention of rational beings, that poetry is not 'as good as pushpin', as Jeremy Bentham claimed, but a good deal better. It thus seems to make possible those statements about qualitative differences between human activities that John Stuart Mill was keen to argue for. And for educationists, it seems to make possible objective assertions about subject hierarchies, clear statements of what should be included in the curriculum and what should not or need not.

This is why before we consider the difficulties this kind of theory raises, it may be worth while to consider in a little more detail the claim that Richard Peters' 'transcendental argument' (1966), which is at the root of his view of education as initiation into intrinsically worthwhile activities, is in fact a repetition of Kant's argument, that Richard Peters is in many ways a reincarnation of Kant, not least in that he is one of the very few among those who have laid claim to being 'philosophers of education' who, like Kant, has recognized the need to begin any kind of philosophical enquiry with some attempt to establish a sound epistemological base for that enquiry, or at least to make it clear from what kind of epistemological base the enquiry was being undertaken.

Peters explicitly reformulates the Kantian argument as it applies in the moral sphere.

> It has been assumed that a differentiated form of discourse has emerged which has the practical function of guiding people's behaviour by the giving of reasons. Men make use of it when they ask what they ought or ought not to do and when they judge things good or bad. The problem to which the classical ethical theories provided no satisfactory answer is that of justifying the principles which make such reasons relevant . . . One of the obvious comments to be made about the classical theories is that they treat the individual too much as an isolated entity exercising his 'reason', 'feeling', or 'intuition' as if he were switching on some private gadget. What they ignore is the public character of the situations in which such exercises occur together with *their public presuppositions in the form of abstract principles* [my italics] (1966, p.114).

This quotation reveals that the essential characteristics of Kant's critique of knowledge are accepted by Richard Peters — the notion that values and valuing are not private activities but are public exercises which involve using 'a public form of discourse' (op.cit., p.115) and 'probing public presuppositions' (ibid.). Furthermore these public presuppositions are 'abstract principles'. Rationality requires of us, therefore, not only that we accept the standards and the discourse of rational public debate but also that we accept that, beginning from certain concepts which constitute what rationality itself is, that debate will lead to conclusions, even in the realm of values, which will have an equally public, and thus universal, character. Again, the assumption is that moral reasoning, along with reasoning in all spheres of values, is in a fundamental sense the same kind of activity as scientific reasoning and will be productive of conclusions of a similar universal validity and status.

Of far more importance are arguments pointing to what any individual must presuppose in so far as he uses a public form of discourse in seriously discussing with others or with himself what he ought to do. *In a similar way* [again my italics] one might inquire into the presuppositions of using scientific discourse. These arguments would be concerned not with prying into individual idiosyncracies but with probing public presuppositions. They might draw attention to considerations of *meaning* in the sense of the established relationship between concepts within the form of discourse . . . Arguments might be drawn from considerations about what conditions must obtain for anything said within a form of discourse to be established as true . . . If it is meant to have *application* in this world some truth conditions must be presupposed (ibid.).

He goes on to argue that while 'it would be open for anyone to say that he is not so committed because he does not use this form of discourse or because he will give it up now that he realises its presuppositions . . . *it would be a very difficult position to adopt in relation to moral discourse* [my italics]. For it would entail a resolute refusal to talk or think about what ought to be done . . . No adducing of reasons for the guidance of conduct would be permissible thereafter' (op.cit., pp.115—116). The implication that acceptance of the presuppositions must lead to acceptance of the conclusions drawn from them is clear. Nor would one wish to quarrel with this as a basic principle of logic or of rationality. It is also clear however that the assumption is being made — certainly in the moral sphere — that there is only one set of presuppositions to moral discourse and that to reject those is to reject moral discourse itself. It is also clear that the final test for Peters, as for Kant, is that of 'respect for persons'. It is this which not only reveals Peters' indebtedness to Kant but also reveals a central weakness in this doctrine.

However, it is this basic conviction that rationality provides not only public presuppositions and concepts which it is irrational to reject but also that these presuppositions and concepts lead to conclusions of a comparable validity, which underlies not only Peters' view of morality but also, and inevitably, his view of education. For much of *Ethics and Education* subsequent to the passages quoted above is directed at demonstrating how, on this basis, decisions concerning the selection of knowledge and subjects for inclusion in the curriculum can be made with relatively few qualms, how subject hierarchies can be justified in terms either of their contribution to the development of rational faculties in pupils or their own level of rationality or both. These are weighty decisions and their basis must be more fully explored. Certainly, this kind of transcendental argument must not merely be accepted at its face value, so that we must now consider some of the difficulties and problems it raises.

Some problems and difficulties of the transcendental argument

The difficulties of this form of argument emerge especially clearly when one considers the conclusions it leads to in the realm of political and other values. Inevitably, therefore, it is on that that we must concentrate, not least because the main focus of our interest is on education, in itself a highly political activity.

It is worth noting first, however, some of the difficulties which have emerged from recent developments in knowledge in less controversial fields. The present century has, for example, seen a number of developments in mathematics resulting from the adoption of alternative, so-called 'non-Euclidean', forms of geometry, and these kinds of development have cast a good deal of doubt on rationalist claims concerning the validity of knowledge even in the mathematical sphere. Similarly, in the realm of the physicist, recent developments have led to a questioning of many scientific hypotheses which might once have seemed to enjoy the status of universal truths. These sorts of development have made it much more difficult to maintain a view of knowledge such as that of rationalism even in the 'scientific' sphere. In criticizing the use of transcendental arguments as a basis for contemporary curriculum planning, Wellington (1981, p.21) summarizes the situation succinctly:

> Kant and his contemporaries strongly believed that the mathematics and physics of that time, and even the moral code, were true beyond all doubt. Kant thus assumed that the schemata employed in mathematical, physical and moral thinking were unique and could not be otherwise. In 1981 we have non-Euclidean geometry, Einstein's relativistic view of the space-time continuum, Heisenberg's 'uncertainty principle' and the knowledge that Newtonian physics only applies to slow-moving objects. Kant's category of cause and effect has been replaced by the statistical probability that one event will follow another, while modern physicists assure us that 'matter' (Kant's category of substance) is mostly empty space, and particles often behave like waves.
>
> In the light of these alternative 'categorial schemata' or ways of understanding the world [Kant's *Anschauang*], who would be bold enough to ever attempt such a transcendental deduction today?

Even in the realm of 'scientific' knowledge, then, a rationalist epistemology is now difficult to maintain and adhere to.

We may note too a second point which emerges from this. In a situation in which alternative forms of this kind are possible, and, indeed, productive, in which a complete overhaul of basic axioms and/or a direct challenging of previously accepted hypotheses are not only permissible but perhaps even essential to the continued development of knowledge, a dogmatic clinging to presumed universal truths will be positively counter-productive to development in all fields, including that of education. For it will hamper not only the educational growth of the individual towards autonomous thinking, but also the development of knowledge itself. One is thus reminded of John Stuart Mill's case for freedom of thought, that without the clash of contrary opinions there can be no development towards truth of any kind.

Again, therefore, one can see the intellectual dangers that we risk from an acceptance of the dogmatic assertions of the rationalist.

It is perhaps when this view of knowledge is extended into the political sphere, however, that the problems it presents begin to emerge most starkly. There is nothing contingent, however, about its extension in this direction, since a theory of morals is essentially a theory of how men ought to live with one another, so that such a theory necessarily involves or entails a certain view of society, and thus of politics. Consequently, a moral theory which claims that there are certain moral principles which by virtue of their rationality are absolute and universal must accept that it will thus provide the same basis for claiming the objectivity and universality of certain political principles.

This emerges most clearly from the work of Hegel (1770-1831), the second major figure in the German Idealist movement. A number of 'philosophers of education' have freely admitted their ignorance of Hegel's work and/or their inability to understand it. It must be admitted that Hegel's ideas, even in translation, are difficult to comprehend, but this is a serious and disturbing confession. For, if they had understood what Hegel was saying, they might have had a clearer view of the direction in which their too ready acceptance of a rationalist epistemology was leading them.

For, taking Kant's concept of rationality, Hegel argues that the whole development of human knowledge must be seen as a slow process of evolution towards what he calls the 'Absolute', the final and perfect manifestation of rationality. For Hegel, rationality develops, as knowledge develops, by a dialectical process of *thesis* (existing knowledge), *antithesis* (contradictory evidence) and *synthesis* (the new knowledge which emerges from the accommodation of the antithesis within the thesis). This synthesis in turn becomes the new thesis, and so the triadic process continues. The movement is towards ever higher levels of rationality and the imperfections of existing knowledge are explicable in terms of their being early stages on a road leading inexorably towards perfection. It is a non-theistic version of Aquinas' doctrine of revelation, and the 'Absolute' is in substance a sophisticated reassertion of Plato's form of Beauty, Truth and Goodness. For the basic notion again is of all knowledge welded into one complete and rational totality.

Inevitably, therefore, history plays an important role in Hegel's philosophy. For it is essentially a historical process he is describing. Thus the idea of history as exhibiting broad patterns of development of this kind is reasserted and, reinforced by Darwinism, this becomes an important ingredient of nineteenth century thought in a wide range of disciplines. The historical process is seen as a rational process, as the continuous unfolding of rationality. 'The only idea which philosophy brings with it,' he tells us, 'is the simple idea of reason, that reason dominates the world and that world history is thus a rational process.' However, that rational process which is world history must be that same dialectical process we described earlier, a process of conflict between thesis and antithesis and that conflict is manifested on the stage of world history in the form of conflict between nations and states — i.e. war.

One result of this, of course, is that one can make no moral judgements about this process. It is neither more nor less than the manifestation of that process of rationality which is all-pervading in human affairs. It would thus be irrational to criticize it as immoral. It is neither good nor bad, it just *is*. 'The insight to which . . . philosophy is to lead us is that the real world is as it ought to be.' The judgement of history is a moral one. 'The history of the world is the world's court of justice.' 'What is, is right, because it is.'

It is not difficult to see here the seeds of a highly sinister political theory, the source of fascism in general and Nazism in particular (albeit as a result of a serious misunderstanding or misinterpretation or even distortion of Hegel's true intent). Nor is one surprised to learn that Hegel's philosophy was the subject of Mussolini's doctoral thesis. As Sir Percy Nunn once wrote (1920, p.3), 'From the idealism of Hegel, more than from any other source, the Prussian mind derived its fanatical belief in the absolute value of the State, its deadly doctrine that the State can admit no moral authority greater than its own, and the corollary that the education system, from the primary school to the university, should be used as an instrument to engrain these notions into the soul of a whole people.' It is here that nationalism can be seen to have its roots — in what Hobhouse (1918) called the metaphysical theory of the state.

What is of prime concern to us here are the implications of this theory for morality, for the role of the individual within the state. If everything which exists is right merely because it exists, if everything which exists is the embodiment of reason, if world history is the unfolding of reason, then it follows that the state must also be the embodiment of reason. This is the basis of Hegel's metaphysical theory of the state, a view of the state as an entity which has developed by this same rational process which history reveals in all forms of development, a view which is only tenable in terms of this philosophy of history. This is also the base for those positivist approaches to the study of society which dominated early sociological studies and whose residue is still to be seen in certain areas of that discipline. It advises us that if the state is the embodiment of reason, our task is not to attempt to devise the 'ideal state' but to study it as it is.

Furthermore, in studying it as it is, our concern must be with the whole, the totality. The state has developed as an organic and rational whole and, if we are to understand it, we must attempt to discover the unifying 'idea' behind the separate processes of human thought and of history. This 'idea' of the totality, like Plato's 'forms', because it is the embodiment of rationality, is completely objective and free of all subjectivity. Not only then is it possible to see history as the unfolding of objective rationality, it is also possible to see the state as embodying the same kind of objective reason. Great historical figures, such as Julius Caesar, he tells us, were great precisely because their 'own particular aims involved those large issues which are the will of the World-Spirit'. In other words, their greatness lies in the fact that they have had a clear vision of the underlying rationality of both state and history and they have gone with it.

Conversely, and this is the crucial point of Hegel's moral theory, those who go against it are wrong — in every sense of the term. They are wrong because they are bucking against the process of rationality and they are wrong because *ipso facto* that means they are kicking against the laws of universal morality. Thus Hegel makes great play, like Kant before him, of the concept of 'will'. For Hegel there is the particular will of each individual and the universal will. If there is conflict between the two, the particular will must be wrong because it is rejecting the concept of will as the universal principle of rightness, i.e. it is behaving irrationally. The moral will for Hegel, as for Kant, is that will which is in harmony with the universal will, so that its freedom consists of its ability to identify itself and harmonize with the universal will. This Hegel calls 'the realisation of freedom, the absolute fixed purpose of the world'. Thus the duty of every individual is to conform to the universal will. Once one gets beyond one's own selfish concerns, one sees that what is really in one's interests is what the state commands. To do otherwise, to oppose the state, to be in any sense revolutionary, is to be wrong because it is *ipso facto* to oppose reason — that reason of which the state is the embodiment.

It is here that Hegel introduces the concept of alienation — a very different concept from that in current sociological theory, or even in Marxist theory. The concept of alienation for Hegel is rather more like that contained in the opening words of Rousseau's *Social Contract*, 'Man is born free; and everywhere he is in chains.' Man is unhappy because he is at odds with society;

he sees the state as something alien to him; he sees himself as subject rather than citizen; he doesn't see himself as a part of the state. He can only overcome this state of alienation by the rational process of coming to understand his situation, identifying himself freely with the state and freely getting into line with the general or universal will. A similar line of reasoning led Rousseau to suggest that men must be 'forced to be free'. Hegel is attempting to avoid that kind of view by emphasizing that freedom consists in this freely adopted identification with the universal will. Whether he succeeds or not, whether to have this particular cake and to eat it is possible or not, is another question.

One is reminded of the Buddhist concept of nirvana, that state of beatitude which comes from the extinction of individuality and absorption into the supreme spirit. It is thus clear that such a theory, when applied to education, cannot sustain any notion of individual autonomy cheek by jowl with such a view of knowledge and values. It will be clear too that there is an inherent contradiction between this view of knowledge and Kant's notion of the autonomy of the will. Hegel's view of this is the only view which is consistent with the basic tenets of rationalism. It is a lack of awareness of Hegelianism which has led to that inconsistency being allowed to reappear in current educational theory.

What this rationalist epistemology has led to then, entirely because of its attempt to establish certainty of knowledge in the areas of values — moral, aesthetic and political — is the elevation of society above the individual, the collective above the particular. This is an inevitable consequence of a rationalist theory of knowledge. For if there is only one form of right — in morals, in aesthetics, in politics, in education — whatever form of right it is, the individual's choice is merely to identify with it or not, and the only *moral* choice is the former. What is more, there is every justification for using whatever measures and devices are necessary to ensure this kind of conformity. There is no room for shades of opinion in any of these spheres; such shades of opinion can only be graded versions of irrationality, of unreason, of immorality. There can be no pluralism of values. There is only one absolute universal reason. It is as if the world were one great perfect syllogism which we can as yet appreciate only imperfectly, and which indeed may as yet only manifest itself in part, since the Absolute, like God, moves in a mysterious way. It was for this reason that it was suggested earlier that Hegelianism is a kind of non-theistic version of Aquinas' revelation. Rationalism of any form must lead to some kind of totalitarianism.

It is perhaps worth noting briefly here the different form of totalitarianism the same kind of theory led Karl Marx to. For Marx accepted Hegel's view of world history as revealing the progressive unfolding of rationality; he accepted too the notion of this as a dialectical process. For Marx the dialectic was a materialist dialectic, a conflict of classes rather than states but it represented the same kind of progress towards perfection, towards the 'classless society'. His theory thus reveals the same metaphysical features as Hegelianism, the same rationalist epistemological base, the same confidence in *a priori* knowledge, and thus the same preference for the collective over the individual. Morality again consists in identification with the movement of history; immorality in opposing that inevitable process. It is for this reason that Marxism is an odd bed-fellow for those 'new directions' in the sociology of education we shall examine in Chapter 4.

It will perhaps now be clear why many people have eschewed this kind of rationalist theory of knowledge and have challenged both its epistemological assumptions and the kind of moral and social philosophy it gives rise to. It may also be emerging why the present writer is opposed to its uncritical adoption within education theory. It will be worth dwelling a while, however, on two major forms this rejection has taken — the rise of existentialism and the reappearance in the present century, especially in Britain, of a more fully developed version of empiricism.

One of the more interesting and encouraging phenomena of human life and society is that creative persons quite often are to be seen making important, if oblique, moral, social and political points, long before the scholars, the philosophers and the sociologists get there. There is much evidence in the history of philosophy to support the dictum that what the artist grasps intuitively today the philosopher makes explicit tomorrow, and the reaction against rationalism is a good example of this.

For the *reductio ad absurdum* of the application of reason to all aspects of existence was provided by Jonathan Swift (in 1726, when Kant was but a two-year-old) in his description of the life-style of the Laputans, whom Gulliver met on one of his travels. These people are caricatures of Plato's ideal man and their behaviour may be seen as similarly caricaturing life in the kind of community envisaged by Kant and Hegel, and even Marx. They live on an island which floats in the air; their garments are decorated with mathematical and astronomical symbols and are cut to measurements taken by sextants and other such measuring devices, so that they never fit the wearer; their food is cut into geometrical shapes of all kinds, symbolizing their desire to put all human experience into a form that can be understood by the use of mathematical categories; they find intercourse with each other difficult since they tend very readily to withdraw into contemplation even during a conversation (for what is there to talk about if everything conforms to one rational scheme?) and they employ servants to rattle bladders filled with pebbles to recall them on such occasions.

Swift's caricature of rational existence is very plain and he was perhaps the first to launch this kind of explicit attack on rationalism. However, the whole Romantic movement which swept European art in the century which followed can be seen as a similar portent. Man's natural life seemed to be threatened by the growth of the industrial society and individualism seemed to be threatened by the rationalism on which that society appeared to be based. In the works of Blake, of Wordsworth, of Coleridge, of Goethe, of Dostoevsky, of Tolstoy, this theme has been constantly developed and the development continues today in the writings of such as Camus, Sartre and Hesse. Herman Hesse's *Glass Bead Game*, for example, is a powerful attempt to caricature this kind of worship of rationality, and his *The Prodigy* describes compellingly and depressingly some of the effects of building a form of education on rationalist principles of this kind.

Such protest, however, was not left for ever to the artists. The nineteenth century saw not only the full development of rationalism in the hands of Hegel, Marx and others, it also saw the beginnings of revolution within philosophy itself — or rather two kinds of revolution, one existentialist, the other a modified empiricism.

The existentialist revolt

A distinction was drawn by the German philosopher Schelling (1775-1854) between what he called negative philosophy, which concerns itself only with concepts and essences, and positive philosophy, which is concerned with existence. Taken by itself, this can be seen as no more than a reaffirmation of a distinction long made in Western philosophy between essentialism and existentialism. But now the problem was to be taken up and the positive philosophy, the existentialist position, was to be developed. Hegel had given the rationalist, essentialist philosophy possibly its fullest statement and it was that which called forth the existentialist response.

It is always dangerous to place labels on philosophical movements. For labels emphasize similarities and obscure differences, and it is often the differences which are most significant for an understanding of particular philosophies. This is nowhere so evident as in a consideration of the many versions of what has been called existentialism. However, with that *caveat*, since it is neither appropriate nor necessary in this context to explore these versions in detail, it may be permissible to pick out one or two relevant general features of existentialist philosophy.

The most important point that needs to be made here is that those philosophies which have been dubbed 'existentialist' during the last century or so have for the most part been explicitly opposed to the kind of essentialist, rationalist views we have been attempting to elaborate. Indeed, one of the first philosophers to be labelled in this way, Arthur Schopenhauer (1788-1860), was so explicit in his opposition to the work of Hegel that he fixed his own lecture times at Berlin University to coincide with those of Hegel. The fact that he soon had to give up lecturing through lack of an audience does not detract from the significance of the gesture (although it may well tell us much else).

Fundamentally, the concern has been to re-establish the claims of the individual to be considered as an individual and not as part of any kind of collective, whether class, state or even mankind as a whole. It follows from this, then, that each person must be defined as an individual and not as a representative of some species or class. This is what is meant by the claim that existence precedes essence, a premise accepted implicitly by all existentialists and stated quite explicitly by Jean Paul Sartre.

Rationalist philosophy, since Plato, had concerned itself with essences, with attempts to define things, and especially to define man, as a basis for — quite illegitimately — deducing prescriptions from these definitions. This had thus, as we have seen, led inevitably and inexorably to a view of existence as in some way to be directed towards the ideals implied in these essences, towards the perfect man and the perfect state as defined by Plato, towards the perfect man as defined by Christian theology, towards the moral imperative of Kant, towards the unfolding rationality of Hegel's 'Absolute'. The significance of the existentialist revolt against this movement lies not just in the fact that it represents a different conception of and approach to philosophy, but also that it offers a quite different view of existence and of morality. For if, as the existentialists claim, man's existence precedes his essence, then man must be seen as first existing and then making of himself what he is or what he becomes; he creates his own essence; he is responsible himself for what he becomes. As Sartre (1948) tells us, 'There is at least one being whose existence comes before its essence, a being which exists before it can be defined by any conception of it. That being is man, or, as Heidegger has it, "the human reality".' And again, 'Man first of all exists, encounters himself, surges up in the world — and defines himself afterwards. If man as the existentialist sees him is not definable, it is because to begin with he is nothing. He will not be anything until later, and then he will be what he makes of himself' (op.cit.).

This view of the personal responsibility of every individual for his/her own essence is the keynote of all versions of existentialism. Existence is seen as an individual matter and the truly moral obligation is that we freely work out our own values and our own individual solutions to the moral issues which face us, not that we find some kind of spurious freedom by identification with the general laws of some kind of collective imperative.

An important corollary of this view is that man is viewed as man, as 'the human reality', and not as an embodiment of rationality. Thus this kind of view does not experience those difficulties which, as we saw earlier, rationalism encounters over accommodating the emotional, affective dimension of existence. Far from being forced to regard the emotions as some unfortunate accretion, whose effect is to inhibit the proper and desirable workings of rationality, existentialist philosophies, of whatever form, are able to take full account of man as a feeling, as well as a thinking, being. After all, it is the emotions as much as, and perhaps more than, rationality which makes us all what we are.

This, then, was one kind of revolt against the developed versions of rationalism which emerged from the German Idealist movement of the last century. In itself, it highlights some important difficulties of the view of knowledge which was fundamental to that movement, and particularly of its approach to values – moral, aesthetic and political.

The reaffirmation of empiricism

It is this view of values which was the focus of the second kind of reaction against rationalism, the reaffirmation, albeit in a modified form, of empiricism. This is the essential feature of that 'revolution in philosophy' which the present century has seen, especially in British philosophy, a revolution which has led the philosopher away from the search for universal truths towards the pursuit of clarity through conceptual analysis of various kinds, and has stressed the latter as his/her proper function. It is this kind of activity, incidentally, that most 'philosophers of education' have claimed to be engaged in while they have been propounding their rationalist theories of knowledge. It is my concern to argue that this represents a serious contradiction, in fact a total muddle which has confused the education debate for too long.

For conceptual analysis may reveal the meanings people actually give to words and it may reveal nuances of meaning and differences, sometimes quite subtle, between concepts. Thus it can demonstrate, for example, not only that people give different meanings to members of families of related words, such as 'education', 'training', 'instruction', 'indoctrination' and so on, but also that there are important conceptual differences here – whatever terminology people use. What it cannot do is to reveal meanings, or essences, in any absolute sense, in any metaphysical or essentialist sense, in any sense in which philosophers prior to the twentieth century could be seen seeking for essences, in any sense which offers a basis for prescriptions. In mainstream philosophy it is a radical alternative to essentialism not a new version of it. It is the failure to recognize this that has vitiated much recent 'philosophy of education' (with some notable exceptions such as the work of D. J. O'Connor (1957), Pat Wilson (1971) and Keith Thompson (1972)), shows it to be rooted in an outmoded methodology and encourages one to claim that much of it has been neither good philosophy nor good education theory.

The study of philosophy as conceptual analysis represents an attempt to establish a radical alternative to traditional, essentialist and rationalist approaches. We saw earlier that rationalism claims that it is possible and valid to make important and wide-ranging assertions which are *a priori*, independent of experience, and that such assertions are also possible in the sphere of values. In fact, it is in this area that the issue is most controversial and thus crucial. Such claims and such assertions are essentially metaphysical and this is clearly the point of attack for the empiricist. The focus of much philosophical activity in recent times, therefore, especially in Britain, has been on the issue of the status of such utterances. What is the logical and epistemological status of value assertions? Is there such a thing as moral knowledge? Are there such things as moral truths? Does it make sense to seek for truths in any area of values – moral, aesthetic, political or educational?

In general, although again a number of different answers have been given to these questions, many have responded to the difficulties of the rationalist, metaphysical position by answering these questions with a negative. Some, such as the logical positivists (Ayer 1936), have even gone so far as to claim that all value utterances are 'literally meaningless', that they do not assert anything, that they merely express the feelings and attitudes of the person uttering them, that if I say 'Pre-marital sex is wrong' or 'Beethoven's "Moonlight Sonata" is beautiful' or 'Socialism is the only proper form of political organization' or 'Science is a more important curriculum subject than Dance', I am merely expressing my own values and attitudes on these questions, and expressly not asserting any universal truth, nor indeed any kind of truth at all.

This, of course, is a view which finds it much easier to accommodate such clearly observable features of present-day society as cultural and value pluralism. For whereas the rationalist can only explain this in terms of some people having got it right and others wrong – an assumption clearly implicit in concepts such as that of 'high' and 'low' culture – an empiricist epistemology can explain it as evidence of its fundamental claim that in the area of values there are no truths. And, whereas the rationalist, because his fundamental claims are *a priori*, metaphysical, independent of experience, has the greatest difficulty in identifying which groups in society have got it wrong, as is evidenced by the arguments of educationists like Richard Peters (1965, 1966), Paul Hirst (1965, 1974), both separately and together (1970), John White (1973), and Denis Lawton (1973, 1975), the empiricist view has no such problem because it regards the question as not a proper question at all, and certainly as not a question which can be properly addressed by philosophy. Thus, while at one level we have here again a difference of opinion as to what the proper function of philosophy is, it is a difference of opinion which has crucial implications for large areas of human experience and, most importantly in the present context, for educational planning.

In general, current empiricist epistemology will view all knowledge as tentative, as hypothetical, pointing to recent developments in areas such as those of mathematics and science as evidence of this, and will go on to claim that, if this is so even in these areas, our 'knowledge' in the area of values of all kinds must be so tentative as not to constitute knowledge at all. Thus knowledge of all kinds is seen as provisional, and not as consisting of those certain, universal truths that the rationalist has been seeking to establish, and values are seen as highly problematic and not susceptible to any kinds of claim for certainty or assurance.

Such a view clearly has crucial implications for educational planning, since it removes the base for the many assumptions we suggested earlier are built into much discussion of education. It encourages us to see knowledge itself as problematic and, in particular, to recognize the problems raised by the values which are an integral part of all forms of knowledge and which come into play immediately one begins to select which knowledge shall be part of one's curriculum.

It is here the sociologists in recent times have picked up the ball and, as was suggested earlier, it is a sad reflection on 'philosophy of education' that it was left to them to do so. For the essence of those 'new directions' in sociology which the last two decades have seen and which was given its first clear statement in Michael Young's seminal work, *Knowledge and Control* (1971) (if one can ignore the inconsistencies of the attempt of many of these to embrace also a Marxist — and thus metaphysical and rationalist — perspective in order to be able to claim certainties of a different kind), is that to fail to recognize the problematic nature of the values implicit in any form of curriculum planning is to fail to recognize the degree to which these values will be communicated to the recipients of the curriculum so planned. At best, therefore, this will result in some kind of unconscious indoctrination of pupils into the value systems of their teachers or the curriculum planners, at worst to the deliberate use of control of the curriculum to bring about this kind of indoctrination and social control — the control of people's attitudes and values through decisions concerning what they are to be exposed to via the curricular provision made for them. In short, they have been picking up those sinister political implications of rationalism which we saw earlier in the work of Hegel.

The rationalist would argue, indeed must argue, that these values have some kind of objective status and that educational planning in terms of 'intrinsically worthwhile activities' or whatever is an imposition not of a particular person's or group's values but of values which have the kind of transcendental status that form of epistemology claims. An empiricist epistemology, regarding values as problematic, must lead to the sinister conclusions sociologists have recently drawn our attention to. It will perhaps now be clear why it is being argued that the issue of what constitutes human knowledge, and especially the question of its scope and limitations, is fundamental to any discussion of education and of the curriculum. It will also be clear why it is being claimed that to make bland, uncritical, unquestioning assumptions in this area, and to base important prescriptions on these, is a quite unacceptable manner of proceeding if a proper form of educational planning is what is desired.

Summary and conclusions

An attempt has been made in this chapter to show how the question of the status and validity of human knowledge, raised in a somewhat simplistic form by the theories explored in Chapter 1, have been pursued in the more complex theories of recent philosophical thought. The purpose was to illustrate, first, that, in spite of the increased sophistication, the issues remain fundamentally the same, and secondly, that they continue to be central to educational planning.

An outline of the modern forms of rationalism was offered not only to reveal its essential features but also to show how, albeit often implicitly rather than explicitly, it has pervaded much of the recent and current educational debate. A discussion of some of the reactions against that kind of epistemology, and the features of it which prompted them, was then undertaken both to highlight the problems it creates, especially in the field of educational planning, and to suggest that these problems are sufficiently important to require careful exploration and not to be taken as assumptions which need not be questioned.

It is clear that this discussion has left us with a dilemma. For on the one hand rationalism offers us a kind of certainty which would be highly reassuring, both in general and in the specific context of curricular planning; on the other hand, such certainty can only be bought at a price which many of the reactions against it would suggest is too high, and these reactions offer us no certain base of any kind for our planning. It is possible to see the philosophical theory known as pragmatism as an attempt to resolve this dilemma. It is to a discussion of this that we now turn in Chapter 3.

CHAPTER 3

PRAGMATISM AND EDUCATION
— A PARTICULAR FORM OF EMPIRICISM

I will come. But in future you will have to go by yourself. Education is
experience and the essence of experience is self-reliance.
(T.H. White, *The Once and Future King*)

There are several reasons why a discussion of the basic tenets of
pragmatism forms an appropriate culmination to an exploration of
epistemology and its relevance to educational theory such as that
undertaken in this first part of this book. The first of these is that in the
work of John Dewey (1859-1952), the most influential figure in the development of this kind of philosophy, the two issues are conflated,
philosophy and education being regarded, as it were, as two sides of the
same coin. For in Dewey's view, 'the most penetrating definition of
philosophy which can be given is . . . that it is the theory of education in
its most general phases' (1916). For, 'education offers a vantage ground
from which to penetrate to the human, as distinct from the technical,
significance of philosophic discussion' (op.cit.). Thus it is largely through
the work of Dewey that an empiricist epistemology has entered
educational thought, and his work has that quality, which this book is
concerned to argue as a great merit, indeed a *sine qua non*, of productive
educational discussion, of recognizing that such discussion must begin
with and from a critique of knowledge.

Secondly, pragmatism, certainly in the form in which it was developed
by Dewey, can be seen as an attempt to resolve that dilemma with which
we concluded Chapter 2. For it is Dewey's aim to explain how knowledge
can be viewed as tentative, as uncertain, as changing and evolving, while
at the same time not necessarily being seen as relative, subjective, personal
and incapable of being expressed in any generally agreed form. The

conclusion of some of those who have rejected the universal certainty of rationalism, such as many of the leading existentialists, has been to assume that, since all experience is personal and subjective, all knowledge must be so too. And this line has also been argued more recently by that movement within sociology known as phenomenology. It is Dewey's concern to break down this polarity and to argue that lack of certainty over human knowledge need not lead necessarily to lack of agreement. (The influence of Hegelianism on his thinking is nowhere more apparent.) Pragmatism can be seen, therefore, as an attempt to find a solution to what we have been suggesting is the educationist's major and first problem, that of finding a basis for judgements of educational values which are neither misleading in their assumptions of certainty nor unhelpful and even dangerous through their narrow subjectivism.

Thirdly, in its attempt to develop a theory of education built on empiricist foundations, pragmatism can be seen as an important counterblast to those rationalist assumptions which we are claiming have gone too long unchallenged in the education debate. It thus illustrates very effectively the general theme of this book. For it has led to the emergence of a quite different theory of education and a quite distinctive approach to the practice of education. Its view of both the theory and the practice of education, however, has constantly been analysed, reviewed and criticized from a completely inappropriate rationalist perspective. It has been seen as a distinctive theory of education but not at the same time, and more fundamentally, as a distinctive theory of knowledge. Nowhere is this more apparent than in that muddled debate which continues to bedevil the development of Primary education in this country, as we shall see more fully in Chapter 5. For it is in this sector that pragmatism has been most significant in influencing educational practice and yet the practices it has led to have constantly been evaluated in terms of those rationalist assumptions about knowledge we have set out in earlier chapters. There is little evidence of any appreciation that, to be effective, or even to be coherent and relevant, the debate must be conducted at a much deeper philosophical level. Nowhere is the central problem this book addresses itself to more clearly revealed.

For all of these reasons, then, a discussion of pragmatism represents the most appropriate culmination to our brief exploration of epistemology and the most effective bridge to those specific areas of the educational debate to which we turn in Part Two.

The origins of pragmatism

General influences

Pragmatism was not born, fully developed, from the head of Dewey. Like all philosophical theories it evolved. And an understanding of its evolution is crucial to an appreciation of its major features. There are two aspects of that evolution which are important. First, there are some general influences, both those which are characteristic of the intellectual climate of his time internationally and others which may perhaps be seen as particular to the American scene. Secondly, there are the specific theories of Dewey's forerunners, and in particular two men, the philosopher, Charles Sanders Peirce (1839-1914), who was the first to use the term 'pragmatism', and William James (1842-1910) who developed (Peirce would have said 'distorted') some of Peirce's basic concepts in a biological/psychological context. Each of these influences we must explore in turn, the second in rather more detail than the first.

Mention was made in Chapter 2 of the massive influence of the German Idealist movement on the development of philosophy in the nineteenth century. That influence is clearly at work also in the growth of pragmatism. In particular, the view, perhaps most clearly expressed by Hegel, of the universe and all aspects of human existence as explicable in rational terms is a major underlying theme.

This is reinforced, or, rather, modified, by a second major feature of the intellectual scene in the second half of the nineteenth century. In 1859, the year in which Dewey was born, Darwin published his *Origin of Species* and, while one does not want to suggest that the young Dewey sat in his cot avidly reading a first edition of this highly influential work, it must be stressed that the general notion of evolution which that work expounded had a profound effect on many aspects of intellectual development for the rest of that century and, indeed, well into the present century. The idea that all aspects of the universe can only be properly understood if seen in terms of a continuous state of evolution is another fundamental theme of Dewey's pragmatism.

Darwin's theory is different from that of Hegel and the other German Idealists in a fundamental way. For it does not claim that the process of evolution which it posits is any kind of unfolding of reason or rationality or the Absolute or any other kind of metaphysical entity or notion. It does not view it as a process towards an ultimate state of perfection but merely as a continuous process of change. It thus rejects that rationalist metaphysical perspective which we have seen is central to Hegelianism and opens the way for an empiricist version of evolution, again another basic feature of pragmatism. As Dewey puts it (although in doing so he reveals a major dilemma of his work), 'not perfection as the final goal, but the ever-enduring process of perfecting, maturing, refining is the aim of living . . . Growth itself is the only moral "end".'

This in turn reflects another major influence on his work, the prevalent belief in the superiority of scientific knowledge. It is clear throughout that Dewey's model for all knowledge is the experimental knowledge of the natural scientist. Indeed, pragmatism itself is often referred to as 'experimentalism'. For Dewey, as we shall see in more detail later in this chapter, knowledge develops through the framing and testing of hypotheses, and he believes that it is by this same method that we can attain knowledge in all fields — not only in the field of science but also in those of morals, aesthetics, politics and education. It is here that we see encapsulated that fusion which his philosophy attempts between rationalism and empiricism, the solution he offers to the dilemma of values. In brief, his claim is that all aspects of human life are explicable in rational and objective terms, as Hegel had claimed, but their explanation is not to be found in any metaphysical theory nor in any concept of rationality *per se* but by the extension and application of the observational methods of the natural scientist, by the framing and testing of hypotheses. Furthermore, such knowledge will not be characterized by the certainty claimed by the rationalist; it will be tentative, hypothetical and subject to continuous change and evolution. Nevertheless, at any given point in time, knowledge in all spheres, including those problematic spheres of values, will have an, albeit tentative, objectivity. There will be agreement amongst all who view the world rationally as to what constitutes the agreed knowledge of any one time.

To these general intellectual influences on the development of pragmatism must be added the more specific effects of the American society in which Dewey lived and worked. Pragmatism has rightly been described as 'in a real sense an expression of American culture' (Childs 1956, p.3). That culture, throughout his lifetime, was in a constant state of flux and turmoil. The same has been true in many ways of all societies, especially during the last few decades, but from the middle of the last to the middle of the present century it was a particular characteristic of the USA. Furthermore, the rapid change experienced there was not only industrial and economic, it was, consequentially, social and moral too.

Values, standards, ways of life were changing rapidly in a manner with which we are now all familiar. In such a context, it was difficult to propound any theory of permanence and stability of values. The notion of social change and evolution had to be built into any theory of social living which was to have any kind of claim to credence. Thus Dewey argues that, in a society whose values are changing so rapidly, a complete overhaul is needed of our ways of thinking, a total reappraisal of our habits of thought. Social and moral problems must be faced not with the concepts and the modes of thinking we have inherited from the ancient world but with new patterns of thought evolved to meet present-day needs, with the kind of knowledge 'with which we operate our machines' (Nathanson 1951, p.86). Again we see him being urged towards that extension of scientific method we noted just now. Our approach to all problems must be a scientific approach, but it must be properly scientific in that, like all science, it must be open-ended — open to change, to modification, to continuous adaptation. Social and moral evolution must be acknowledged and responded to in the same way as all other forms of evolution.

These, then, were the main general influences on the development of Dewey's pragmatism. We shall see them all reflected and reinforced in the specific influences of Charles Sanders Peirce and William James to which we now turn.

Charles Sanders Peirce (1839-1914)

C.S. Peirce was a logician and his prime interest was in questions of meaning. The theory for which he coined the term 'pragmatism' was a method of logical analysis he had devised to determine 'the meanings of intellectual concepts, that is, of those upon which reasoning may hinge' (quoted Gallie 1952, p.11). It was a method devised to clarify, and sometimes to eliminate, some traditional metaphysical questions and he developed it into a systematized theory of logic. His original formulation of it took the form of this maxim: 'Consider what effects, that might conceivably have practical bearings, we conceive the object of our conception to have. Then, our conception of these effects is the whole of our conception of the object' (quoted ibid. and Childs 1956, p.47). In short, meaning is a matter of consequences and we are reminded here of the notion of 'meaning as use' which G.E. Moore and Wittgenstein were to offer a good deal later. We must consider this a little more fully in order to see its main implications for the later theories of John Dewey.

Peirce is concerned to develop a theory of meaning of a kind sufficiently sophisticated to provide a base for major scientific advance. In particular, he is critical of the theory of meaning of Berkeley which suggests that a term only has meaning if we can frame an idea which corresponds to it (Gallie 1952). By 'idea' Berkeley means something like a mental image. Peirce regards this as a very limiting definition of meaning and argues that many concepts of great value in the development of scientific knowledge cannot be shown to have meaning on this definition. If this had been used in mathematics, he says, 'if everything about negative quantities, the square root of minus terms, and infinitesimals, had been excluded from the subject on this ground that we can form no idea of such things, then science would have been simplified no doubt, simplified by never advancing to more difficult matters' (quoted Gallie op.cit., p.14). Peirce offers us a more sophisticated formula for discovering if an abstract term has meaning, a formula based on use. An abstract term has meaning if, and only if, we can use it productively. The meaning is to be found in the practical effects our conception has. 'If I have learnt a formula in gibberish which in any way jogs my memory so as to enable me . . . to act as though I had a general idea, what possible utility is there in distinguishing between such a gibberish formula and an idea' (quoted ibid.). If a concept has a practical effect, it has meaning; and if two concepts have different effects, then they are to be distinguished.

Pragmatism, then, is for Peirce 'an instrument of logical clarification and analysis' (op.cit., p.17) and it is neither necessary nor appropriate in this context to pursue his statement of it further. It is important, however, to identify several aspects of his views which have significance for an understanding of those of Dewey.

The first of these is that, in developing a new theory of meaning, Peirce is concerned not merely to provide a formula by which we can ascribe meaning to complex intellectual concepts; he is also concerned to offer a device for demonstrating the meaninglessness of many abstract concepts, especially in the field of metaphysics. In other words, although by no means an out-and-out empiricist, he is attempting what others were later to take to extremes, a challenge to many of the metaphysical claims and notions of rationalism.

Secondly, it is important to note that Peirce is led to the particular theory of meaning he offers us by his belief in the experimental method of science as the only satisfactory way of pursuing knowledge or of seeking security of belief. Scientific method rejects private and purely arbitrary opinion and looks to the test and the criticism of others and this method of experimental inquiry is, he claims, superior to all others because of its objectivity. 'Though the object of the final opinion depends on what that opinion is, yet what that opinion is does not depend on what you or I or any man thinks' (quoted Childs 1956, p.44).

Thirdly, we must note that Peirce's theory of meaning is a result of precisely this kind of the application of scientific, experimental method. 'All pragmatists will further agree that their method of ascertaining the meaning of words and concepts is no other than that experimental method by which all the successful sciences (in which number nobody in his senses would include metaphysics) have reached the degrees of certainty that are severally proper to them today; this experimental method being itself nothing but a particular application of an older logical rule, "By their fruits ye shall know them" ' (quoted op.cit. p.46). This idea that we must look to results, to consequences, to 'what works' is central to pragmatism for reasons which will become clear as we turn to a consideration of the contribution of William James to its development.

William James (1842-1910)

William James was a psychologist/biologist (the distinction being nowhere near as clear at the end of the last century as it is today). His early work led him to the belief that mental processes can best be understood by reference to biological needs and functions, that certain biological interests underlie all thinking, that thinking is directed at satisfying the needs of the organism. The emphasis is thus on the personal nature of thought. A person thinks in order to solve the problems that face him or her. Thought is the instrument used by the individual to solve problems and to adapt to new situations. For this reason, we sometimes find this view called 'instrumentalism'. This notion of thought, and indeed knowledge, as an instrument for problem-solving is a major feature of Dewey's philosophy, as we shall see.

First, however, we must note a further aspect of James' theory, one with which Dewey profoundly disagreed and which is crucial to a proper understanding of Dewey's philosophy. For James took the further step of claiming that, if thinking is undertaken and knowledge is developed to solve problems, then that knowledge is true which solves these problems satisfactorily. Thus he introduces the very important notion that truth is a human construct, a property of our assertions about things and not of those things themselves, and this clearly is a crucial point of disagreement with the rationalist, a point which it is equally crucial to be clear about in discussions of education. 'An idea,' says James, 'is "true" so long as to believe it is profitable to our lives' (quoted Russell 1939, p.844); 'the true is only the expedient in the way of our thinking' (quoted ibid.); 'our obligation to seek truth is part of our general obligation to do what pays' (quoted ibid.); 'most of our intellectual beliefs can be justified only on grounds of their social, moral and biological utility' (quoted Gallie, p.21). This is the source of that view of truth as 'what works' which is a central tenet of pragmatism, but which has been much misunderstood and misinterpreted by critics of pragmatism, especially those exploring its implications for education.

For, clearly, there are two major interpretations one can make of this view. The first, that of James, which Dewey totally rejected, is that thought, knowledge, truth become totally personal and subjective concepts. Each organism is faced with its own peculiar problems; it thinks, frames hypotheses and acts on them, in order to solve these problems; successful hypotheses, those which work, are stored up for future reference. This is how knowledge is developed – at a completely individual level – and truth is what works for me. If it does not work for you, then it is not for you a truth. James, for example, applied this theory to the question of the existence of God and concluded that since the hypothesis that God exists works satisfactorily for some people, then for those people it is true; for others, it is not.

This view of the individual nature of knowledge and of truth is comparable to the view expressed currently within phenomenological sociology, although here it is reached from an awareness of the individuality of our perceptions rather than from a theory about the problem-solving nature of thought. In essence, however, it is much the same and its implications not only for the generation of any coherent body of knowledge but also for the development of a satisfactory theory of education are far-reaching. It is this, therefore, which has attracted the critics of pragmatism, especially as a theory of education, so that it is important to be clear that this is not the view of Dewey – nor indeed is it that of Peirce who, on discovering what James was using the term pragmatism to describe, decided to call his own theory 'pragmaticism', a name, he said, ugly enough to be safe from kidnappers.

For Dewey, as for Peirce, the supreme method of knowledge-getting is the experimental method of science and the essence of that, as we saw in our discussion of Peirce's views, is its objectivity. Dewey accepts James' claim that truth is a human construct, a property not of things but of our assertions about things. A belief is a kind of prediction; both are true if they produce satisfactory consequences when acted on. Dewey, however, will not accept James' interpretation of 'satisfactory' as extending to situations in which our ideas, beliefs or predictions 'tend to produce emotional consequences that are deemed "satisfactory" ' (Childs 1956, p.142). He restricts his definition of 'satisfactory', and thus of 'truth', to those situations in which our beliefs or ideas are confirmed by 'observed events which follow from our acts or experiments' (ibid.). In other words, Dewey does not accept the kind of subjectivist conception of truth adopted by James. Ideas or beliefs must satisfy objective criteria. A term he uses is 'warranted assertibility'. They must be warranted or verified by data and consequences which are public in nature. Truth and knowledge can only be based on a kind of 'public empiricism'. As Dewey says, 'the best definition of *truth* from the logical standpoint which is known to me is that of Peirce: "The opinion which is fated to be ultimately agreed by all who investigate is what we mean by the truth, and the object represented by this opinion is the real"' (Dewey 1938a). The point is put more succinctly by Peirce in a letter to James in which, after appealing to him 'to try to learn to think with more exactitude' he goes on to tell him that 'truth is public' (quoted Gallie 1952, p.29).

Thus both Peirce and Dewey maintain their commitment to the experimental method of science and their confidence in this as a source of objective knowledge. Both, however, accept a weaker indefinition of 'objectivity' than that of the rationalist. For, while they claim 'that meaning and truth are empirical affairs to be developed and tested by operational or experimental procedures' (Childs 1956, p.143), they also recognize that those procedures are self-correcting, so that all the knowledge they generate has to be recognized as being tentative, provisional, hypothetical and thus subject to tests of further experience. Knowledge, for the pragmatist, consists not of the eternal truths of the rationalist, but must be seen as temporary, if not actually ephemeral.

This examination of James' notion of truth and especially of Dewey's reaction to it has taken us some way towards an understanding of Dewey's developed theory of knowledge. We must now attempt to elucidate this in greater detail. In doing so, we will also be exploring his theory of education, and, indeed, his theories of man and society, since for Dewey these are inseparable in any philosophical system.

John Dewey's pragmatism

The view of truth which we have just seen adopted by Dewey and his wholehearted acceptance of the concept of evolution, to which we referred earlier, form the two pillars of his theory of knowledge. For his view of knowledge, truth, and indeed intelligence, is not only instrumental and experimental, it is also evolutionary. Truth, for him, is not something fixed and final but is subject to constant change and development. Truth evolves since it is not a matter of some kind of correspondence; it is a matter of what works in a changing and evolving situation. Knowledge is not a body of facts which grows bigger and bigger as we come to discover more and more about the world about us, or have more and more revealed to us by God; knowledge itself evolves as we find different solutions, and indeed different problem-solving techniques, for the ever-new problems we have to face. And man's intelligence evolves as he develops it to overcome the obstacles and to solve the problems presented to him by his ever-evolving environment.

This he does, however, by developing a public body of knowledge, an agreed corpus of hypotheses which enjoy general current acceptance but which must be recognized as tentative, as hypothetical, as subject, therefore, to constant review and modification.

This theory of knowledge is the foundation of his philosophy and provides the clue to an understanding of his views on morals, on aesthetics, on politics and on education. For it will be clear that the kind of epistemological theory Dewey offers is the result not of any metaphysical exploration of knowledge as an abstract entity, with a status independent of the knower, of the kind envisaged by the rationalist, but of an examination of knowledge as a social phenomenon, as something which is socially constructed, created by man rather than discovered by him or revealed to him. And so this is not merely a theory of knowledge, it is also and at the same time a theory of man, a theory of society and a theory of education. This is why, as we saw earlier, he regards philosophy and the theory of education as virtually identical. This is why it is not possible to examine productively his views in any of these spheres in isolation from each other. And this is why much of the criticism of Dewey's theory of education, and of its practice, has gone badly wrong, since it has failed to consider that theory of education in the context of its underpinning epistemology and has, like so many of the criticisms this book is concerned to identify, made the crucial category mistake of evaluating it against a totally inappropriate set of criteria, culled from a quite different epistemological tradition.

The theory of education which Dewey builds onto, or perhaps into, this kind of epistemological foundation begins inevitably with the notion of education as experience. It cannot be seen in terms of the acquisition of bodies of fixed and largely inert knowledge. If knowledge itself is in a constant state of evolution, then the process of education must acknowledge and allow for this; it must therefore be seen in terms of the developing experience of the educand. For knowledge as Dewey defines it cannot be attained by the assimilation of information, it can only be gained by involvement in the process of knowledge-using and thus of knowledge-getting, by the experience of developing knowledge in order to solve problems. Educational planning, therefore, must start not with a statement of the bodies of knowledge to be acquired but with the devices and strategies by which this kind of experience can be made available to each individual pupil. Education is not a matter of assimilating what is currently accepted as the corpus of human knowledge (Warnock 1977), it is a process of developing the powers and the attitudes of mind which make possible the continued evolution of that knowledge. If knowledge is evolving we must not merely learn what is currently accepted, we must learn also how to develop new knowledge. This can only be done if pupils have genuine experiences, if they are faced with genuine problems and assisted to develop the abilities needed to solve them, in particular by the framing and testing of hypotheses. Thus the emphasis is on education as a process of development in which the quality of that development is crucial rather than the quantity of obsolescent information stored. 'Not knowledge but self-realization is the goal' (1902).

It is here, of course, that one begins to see the link between this view and the Hadow/Plowden philosophy of Primary education in England, a link we will pursue more fully in Chapter 5. We can also see here the basic rationale for some recent curriculum projects, such as the Schools Council's Learning Through Science Project. For essentially the notion is that of development *through* the acquisition of knowledge and not merely such acquisition itself. The emphasis is on the quality and nature of the learning experience rather than its content.

It will also be clear that a strong argument in support of this view comes not merely from this particular theory of knowledge but also from a consideration of that process of rapid economic and social change to which reference was made earlier as a major influence on Dewey's thinking. It is clear not only from an analysis of knowledge but from the most casual glance at current and recent developments in society that today's knowledge is unlikely to solve tomorrow's problems any more than today's problems can be solved by yesterday's knowledge. Hence, as Carl Rogers (1969, p.104) has said,

> We are . . . faced with an entirely new situation where the goal of education, if we are to survive, is the facilitation of change and learning. The only man who is educated is the man who has learned how to learn; the man who has learned to adapt and change; the man who has realized that no knowledge is secure, that only the process of seeking knowledge gives a base for security. Changingness, a reliance on process rather than upon static knowledge, is the only thing that makes sense as a goal for education in the modern world.

One cannot but be amazed at how long this message is taking to reach people, even the so-called professionals, at how tightly people cling to traditional viewpoints, even when they have become demonstrably inappropriate.

If education must first be viewed as experience, its second major characteristic must be that it is a process of growth. There are two important aspects of this claim. The first is that education must be seen as a continuous lifelong process, not as a means to some extrinsic end. One of the fallacious ideas of traditional approaches to education which Dewey criticizes is that 'growth is regarded as *having* an end instead of *being* an end' (1916). 'Since in reality there is nothing to which growth is relative save more growth, there is nothing to which education is subordinate save more education' (op.cit.). 'The educational process has no end beyond itself; it is its own end' (op.cit.). Education then must be seen and planned as a process and not in terms of any assumed products. Out, therefore, goes the product model of educational planning along with the content model.

Secondly, as a corollary of this, growth itself becomes the only criterion by which we can evaluate educational success. We cannot evaluate this kind of education in terms of the content assimilated nor in terms of the extrinsic objectives attained. It can only be evaluated in terms of the process it claims to be. Again, therefore, we see how wrong it is to evaluate this kind of education in terms inappropriate to it. If education is a process of growth, we can only evaluate it in terms of the quality of that growth and we can only define what we mean by quality of growth in terms of its contribution to further growth. Dewey has often been criticized on the grounds that his philosophy will not allow him to make qualitative judgements between different kinds of knowledge and activity, between reading Shakespeare and pulling legs off flies (this seems to be a popular example) or between learning to be a research chemist and learning to be a burglar. Such criticisms completely fail to understand his philosophical position, which, as was suggested above, sets out to establish objective criteria of judgement. They also fail to appreciate what he means when he claims that it is the quality of growth rather than its direction that is the criterion by which we must assess its worth.

That a man may grow in efficiency as a burglar, as a gangster, or as a corrupt politician, cannot be doubted. But from the standpoint of growth as education and education as growth the question is whether growth in this direction promotes or retards growth in general. Does this form of growth create conditions for further growth, or does it set up conditions that shut off the person who has grown in this particular direction from the occasions, stimuli and opportunities for continuing growth in new directions (Dewey 1938b).

Education is not to be equated with experience. It does not consist of any old experiences. 'Some experiences are miseducative' (op.cit.), not in that they are regarded as immoral nor in that they consist of the acquisition of knowledge which is not felt to measure up to some assumed standards of quality, but in that they are blind alleys, they are likely to inhibit rather than promote further growth. This is what Dewey calls the 'experiential continuum' (op.cit.) and it is a far more useful criterion of educational measurement than has often been allowed, although one can see why people shy away from its subtleties and complexities.

The role of the educator in this process of growth then is that of facilitator of the process. He or she is not there to direct the learning towards those experiences regarded as worthwhile in any rationalist or intrinsic sense, but to offer guidance to the educand in his or her development towards continued and continuing experience.

For to be directive over the content of pupils' learning is not only to restrict them to that knowledge which is currently accepted as valid and thus to hinder them from developing a proper awareness of the evolutionary nature of knowledge, it is also to impose the current system of values upon them and to prevent them from recognizing that values too change and develop. It is thus a form of indoctrination, the imposition of those values which have current acceptance; it is precisely what recent developments in the sociology of education have drawn our attention to — the use of knowledge as a means of social control. True education, in the context of the pragmatist's theory of knowledge, cannot be a matter of the imposition from without of adult values, whatever the source and presumed status of those values.

Many critics of this view have assumed that if adults are not to decide on the content of pupils' education, the only alternative is a free-for-all in which pupils are permitted to do whatever they wish. However, the relationship between the content and the process of education is infinitely more subtle than this kind of criticism appreciates. Again Dewey's answer is to be found in the notion of 'guidance'. Education is the process by which the individual is led towards the development of new knowledge and new values. And that is a far more sophisticated process than has usually been recognized.

> The fundamental factors in the educative process are an immature, under-developed being; and certain social aims, meanings, values incarnate in the mature experience of the adult. The educative process is the due interaction of these forces. Such a conception of each in relation to the other as facilitates completest and freest interaction is the essence of educational theory. But here comes the effort of thought. It is easier to see the conditions in their separateness, to insist upon one at the expense of the other, to make antagonists of them, than to discover a reality to which each belongs (Dewey 1902). There are those who see no alternative between forcing the child from without or leaving him entirely alone. Seeing no alternative, some choose one mode, some another (op.cit.).

This quotation encapsulates a problem which has been central to the education debate for many years — at least, since the publication of Rousseau's *Émile*. It also states clearly Dewey's attempt to resolve the problem by suggesting we cease to see it as a dichotomy and begin to search for a more sophisticated solution.

It is also clear, however, that such a solution will only be found if the search begins from a looser view of knowledge than that of the rationalist, a view that acknowledges the impossibility of achieving certainty in any area of human experience and one which, especially, is prepared to recognize this as true in the realm of values. For, even if one is inclined towards a view of knowledge in the 'scientific' sphere as reasonably solid or certain, it is increasingly difficult to accept the rationalist view of knowledge in the moral sphere as being fixed and static. Moral values have evolved detectably in our own lifetime and it is now very difficult to maintain with the rationalist that this represents either a deterioration from some absolute standard or a movement towards some kind of future absolute perfection. It makes much more sense to see values as socially constructed and as relative to particular societies and even to particular groups in society, so that some would want to argue, as we have seen, that 'knowledge' is not an appropriate word to use in the sphere of values.

This is one point, however, at which the Hegelian influence on Dewey is most apparent. For, although he accepts, indeed insists, that values — moral, aesthetic, political — evolve along with all else, he also wishes to claim that it is possible to attain that status of current acceptance in this area that we have seen him arguing for in the area of 'scientific' knowledge. Values, for Dewey, are exactly like other probable empirical hypotheses. They are to be tested by the criterion of whether they 'work' or not. And again this is a question not of whether they work for you and me as individuals, but of whether they work for everyone collectively, whether they are such as to be accepted generally as currently valid. Values in all spheres are as much a matter of experimentation and evidence as knowledge in any other area.

Here again we see that Dewey is attempting a reconciliation of that dilemma we identified earlier, that polarity between the absolute values of the rationalist and the total relativism of extreme versions of empiricism. Whether he succeeds is a matter for debate and this is not the place to pursue that issue.

One thing we must note, however, as emerging from this, and that is the clear indication that for Dewey all knowledge is of the same kind. There is no basis for any claim of the kind pressed upon educationists by Paul Hirst (1965) and Philip Phenix (1964) that human knowledge is divided into several discrete logical categories. Thus, just as there is no basis in pragmatism for arguing for a certain fixed content to the educational curriculum, there is equally no basis for claiming that that content should include those several different subjects or disciplines into which knowledge is said to be divided.

Again we see that such arguments derive from an assumed rationalist perspective. If one rejects that perspective they fall, so that to criticize, for example, a curriculum developed along pragmatist lines, such as that still to be found in many Primary schools, on the grounds that it fails to ensure the exposure of pupils to or their initiation into all forms of knowledge (Dearden 1968, 1976), is to miss the point completely. It is another example of that category error, which this book is concerned throughout to highlight, of evaluating particular forms of education in terms totally inappropriate to them.

Dewey recognizes that knowledge is in fact organized into separate subjects or bodies. He does not, however, regard these as based on logical differences but merely as matters of practical convenience, as social constructs. Furthermore, he stresses too that the divisions, since they have a practical rather than a logical justification, must themselves be permitted to change and to evolve. There is a good deal in our recent experience of the evolution of knowledge to support this view. What it means for the curriculum is that subject divisions must only be allowed to emerge and develop when they make sense to the child in the organization of his or her own knowledge. Otherwise, they will again represent an imposition of adult categories on the next generation and thus act as inhibitors of continued evolution.

Mention must be made finally of the social dimension of Dewey's theory. We said earlier that it is a theory not only of knowledge nor even of education but of man, morals and society. It will be clear that, to be consistent to his basic position, Dewey must recognize that like knowledge, like man, like values of all kinds, society also evolves. It must, therefore, be open to and accepting of change and development. Thus he must be opposed to all forms of totalitarianism, which by definition are concerned to preserve the *status quo,* or at least to ensure development along predetermined lines.

For him 'democracy' is the term which describes the only kind of society which is open to and welcoming of continuous evolution and development. But he does not have in mind any particular form of political organization or set of procedures. 'A democracy is more than a form of government; it is primarily a mode of associated living, of conjoint communicated experience' (Dewey 1916). 'Universal suffrage, recurring elections, responsibility of those who are in political power to the voters, and other factors of democratic government are means that have been found expedient for realising democracy as the truly human way of living. They are not a final end and a final value' (Dewey 1915). The notion of democracy itself must be open to the same kind of modification and change as all else in a world of continuous evolution. And this in many ways is the coping-stone of his theory.

> The very idea of democracy, the meaning of democracy, must be continually explored afresh; it has to be constantly discovered and rediscovered, remade and reorganized; while the political and economic and social institutions in which it is embodied have to be remade and reorganized to meet the changes that are going on in the development of new needs on the part of human beings and new resources for satisfying those needs. No form of life does or can stand still; it either goes forward or it goes backward, and the end of the backward road is death. Democracy as a form of life cannot stand still. It, too, if it is to live must go forward to meet the changes that are here and that are coming (1916).

If this is the culmination of his social theory, it is also a keystone of his education theory. For it is here that we see the interlinking of his view of education and his view of society in its wider aspects. An open, democratic society is necessary for the development of the kind of open system of education he advocates. But, similarly, that open system of education is vital to the continued development of democracy. Schools must be themselves democratic communities; they must have their own 'embryonic community life'. They must be places where pupils can grow and develop through experiences which are genuinely their own but which are at the same time shared with others and which lead to the development of knowledge and of values which are shared and accepted by others. They must not be places where 'anything goes' nor must they be places where pupils are required merely to assimilate the knowledge and the values of their elders.

Thus we see that it was Dewey's concern to develop a theory of knowledge which would avoid both the total certainty of the rationalist and the scepticism of extreme forms of empiricism, a theory of values which would avoid the dogmatism of rationalism and the complete relativism to which empiricism appeared to be leading, and a theory of education which would avoid the 'transmission', and thus 'imposition', model to which rationalism inevitably leads and the complete 'laissez-faire' approach which has been many people's interpretation of the educational advice of Rousseau and many of his equally illustrious successors.

Whether he has succeeded or not is a major question, but it is another question. It is not one which it is the intention of tackling here. Certainly, there are many points at which one might direct a critical appraisal of this theory, perhaps especially at his attempt to establish a non-rationalist basis for an objective theory of values. The concern here, however, is merely to make three points. The first of these is that any critical appraisal must be made in the context of the theory of knowledge which is the foundation of his theories of man, of values, of politics and of education. Criticisms which are not mounted within that context and fail even to recognize and appreciate that context have no force whatever; they are discussions which go on in a different world, in fact in a vacuum. Secondly, it must be stressed that such weaknesses as this theory undoubtedly has are no greater than those we have seen in other epistemological theories and probably a good deal less serious than those apparent in the rationalist's epistemology. Thirdly, the prime concern here has been to establish clearly and beyond any doubt that there are several views of knowledge which can legitimately be taken, that none of these is without its difficulties, that none, therefore, has any claim to be accepted as supreme, that the same is true consequently of the different theories of education to which they lead, and that not to acknowledge this in discussing and evaluating these theories is to be guilty of either a sinister form of intellectual arrogance or an even more dangerous form of ignorance.

However, it must also be made clear that a further purpose of this discussion of Dewey's theory of education has been to reveal that it is a theory which, while allowing for its imperfections, it is very difficult for one not to see as offering far more attractive possibilities than the rationalist view which it attempts to replace. It is a theory which acknowledges those changes and developments in human knowledge, even in the 'scientific' sphere, which we saw in Chapter 2 rationalism cannot accommodate. It is a theory which, while recognizing the importance of the individual in a democratic social organization, attempts to reconcile that individualism with membership of a larger group or groups, not by demanding the denial of individuality but by insisting on the acceptance of joint and collective responsibility for continued evolution and development. It is thus a theory which lends itself better to the planning of education in any society which lays claim to offering its members freedom and/or equality.

Summary and conclusions

This chapter has attempted to identify the main features of the philosophical theory known as pragmatism both as a theory of knowledge and as a theory of education and society, first, by exploring its origins and the historical factors which seem to have exercised a major influence on its development and, secondly, by picking out the key elements in the developed theory of pragmatism we have been offered by John Dewey.

Those key elements were seen to include an acceptance of the concept of evolution and of all that that entails not only for the rationalist's view of knowledge as fixed and static but also, and consequentially, for the planning of educational provision. For we saw that this notion leads us away from that confident conviction, still displayed by many, both professional and lay, that we can plan education merely by making statements of the knowledge content to which pupils must be exposed, towards a recognition of the fact that education is a far more subtle process than this, a process of guided growth and development, and that the role of knowledge-content in that process is both far more complex than is often acknowledged and subsidiary to other considerations.

A second major feature was its preference for scientific method as the source of the most secure kind of knowledge we can ever hope to attain.

The only way to knowledge, it was claimed, is via the framing and testing of hypotheses, and the essential test of any hypothesis is that of whether it works or not. We noted further, however, that this question of whether a hypothesis works or not is to be interpreted in an objective, impersonal sense rather than in that subjective sense that William James wished to give it and which has been the focus of much subsequent criticism.

A third important element in this philosophy is its view of values. For, while recognizing the problematic nature of values of all kinds and stressing the need to acknowledge that values, like everything else, must be seen as constantly changing and evolving, this philosophical theory attempts also to establish some security in this sphere by arguing that 'knowledge' in this area can be or can become at least as secure as knowledge in other fields, that value hypotheses can be framed and tested and shown to be valid in the same way as other hypotheses of a more straightforwardly 'scientific' kind. In this we saw a difficulty, but we also suggested that it was a gallant attempt to strike a balance between the dogmatic certainty of rationalism and the negative uncertainty and scepticism to which other empiricist positions appeared to lead.

We then noted that the final interlocking piece of this jigsaw puzzle was the notion of an evolving democratic social organization, one which by being open to continuous evolution itself would permit the continuous evolution of everything else — of knowledge, of values, of man, of education. Again it was suggested that this could be seen as an attempt to avoid, on the one hand, those totalitarian political solutions to which rationalism has seemed to point and, on the other hand, the complete nihilism to which some empiricist theories appear to lead.

The main concern in this chapter, however, has not been either to advocate or to criticize these views. It has been that of the book as a whole, namely to establish that different views of knowledge can quite legitimately be taken, that these will lead to different beliefs as to how educational provision should be planned and organized and that these different beliefs must be acknowledged and evaluated in their own terms and not by reference to criteria which are inappropriate to them.

An attempt has been made in these first three chapters to suggest that there are at least two fundamentally different theories of knowledge and that they will lead to at least two very different theories of education. Other views may be taken of education too which are not essentially interwoven with any theory of knowledge; we might, for example, see education in purely instrumental terms as the provision of knowledge and skills which can be employed for economic productivity regardless of any concern with the validity of knowledge or values or with the effects of such learning on the individual. What has perhaps emerged from this chapter, however, is the peculiar suitability of the kind of educational theory Dewey has outlined to any society which is genuinely concerned with the quality of the life of its members, with ideas of freedom and/or equality and thus with the nature of the learning and the development which education should be concerned to promote.

It is this kind of thinking, and in particular this view of knowledge, which has been at the root of those attempts to plan education in terms of the development of pupils rather than the transmission of knowledge, to see educational processes as more important in curriculum planning than statements of curriculum content, and thus to avoid that imposition of values which, once one concedes that these must be, if not totally subjective, then at the very least impermanent, must be seen as counter-productive to the notion of education as individual development and as incompatible with the idea of democratic living.

We now turn to a consideration of some further reasons for adopting this view of education. For Chapter 4 will attempt to provide a summary of some of the different positions which can be taken on the question of the nature and validity of knowledge and of the different views which can consequentially be taken on education. This will be offered as a basis from which we can explore and evaluate in Part Two some major aspects of the current debate over educational provision, which seems to reveal not only serious misunderstanding in this area but also important and disturbing deficiencies when viewed in the light of the kind of approach to education this chapter has outlined.

CHAPTER 4

KNOWLEDGE, VALUES AND CURRICULUM PLANNING — SOME OTHER PERSPECTIVES

There is nothing either good or bad, but thinking makes it so.
(Shakespeare, *Hamlet*)

The previous chapters have been largely philosophical in their content, although every attempt has been made to retain as far as possible the focus on education and to point up the implications of the philosophical debate for major educational issues. It is now necessary to shift the focus more directly onto those educational issues. The purpose of this concluding chapter to Part One, then, is to summarize the debate over knowledge, to reveal its particular relevance to questions of values and to highlight its major implications for education, so that Part Two can explore in greater detail certain issues of current importance for education to which the problem of knowledge is crucially relevant.

This we will do, first, by summarizing the major positions which can be, and have been, taken on the matter of knowledge, secondly, by revealing the quite different consequences all these have for questions of values and thus of education, in both its theory and its practice, and, thirdly, by looking at some of the criticisms, explicit and implied, of the rationalist and objectivist positions on knowledge and values which have emerged from two other sources, the 'new directions' in the sociology of education and the similarly new pointers offered by developmental psychology. The first of these will be used as a stepping-off point for a discussion of the politics of knowledge, the second for what will be a major theme of Part Two of this book, that notion of education as development rather than as the transmission of knowledge which was a major theme of the educational philosophy of John Dewey which Chapter 3 has just outlined.

With that in view, it may well be worth while beginning this chapter with a brief analysis of the concept of education or, since that may seem too much like claiming some kind of objective definition for what is essentially a value-laden activity, with a brief statement of what the writer sees as being the central components of education, the value positions, the principles from which all that is said about education in this book derives, and which he also believes can be detected in much that is said and written about education even when this claims to begin from different, and even incompatible, positions.

The concept of education

The reader may already have noticed that this book is peppered with phrases such as 'real education', 'true education', 'education in the full sense of the term'. The time has come to explain what is implied by such phrases.

The term 'education' is used very loosely by many people in many contexts and is thus used to refer to a wide variety of practices. People speak of 'liberal education' and of 'vocational education'; yet a moment's thought will reveal that there must be major distinctions between these concepts, so that it may not be especially helpful nor conducive to clarity of thought to use the term 'education' of both. Similarly, many current pronouncements by politicians and in official documents use the term to denote all that goes on in schools without attempting any finer distinctions between the many qualitatively different kinds of activity schools are concerned with. It will be helpful here to try to identify some of these finer distinctions, since their significance has underpinned much of our earlier discussion of knowledge and education and an awareness of them will be important for the discussions we are about to undertake in Part Two.

First, it is clear that teaching can take the form of simple instruction, the purpose of which is to communicate some kind of skill or knowledge of a 'factual' kind, and that this can be contrasted with the kind of teaching which is designed to promote understanding, a knowledge not only of *what* might be the case but also of *why* this is so. It might be claimed, and indeed it has been claimed (Peters 1965, 1966), that it is only of the latter kind of teaching that we normally use the term 'education'.

Secondly, and related to this, a distinction may, and indeed must, be drawn between teaching concerned with, or even deliberately designed to ensure, the uncritical acceptance of that which is the substance of such teaching and that which is framed in such a way as to encourage some kind of critical appraisal of what is being offered and thus intended to promote in the individual certain powers of critical appraisal and awareness. Some would argue that the former kind of teaching is a form of indoctrination, whether uncritical acceptance is the intention or merely the effect of such teaching. There is an important debate there. What is important here, however, is that few would be prepared, if encouraged to reflect on the usage, to use the term 'education' of such teaching but would rather reserve that term for the kind of teaching whose explicit purpose is to promote critical awareness in pupils. Another way of expressing this is to suggest that 'education' is a term only to be used of the kind of teaching which is genuinely aimed at producing autonomous human beings, people whose education has helped them to acquire the power to think for themselves and to make their own judgements.

Thus one major feature of what some people would claim to be essential components of any teaching which is to be called 'education' is that it should concern itself not merely with the acquisition of knowledge but with certain forms of intellectual development. At the very least it has to be accepted that there is an important distinction to be made here, whatever terminology we wish to use to describe it. Another way of looking at this is to view it from the other end, as it were, and to suggest that the educated person is not someone who has acquired a great store of knowledge but someone who has learnt to think for him or herself, to evaluate all things in an informed and properly critical manner, someone who evinces true understanding rather than mere knowledge. As Alfred North Whitehead suggested a long time ago, 'a merely well-informed man [we must now, of course, include woman in this stricture] is the most useless bore on God's earth' (1932, p.1). For 'education is the acquisition of the art of the utilisation of knowledge' (op.cit., p.6).

We may take this a little further and foreshadow what will be a major theme of Part Two by suggesting that this stance implies that education, as we saw Dewey suggesting, should concern itself much more with the development of the pupil than with the transmission or the acquisition of knowledge. There are two aspects of this which it is worth stressing here.

The first of these is the distinction which is often made between those things — activities, subjects, bodies of knowledge — which are pursued or which are included in the curriculum for their own sakes, those things which Richard Peters (1965, 1966) has called 'intrinsically worthwhile activities', and those whose justification is instrumental, utilitarian, even vocational, those things whose presence in the curriculum is justified not in terms of any intrinsic value it may be claimed they possess but in terms of the things they are intended to lead to — examination success, entry into further levels of the education system, access to a lucrative career, the enhancement of the economic well-being of society or whatever. There is no doubt that this is an important distinction nor that, again, most people would reserve the term 'education' for the former kind of curricular offering and deny it to the latter.

We must go a little further here, however. For the concept of an 'intrinsically worthwhile activity' is essentially a product of that rationalist epistemology we are suggesting is an inadequate base for curriculum planning. It is only from a rationalist perspective that one can argue that certain forms of activity possess some kind of value *in themselves*. Without that perspective, one has to acknowledge that value, like beauty, is to be found in the eye of the beholder. One might have to concede, therefore, that education consists only of those activities which individuals pursue because they see value in the activities themselves rather than in their outcome or their products.

It will be a contention of this book, however, that the crucial distinction to be made is not between intrinsic and instrumental justifications for the inclusion of activities, subjects or bodies of knowledge in the curriculum, but rather between activities justified in terms of either their content or their intended outcomes on the one hand and those, on the other, whose justification is to be sought in the contribution they are felt to make to the development of the pupil. The implication of viewing education as growth or development is that only those curriculum activities selected as contributory to those processes of growth and development qualify for the description 'educational'. That which is 'educational', it is being claimed, is that whose justification is to be found not in its utility, nor in the knowledge-content itself, nor even in the ways in which both teacher and taught view that knowledge-content, but in the fact that it represents a genuine attempt to promote the development of its recipients.

Another way of expressing this is to suggest that we must add a third approach to education and curriculum planning to the two which can be readily recognized in traditional views. It is clear that, while some people have wished to argue that education must be planned by reference to the intrinsic value of certain kinds of human knowledge, others have claimed that the only basis for such planning is a concern with the utility of the knowledge which is offered (Woods and Barrow 1975). It is equally clear that many of the current pronouncements from political sources to which

)een increasingly subjected in recent years in the United
attempt to steer an uneasy (and impossible) course between the
at is being suggested here is that there is a third criterion for the
n of the content of our curriculum, the criterion of potential
effec..veness in relation to the educational development of the pupil, that
our choice of curriculum content should be based not on economic or
vocational usefulness, nor on some notion of intrinsic value, but on a
concern with educational effectiveness, the promotion of the kind of
development we have just attempted to describe. A further contention is
that at root this is the concern of those who make claims about the
intrinsic value of certain kinds of knowledge and that the attempt to
maintain both positions simultaneously represents a serious inconsistency
in their views.

There is another aspect of this which will be seen to be important when
we consider some of the political dimensions of this debate later in this
chapter. The view of education which is often taken, and which is
particularly apparent in certain recent official pronouncements on the
curriculum in the United Kingdom, is that of education as the pursuit of
academic excellence. It will be argued later that this is a view which must
inevitably exclude a large proportion of the school population from any
real advantages which schooling might offer them and is a major barrier
to the attainment of anything approaching universal education. What
must be noted here is that it is a view which is rooted in that rationalist
epistemology whose inadequacies we are concerned to demonstrate and it
is a view which is at odds with that concept of education as a process of
growth and development we are concerned to describe. There is an
important distinction to be made between the academic and the
educational. To equate the two is to return to a rationalist view of
knowledge with all that we have seen that implies. The importance of this
distinction will emerge more clearly as our discussion proceeds.

These, then, are some of the distinctions we need to bear in mind when
attempting any kind of evaluation of schooling. It has been the contention
here that our customary usage of the term 'education', what we have
elsewhere referred to as 'education in the full sense', restricts that term to
activities which are not seen as instrumental, and which are designed to
promote the development of certain attitudes of mind, pre-eminent among
which is the ability to look critically at one's world and to reach one's own
conclusions about it, and, indeed, to achieve a measure of control over it.

It must be conceded, of course, that, as was suggested at the end of
Chapter 3, a number of views or theories of education can be legitimately

adopted. At a purely descriptive, and neutral, level what is being said here is that, since this is so, it is important to be clear about the particular theory one is adopting and the particular meaning one is giving to the term 'education'. For a major complaint of this book is that this is too seldom the case and that all too often the term 'education' is used as if it had but a single and universally agreed meaning. It is important to remember, therefore, that there are different views and meanings of education (in spite of what essentialist versions of philosophy might suggest) and that these must be distinguished.

The intention here, however, is to go further than that and to argue, as was done at the end of Chapter 3, that the definition of education which has just been offered reflects and represents a view of education peculiarly fitted to schooling in a democratic society and, indeed, most peculiarly so fitted, and that, conversely, the idea of education as the transmission of knowledge deemed to be objectively worthwhile and/or that of education as an instrumental process for the attainment of certain utilitarian and/or economic aims are inconsistent with and counter-productive to any notion of democratic living and, more specifically, any ideas we may have that education is a process by which individual freedom may be enhanced or social equality achieved. If those are our ideals, we must look for their attainment to the kind of democratic theory of knowledge and of education which we saw in the last chapter Dewey was at pains to advocate.

It is also worth noting here that this is the view of education which is also embraced by those people who have brought a directly and overtly rationalist epistemology into education theory, and it is here that the inconsistency of their position becomes most apparent. Richard Peters (1965, 1966), for example, has offered a most compelling analysis of the concept of education, claiming that what distinguishes it from other kinds and forms of teaching is its concern with the development of understanding, of critical awareness, of individual autonomy, but he seems to have failed to recognize the difficulties of reconciling that kind of definition with the view he also takes of education as initiation into worthwhile activities, activities whose worth is designated not by the autonomous individual concerned in the process but by the dictates of a rationalist epistemology. Similarly, Paul Hirst's (1965) concern that education should initiate pupils into the several different forms of understanding or of rationality is fundamentally a plea that we should see education in terms of certain processes of development (albeit intellectual development only). Again, however, a fundamental commitment to rationalism leads him to view this rather more in terms of the forms of understanding or of rationality themselves than of the processes of development of the pupils.

There are elements of this too in some of the current pronouncements of the politicians and those concerned to give voice, and even practical effect, to these pronouncements. Thus we are told (DES 1981, p.1) that 'what is taught in schools, and the way it is taught, should help all children to realise their potential to the fullest possible extent', that (DES 1980, p.2) 'few people would dissent from the proposition that schools should help pupils to develop lively enquiring minds' and that (DES 1981, p.3) schools should 'help pupils to develop the ability to question and argue rationally'. The emphasis on education as a process by which individual autonomy is developed is again clear. However, most of these documents, along with all the others from the same stable, move quickly into a discussion of curriculum predicated on a subject-based concept of what curriculum is, a view of the curriculum as designed to offer 'a sufficient grounding in the knowledge and skills which *by common consent* [my italics] should form part of the equipment of the educated adult' (DES 1980, p.5). We are told that the Secretaries of State, although recognizing 'that the curriculum can be described and analysed in several ways' (DES 1981, p.6), and in spite of their original statements about the primacy of those processes which we saw just now they include in their 'general aims', 'have thought it most helpful to express much of their guidance in terms of subjects' (ibid.). We are also told, in another document which begins from a statement of the processes embodied in these same 'general aims' (DES 1985, p.37), that 'that which is taught should be *worth knowing* [again my italics], comprehensible, capable of sustaining pupils' interests and useful to them at their particular stage of development and in the future'. Again the emphasis is on content and/or on instrumental justification (in fact there is an unhappy and unsatisfactory confusing of the two), and again the inconsistency of this view with that encapsulated in the earlier quotations is not recognized. Here, indeed, it almost seems as if inconsistency and ambiguity are deliberately and consciously embraced.

It is clear, then, that, even when a rationalist epistemology is explicitly adopted or implicitly assumed, elements of that view of education which derives from quite different philosophical premises are apt to creep in. And this in itself suggests not only inconsistencies but also important weaknesses in the rationalist view of education. These weaknesses will emerge more clearly when we proceed to consider education from other important perspectives.

It is against this backcloth, then, that we now turn to a resumé of what earlier chapters have said about knowledge, as a base from which to consider other important perspectives.

Knowledge and values

It will be clear from the foregoing chapters that there is a broad spectrum of views which can be taken and which have been taken about the nature, the origins and the status of human knowledge. That spectrum ranges from, at the one extreme, the view of knowledge as literally God-given and thus not only certain but also enjoying a status independent of the knower, to, at the other extreme, a complete subjectivity, like that of the phenomenologist, which sees knowledge as so dependent on the personal perceptions of the individual as to be virtually incapable of communication to others let alone of any kind of generalization. In the realm of values, the same spread of opinion will also be evident and it is in this area that the issue has most relevance for education.

It is possible, however, without doing too much violence to the shades of opinion represented, to identify four main stances, four points on this spectrum which can reasonably be claimed to be, if we can pursue the analogy, its primary colours. The first of these is that rationalist view of knowledge which accepts that some knowledge is certain, regards it as in some sense having a status, and indeed an origin, quite independent of individual human beings and believes that this kind of status extends also to the realm of values. Thus, as we saw in Chapter 2, its proponents speak of 'moral knowledge', for example, and regard that as having a status quite independent of individual beliefs and preferences and thus a high degree of certainty.

The second major perspective is that which sees all knowledge as completely individual, personal and idiosyncratic. In relation to all kinds of 'scientific' knowledge, this view, while interesting, is of only marginal importance for educational planning, since its acceptance makes all such planning impossible. If my knowledge is the result of my perceptions and those perceptions are totally private to me, then my knowledge is equally private to me and cannot be communicated to others any more than my perceptions can. In the realm of values, however, this perspective is crucial to educational planning and it is for this reason that we must consider it very carefully. For there is no inconsistency in taking this view of the status of judgements of value without extending it into the area of 'scientific' judgements. In other words, as we have seen, it is perfectly possible and quite reasonable to accept that there is a body or that there are bodies of knowledge of a 'factual' kind in many areas of human experience and that these bodies can be built on, added to and communicated to others, while not accepting that there are comparable bodies of moral knowledge or aesthetic knowledge or social/political knowledge. If one takes this view and regards all utterances in these areas as being totally idiosyncratic, the consequences for educational planning are serious, if not extreme.

Thirdly, there is what we might call the compromise perspective, that which is especially evident, as we have seen, in the work of John Dewey. This is the middle-ground position which says that, although knowledge is not God-given or absolute in any way, although it is man-made, nevertheless it is made by man as a species, that it thus holds good for all men and that this is true in the sphere of values as well as in the 'scientific' spheres. Thus, this view recognizes the tentative and hypothetical nature of human knowledge in all spheres but regards the sphere of values, the moral sphere, the aesthetic sphere, and even the political sphere, as being neither more nor less tentative than any other. It thus makes possible a certain degree of confidence in educational planning and, indeed, in any other form of social planning.

Lastly, we must note a general perspective which is related to both of these last views but which differs from them in one fundamental respect, the perspective of recent developments in the sociology of education, the sociology of knowledge. For this view accepts the view of the pragmatists that knowledge is man-made, but regards it as made not by man as a species but by man as a member of a particular group. It accepts too the view that values are relative and subjective but sees them as relative to particular social groups. On this view, knowledge is socially constructed; but it is 'a product of the informal understandings negotiated among members of an organised intellectual collectivity' (Blum 1971, p.117); different knowledge is generated by different groups and, in particular, different groups within society will develop their own value systems.

These four main perspectives will clearly lead to correspondingly different views of education and we must attempt now to identify the main features of these.

Values and education

It has been asserted several times that it is differences of view over the nature of values and the status of value judgements that is the crucial aspect of the knowledge debate for education. For while disputes over the status of, say, mathematical or scientific knowledge are interesting, and clearly important for education, of much more importance for educational planning are the questions of whether and why such knowledge ought to be included in the curriculum and whether and why it ought to take precedence over other areas of knowledge. It is the concern here, then, to pick out the relevance for education of different views of the status of value utterances. This is what we turn to now in relation to those four perspectives we have just identified and defined.

The view of knowledge that regards certain knowledge as possible of attainment leads to a view of education which has no qualms about making quite hard and fast educational prescriptions. It also leads to a view of education based primarily, if not entirely, on considerations of its content. We saw in Chapter 1 how this view of knowledge led Plato to some very confident assertions about what education ought to consist of and what knowledge the educated person must by definition have attained. This is the kind of view of education which must follow from the adoption of that view of knowledge and, conversely, this view of education must presuppose that kind of view of knowledge. It is this combination of a rationalist epistemology and a view of education as concerned primarily with subject content which we also saw led Richard Peters to define education as 'initiation into intrinsically worthwhile activities' (1965, 1966) and to proceed to a listing of what those activities are. There exists a body or certain bodies of knowledge and it is the task of education to initiate pupils into these. Children are regarded as 'in the position of the barbarian outside the gates' (Peters 1965, p.107) and education is the process of getting them 'inside the citadel of civilisation' (ibid.). The emphasis is thus on the knowledge side of the educational equation rather than on that of the pupil, on what is to be learned rather than on the learner, and educational planning begins from statements of its content.

Clearly, this is a view of education which is not peculiar to Richard Peters. It is that traditional view which dates from the time of Plato. It has been supported and extended by many influential figures in the world of education theory in recent years, by Paul Hirst (1965), for example, in his theory of different forms of rationality as the basis for curriculum planning. And it has the, perhaps too uncritical, acceptance of a good proportion of the men in the street — not to mention those in Elizabeth House and other bastions of educational power. It is the view which underpins the many recent pronouncements on the curriculum which have emanated from that source.

It is not the intention here to explore this view of education in detail. This will be a continuing concern of later chapters of this book. The intention here is merely to draw attention to its close connection with the kind of rationalist epistemology we have been endeavouring to elucidate. Two points are perhaps worth making here, however. The first of these is that it is important to remember that we are discussing here theories of *education*, theories of what must be done to ensure the production of educated men and women, and that this particular theory is one which takes its stand on this being a matter of knowledge content, a matter of *what* must be learned in the process of becoming educated. Where the justification of beginning one's curriculum planning from considerations of content is made in terms of the utilitarian functions of knowledge, the learning of those things which will lead to productive employment for the individual and the promotion of the economic health of society, as we saw earlier, we are dealing not with a theory of education, or, at least, not with a theory of education to which the debate about knowledge is relevant, but with something quite different. The only relevance of this point here is that the distinction is not always understood and the word 'education' is often used even when the concern is with economic utility rather than with educational worth, as has been the case in many of those recent political statements which have been made about schooling and the curriculum.

The second point which must be noted here about this view of education is its attraction for the practitioner. For, as we shall soon see, whatever view one takes about the role of knowledge-content in educational planning, it must be acknowledged that knowledge has some kind of role and that, as a consequence, a selection of knowledge to be included in one's educational provision must be made. Such selection is much easier to make if one adopts some notion of what kinds of knowledge are importantly worthwhile and even superior. Furthermore, there is something in most of us that wishes to accept the idea of the superiority of certain kinds of human activity and achievement. We need some concept of quality in the areas of art and literature, even if we are reluctant to accept it in other areas of values. The rationalist perspective offers us this concept, even if the arguments it adduces in support of it are highly tenuous, and it is no doubt for this reason as much as for any other that it has often been too readily and uncritically accepted. What is crucial, however, is that we do not allow this kind of view, whatever its roots, to lead us to see education as a matter merely of the transmission of such knowledge. This is the weakness of Mary Warnock's advice (1977) that we acknowledge the tentative nature of knowledge but work at the transmission of the currently agreed corpus of knowledge. For it is impossible to identify such agreement, and, as we shall see, to transmit the knowledge is to transmit also the values implicit in it, and if the knowledge is tentative, so too must they be.

This is one of the main aspects of the appeal of the pragmatist perspective on knowledge and on education; to which we now turn. It is not necessary to explore this in great detail here since it was discussed at some length in Chapter 3. What must be done is to point up the distinctive perspective on education which it leads to. For, as we saw in Chapter 3, it regards knowledge as being coherent and objective, at least in the sense of enjoying current general acceptance, but as also tentative and subject to constant revision and modification. We also saw that it regards values in the same way. Thus, while it has no difficulty in making some educational prescriptions, those prescriptions cannot begin from a concern primarily with *what* should be taught, with the content of education; they must concern themselves primarily with *how* things should be taught, with *how* knowledge should be presented to pupils or rather how pupils should be introduced to knowledge, i.e. with the processes of education, of development and of growth, rather than the content and its transmission. For if knowledge is tentative, it must be presented to pupils as such, if values are tentative, we must avoid imposing the values of the present generation on the members of the next generation. Education is seen, then, not as the transmission of certain knowledge in accordance with non-problematic value systems, but as a process of knowledge-getting, of developing new knowledge and, especially, of generating new systems of values.

We thus have a theory of education which is quite distinct from that spawned by the rationalist perspective on knowledge and which is distinctive precisely because it has grown from a totally different epistemological base. It is quite improper, therefore, to attempt to evaluate either theory by using the categories of the other. They are quite different and there is no basis of comparison. Such a base could only be found in the epistemological assumptions themselves and it is at that level that the debate must take place.

However, although giving rise to a distinctive view of education, this perspective shares an important feature with that of the rationalist — the belief that some kind of objectivity is attainable in the realm of values.

This is a belief which it is increasingly difficult to hold to, particularly in the face of the obvious value pluralism of present-day societies. A rejection of this belief is the main characteristic of the third and fourth perspectives we need to identify. These perspectives can also be seen, like pragmatism, as resulting from a feeling of dissatisfaction with the traditional rationalist view of knowledge and education and especially of some of its implications and consequences. We saw in Chapter 2 that an empiricist view of knowledge has been seen by some major philosophical figures, such as A.J. Ayer, as leading inexorably to the conclusion that there can be no objectivity of values, that terms such as 'moral knowledge', 'aesthetic knowledge' and so on are self-contradictory since there can be no knowledge in these fields, and that all value utterances are expressions of attitudes, preference or beliefs and have no status beyond that.

The extreme version of this view is that all valuing is totally subjective and personal. Such a view would seem to make all educational planning impossible. For there is no doubt that the concept of education contains some notion of the value of the process and, if we see all values as completely personal and idiosyncratic, it becomes quite impossible to distinguish education from indoctrination. This thus offers a perspective which eliminates educational planning so that, while it must be noted, there seems little point in pursuing it further here.

More recently, however, as we saw earlier, we have been offered by certain sociologists a different version of this view based on an analysis of knowledge in its social context and on direct criticisms of traditional rationalist epistemology and objectivist theories of knowledge. We must now consider this in rather more detail.

'New directions' in the sociology of education

The last fifteen years or so have seen considerable attention paid by sociologists, especially those concerned primarily with education, to questions of knowledge. A whole spectrum of views can be discerned in the discussions which this has generated and the history of sociology of education during that period is one of argument, debate and disagreement between a number of schools of sociology over questions about reality, about human perception of reality and thus about the status of human knowledge. It is not the intention here to attempt to pick a way through the minefield of that debate nor even to identify its major competing theories. Much of it has been philosophical rather than sociological in that the attention has been focused on questions, such as those about the nature and status of human sense-experience, which have traditionally been the concern of philosophy and which have exercised the minds of philosophers for centuries. It has perhaps, however, a common denominator. For there is an important perspective on knowledge which it has introduced which is distinctively sociological, a view which broadly sees knowledge as socially constructed, a creation of man rather than of God, and thus as something which is properly explained and understood not through an analysis of its own essence but through an examination of the social context in which it is generated. We noted in Chapter 1 that David Hume's rejection of an objectivist stance led him to a sociological view of morals, and it is worth noting here that, once one rejects the epistemological perspective of the rationalist, questions of the nature and status of knowledge inevitably become sociological rather than philosophical, focusing on the social relations through which knowledge develops rather than on features of the knowledge itself.

It is this broad sociological perspective which is the concern here, since it adds a new and important dimension to our discussion and, in doing so, adds weight to our general claim that we must look to empiricism for any adequate theory of knowledge and of education.

Its essence is well summed up in a passage from Geoffrey Esland's paper in Michael Young's *Knowledge and Control* (1971). Esland begins by suggesting that it has been a mistake 'to leave epistemological issues to philosophy' (op.cit., p.70) but that this has been a natural result of positivist forms of sociology, and we might add rationalist forms of philosophy. 'The prevalence in sociological research of neo-positivism has perpetuated a view of man as a dehumanized, passive object' (op.cit., p.71) (precisely the view of man we have suggested is that of rationalist philosophy). This he claims is the inevitable consequence of adopting an objectivistic view of knowledge.

The objectivistic view of knowledge ... is the view represented in traditional epistemology and analytic philosophy. It is also how knowledge is conceived in the reality of everyday experience where the taken for granted nature of the world is rarely questioned. The individual consciousness recognizes objects as being 'out there', as coercive, external realities ... Knowledge is thereby detached from the human subjectivity in which it is constituted, maintained and transformed. Such a view implicitly presents man as a passive receiver, as the pliable, socialized embodiment of external facilities. He is represented not as a world-producer, but as world-produced. We have, therefore, a reified philosophy in which objectivity is autonomized and which does not regard as problematical for the constituency of the object its constitution in the subjective experience of individuals. One finds it difficult to disagree with the claim that this epistemology is fundamentally dehumanizing. It ignores the intentionality and expressivity of human action and the entire complex process of intersubjective negotiation of meanings. In short, it disguises as given a world which has to be continually interpreted (op.cit., p.75).

If this passage sums up what the new sociology is saying about knowledge and education, then it will be seen that it reinforces what is being argued here, that a rationalist, and thus objectivist, view of knowledge leads to an unjustifiable reification of knowledge, to a view of knowledge as 'out there' or 'God-given' and thus to a view of man as a passive recipient to whom this knowledge is transmitted through education. It is the claim here, of course, that this is a result not of all philosophical activity, and not even of analytic philosophy, as Esland claims, but of that which is based on a rationalist epistemology. For our claim is that there is another respectable philosophical tradition which does not lead to this, but rather reinforces the very points which Esland is making. It must also be noted that many of those who have made these claims about the sociology of knowledge have quickly been led into another form of rationalism, that of Marxism, which differs from the kind of rationalism we have been attacking only in the 'truths' it advocates, not in its essence.

It is not only, however, the reification of knowledge and the treatment of man as passive that is being attacked here. It is the fact that this leads to the denial of his right to negotiate meanings, to interpret and reinterpret his own experience and thus to develop his own systems of values. For this kind of sociological analysis suggests also that values and value systems are created by groups and sub-groups in society, that value pluralism is a recognizable feature of modern societies and that there are no grounds upon which one can make valid judgements concerning the relative merits of those value systems (since to do so would be to adopt a rationalist and objectivist view of the status of knowledge and values). It is a view, incidentally, which, as we noted just now, was foreshadowed in the sociological theory of morals which we saw in Chapter 2 was the only kind of moral theory David Hume regarded as compatible with an empiricist epistemology. It is thus a rather different development of Hume's empiricism from that of Ayer. For it suggests that, while there is no philosophical basis for claiming the status of knowledge for any value assertion, it is a recognizable and significant sociological phenomenon that groups of human beings are held together by shared value systems, that, although consensus does not confer validity, nevertheless consensual value systems can be seen to exist and their significance must be acknowledged.

This raises in turn some important political issues and we must consider these now in a little more detail. For, as was stated in the Introduction, it is a central purpose of this book to draw attention not only to the effects on curriculum planning of adopting — and especially of doing so uncritically or unquestioningly — a rationalist view of knowledge, but also, and perhaps more importantly, to the implications of the adoption or the assumption of such a view of knowledge by those who control the educational system of the country. Indeed, this is seen by many as the central issue in the age-old battle for control of the curriculum between central government and the teaching profession — a battle which in the United Kingdom has recently taken on the characteristics of open rather than guerilla warfare.

The politics of knowledge

We saw in Chapter 2 how Hegel's development of rationalism had led him to make political assertions of a kind which were fundamentally totalitarian. This kind of political stance is the inevitable and inexorable conclusion to which one is led from that kind of view of knowledge. For certainty in moral matters must lead to comparable certainty in matters political, the moral, the social and the political being merely different sides of the same (three-sided) coin. Indeed, Dewey once argued that most of German cultural and philosophical thought reached its natural fruition in Hitler. It is always a mistake to regard philosophy as pure thought. We saw too earlier that Plato had been led by the same kind of epistemological perspective to the same kind of political conclusions, albeit expressed in a somewhat more naive fashion. And we have also suggested that the same criticism can be offered of Marxism. Indeed, the three great enemies of the 'open society' identified by Karl Popper (1945) are Plato, Hegel and Marx. What unites them all is a rationalist view of knowledge, and it is important, especially for those concerned with the planning of educational provision, to recognize the political implications of such a view. If values are problematic, then to be dogmatic about them must be politically sinister.

The other educational perspectives we have identified can be seen as the result as much of a rejection of these political implications as of a rejection of the epistemological and educational theories associated with rationalism. For central to Dewey's theory, for example, as we saw in Chapter 3, is the notion of democracy, a term which he would only be prepared to define negatively, as the opposite of totalitarianism. This notion can be seen as the culmination of his views, as encapsulating an idea of the kinds of social condition necessary to the development and continued evolution of knowledge as he saw it. It is also possible, however, to see it as the foundation of his theory, an initial commitment to a view of society (and of man) which in turn leads to certain views of knowledge and education. At all events, it is necessary to appreciate that this notion of democracy, or 'the democratic way of life', is fundamental to his theory, and his views on education lead both into and out of this kind of political view.

Thus different epistemological stances lead not only to quite distinctive views of education but also to equally distinctive views of society.

More recent explorations of this issue have led to the suggestion that this view of Dewey is somewhat naive, mistaken not least, in fact mainly, in its assumption, which we noted in Chapter 3, of some kind of objective status for human values. The rejection of this assumption leads us to quite different, and far less optimistic, conclusions. If the rationalist perspective, along with its associated claim to objectivity of values, leads to totalitarianism, the alternative view, with its acknowledgement of a plurality of value systems and the socially constructed nature of knowledge and values, must alert us to the dangers of forms of social control operated through the control of knowledge and, especially, of the distribution of knowledge through the educational system. If knowledge is ideology, then the ideology which will be promoted and promulgated will be that of the dominant group within society, the group which has control of the educational system and of the curriculum. If values are the creation of social groups, then the dominant social group in any society will use the educational system to impose its values on the rest — whether deliberately or by default makes little difference. For the education system will be in the hands of the dominant social group and thus society and its future will be in the same hands.

The implications of this view for educational planning and the control of such planning are wide-ranging and important. For it is a view which leads, like Dewey's theory, to an awareness of the dangers of education becoming a form of indoctrination. This time, however, the danger is seen not as that of the present generation indoctrinating the next and thus inhibiting the development and the evolution of knowledge; it is the danger of one dominant sector or group in society indoctrinating other groups or sectors and thus achieving political control over them in the here and now. For value systems, the argument goes, are implicit in bodies of knowledge and in the selection of which knowledge should be transmitted in schools. The act of transmitting such selected areas of knowledge, then, becomes the means by which those implicit values are transferred to, indeed forced upon, the recipients. Thus the transmission of knowledge becomes a form of social control, as the dominant group, that group which has the power to make educational decisions, uses that power to impose its values on the rest. This is what Ivan Illich (1971, p.9) meant by 'the institutionalization of values' which he claims, 'leads to ... social polarization and psychological impotence'. The particular areas in which this process is identified as occurring in current societies are those of class, race and gender.

Another important aspect of this argument, and one which may again be seen as fundamental to the case being presented in this book, is that epistemological theories, of whatever stripe, are not in themselves an adequate basis for making decisions about education or curriculum. They may offer important considerations but they establish nothing which is conclusive about educational planning or educational policy. Decisions of that kind are essentially moral and political, and 'education is, first and foremost, a political act' (Harris 1979, p.139). It is the awareness of this that the 'new sociology' has brought to the educational debate.

Its significance is argued very cogently by Kevin Harris (op.cit., pp. 140-1):

... education in a class society is a political act having as its basis the protection of the interests of the ruling class. It is a mechanism (and that word hardly does it justice) for securing the continuation of the existing social relationships, and for reinforcing the attitudes and beliefs that will help ensure that those social relationships will continue to be accepted. Education is thus more than a 'mechanism' — it is an ideological force of tremendous import. On the one hand it is a *lived-ideology* which, in modern liberal capitalist democracies, everyone is compelled to live through for a long period of time. On the other hand it generates theoretical ideology, as all lived-ideologies do, but in the most influential and insidious of ways.... education's very function is to instil in people a particular way of seeing the world; it takes those 'tender, impressionable minds of the new generation' and implants in them the master mental set — *see the world this way*. In this way it brings about the large-scale consensus spoken of previously; and in establishing a mental set it both opens up certain ways of seeing the world, and also closes off others: it both reveals and conceals as it promotes the production of certain knowledge while excluding the production of other kinds. Education is the manipulation of consciousness (a point that must be agreed with even by those who would see 'manipulation' in a non-pejorative way), and it functions largely without serious opposition of any sort.

One major conclusion of this analysis must be that education is and must be counter-productive to the development of that kind of critical awareness and autonomy we have elsewhere claimed to be basic principles of educational planning, central aims of any system of education worthy of the name. Indeed, Walter Feinberg (1975) has claimed that American schooling, even when one accepts that it is 'a liberal institution conceived by liberal theorists and carried out by liberal practitioners' (op.cit., p.v), nevertheless 'from Kindergarten through graduate school operates to reinforce certain basic aspects of the American political, economic and moral structure' (op.cit., p.vi).

It is this that has led some writers, such as Ivan Illich (1971), to suggest the abolition of schools, a 'deschooling' of society, and it encouraged the emergence of a number of 'free schools' both in the United Kingdom and in the United States in the early 1970s.

It has been seen in particular as having serious implications for the ideals of universal education. For it would explain, better than most hypotheses, the massive evidence (see, for example, Bowles and Gintis 1976) of the failure of mass education to provide anything like equality of educational opportunity. It would support Kevin Harris's claims (1979, p.129) that Helvétius was right to assert that 'children are born ignorant, not stupid; it is education that makes them stupid' and that, in spite of the contrary advocacy of men such as J.S. Mill, mass education has been concerned primarily to create 'satisfied pigs and fools' rather than 'dissatisfied human beings and Socrates'. It is also the prime reason why Ivan Illich advocated the deschooling of society, since 'universal education through schooling is not feasible' (1971, p.7) and 'we must recognize that it [equal schooling] is, in principle, economically absurd, and that to attempt it is intellectually emasculating, socially polarizing and destructive of the credibility of the political system which promotes it' (op.cit., p.17).

Such a view is depressingly reinforced by the recent work of people such as Ivor Goodson (1981, 1983, 1985 a & b; Goodson and Ball 1984); who have explored the history of the development of school subjects. For a further and, from the point of view of our theme, very important point to emerge from this recent sociological debate concerns not so much the issue of values, and the political problems which arise from a recognition of their centrality to curriculum planning, as an exploration of the nature of knowledge itself, the history of its organization into subjects and, in particular, the processes by which those subjects become established in the school curriculum.

The rationalist explanation of these processes is framed in terms of features endemic to knowledge itself. Thus it is argued (Peters 1965, 1966; Hirst and Peters 1970) that the curriculum should consist of important, essential, intrinsically worthwhile knowledge, whose cognitive content is greatest. It has also been argued (Hirst 1965; Hirst and Peters 1970) that that cognitive content must be seen as having several quite discrete forms, so that education is seen as requiring not merely initiation into this worthwhile knowledge but also access to all its forms. Education is the development of the rational mind, it is argued, and, since there are several (usually the magic — or magnificent — seven) forms of rationality, education requires initiation into all of these. Thus 'philosophers of education' have explained and justified, first, the presence of certain subjects on the curriculum, and, second, the organization of knowledge into subjects, by reference to properties presumed to appertain to the knowledge and to the subjects themselves.

Recent studies, however, have offered other, more cogent, explanations, framed in terms of the historical and social context of the growth and development of school subjects.

First, a look at the history of the development of the curriculum of schools in England and Wales during the present century reveals that most of the subjects currently to be seen in the school curriculum, certainly at Secondary level, were established there at the beginning of the century. Several further points of interest also emerge. First, its establishment is better explained in terms of the predilections and values of Sir Robert Morant and his influence on the Board of Education than in terms of any intrinsic properties of the subjects themselves. Secondly, however, it is also worthy of note that those predilections and values were based on a conviction of the importance of providing a 'liberal' education and reflected a deliberate attempt to avoid instrumental or vocational forms of curriculum. Thirdly it has also been argued (Gordon and White 1979) that the concept of a 'liberal' education which was employed was that derived from the philosophy of one man, T.H. Green, a man whom we might call the last of the English rationalist and metaphysical philosophers. For most of the HMI employed to oversee the new schools were his ex-pupils and were thus thoroughly imbued with his rationalist perspective.

We may make of this what we will. Certainly, we might begin by identifying this as a possible explanation of how a rationalist epistemology came to be so influential in the development of the curriculum of our Secondary schools. We may, if we wish, even argue that it suggests that curricula are established according to philosophical or theoretical principles. It is equally plausible, however, to see it as evidence that curricula are established according to the values of those with the power to establish them.

The plausibility of that interpretation gains support from recent work which has been done in exploring the historical development of school subjects, what happens to them after they have arrived on the curriculum, work which is essentially an off-shoot or a development of those 'new directions' in the sociology of education we considered earlier. This work too casts considerable doubt on the validity of the view that the organization of knowledge into subjects, and especially the continued presence and form of those subjects on the school curriculum, can be explained in philosophical or epistemological terms, in terms of the properties of the knowledge or the subjects themselves.

The general themes of this work, which has been fully documented in a series of publications and edited collections by Ivor Goodson (1981, 1983, 1985 a & b; Goodson and Ball 1984), are that, while subjects may originally find their way onto the curriculum for pedagogic, or even utilitarian, reasons, they are maintained there by practices and procedures which have little to do with their educational merits — and less to do with their supposed epistemological status — that a large part of these practices and procedures amounts to a process of promoting an academic rather than an educational, or even a utilitarian, justification (a distinction whose importance was stressed earlier in this chapter), and that, as a result, their continued presence on the curriculum necessitates a move away from those things which might be felt to constitute their educational value towards the assertion of those features which seem to give them academic respectability, so that, whatever their initial justification, they soon adopt forms which bear little resemblance to that.

Thus, it is claimed, the explanation of the presence of many, and perhaps all, subjects on the school curriculum is to be found not in their contribution to educational development, still less in the essence or nature of the knowledge they offer, but in the success with which their advocates or proponents have been able to establish their academic credentials and status, and thus their right to resources and territory. And the kinds of device which have proved most effective in achieving this are such things as the creation of public examinations, the acceptance of these by the universities, the establishment of subject associations at a national level and anything else which will create for the subject a real status in the eyes of the public rather than a metaphysical status in the eyes of the 'philosophers of education'.

Three things would seem to follow from this, all of which will prove highly relevant to the discussions we are about to embark on in Part Two. The first is the questions this analysis raises about the validity of those rationalist views of knowledge which have led to quite different, and far less convincing, explanations of the place of subjects in the school curriculum. For there is little evidence for the establishment of any school subject, and less for its maintenance, in terms of intrinsically worthwhile activities or forms of understanding or rationality. Indeed, it even suggests that, while subjects might seek to maintain themselves by appealing to these aspects of themselves, any such appeal is political rather than philosophical, and, furthermore, its success appears to lead to a loss of educational potential rather than any gain.

The second point to note is the doubt it casts not only on the organization and planning of the curriculum in terms of its knowledge-content but, further, on the organization of that knowledge content into clearly defined subject categories, divided each from the other by apparently insuperable and insurmountable barriers.

And finally we must note that the process we have described as that by which subjects establish themselves is one which makes them less accessible to a majority of pupils. If, to establish itself, a subject has to become increasingly 'academic', then by definition it has to become more remote from the experience and interests of a large proportion of pupils. Thus we have further support for those claims we noted earlier that schooling, at least as currently organized, is not an appropriate mechanism for the achievement of universal education, that, in practice, it is counter-productive to its attainment, and that it adds to rather than counteracts the disadvantages of the underprivileged. There is a good deal of significance in this point, then, for the notion of educational equality which we explore in Chapter 7.

If we put this together with what was said earlier about values and ideologies, we are left with a dilemma. If the status of all knowledge is problematic, if, consequently, the status of all value assertions is also and particularly problematic, and if too the existence of school subjects can only be adequately explained in terms of the political activities of their proponents, then all educational prescriptions will be ideological, they will contain implicitly the value assumptions of their authors, their effect will be to communicate those values, in a largely uncritical manner, to those being educated, and they will thus lead to forms of indoctrination rather than education. Furthermore, an educational system which is founded on the values of the dominant ideology in a society will work constantly to the disadvantage of other social groups.

The political context of curriculum planning

It is at this point that we must try to relate this debate to the current political climate in which curriculum planning is being conducted in the United Kingdom and note the interpretation which it must encourage us to place on recent government initiatives in education.

The organization of education in the United Kingdom has been marked during the last decade or so by an escalating political intervention of a direct kind. An ever-increasing volume of publications on curriculum has emerged from official sources and a number of direct initiatives have been taken to increase the control of central and, to a lesser degree, local government over the school curriculum and to render teachers more accountable for their work. We will consider this development in more detail in Part Two and especially in Chapter 9.

We must note here, however, some of the major characteristics of this development, not least because they may be interpreted as illustrating some of the general points we have just been making. First, we must note the growing emphasis on traditional school subjects and the attempts being made not only to reinforce them but to extend their sphere of influence, especially by advocating their establishment in the Primary school curriculum, which traditionally, as we shall see in Chapter 5, has been 'undifferentiated', concerned more with the development of children than with the promulgation of academic knowledge through the teaching of traditional school subjects. This is perhaps best illustrated by the current insistence that all student teachers (including those who will work in Nursery schools) must spend at least two of their four years of preparation for teaching in studying one or two 'subjects'. Second, we must note the emphasis on education as the pursuit of academic excellence, as evinced, for example, by the all-pervading concern with 'academic standards', a view of education which, as we saw earlier in this chapter, is essentially rationalist and difficult to reconcile with the notion of mass education, with education as a means of increasing the control of every pupil over his/her environment. Third, we must note the concomitant concern with the content of education, with education as the transmission of worthwhile knowledge, illustrated perhaps most clearly in the techniques for the assessment of pupils and the appraisal, evaluation and accountability of schools and teachers which are currently favoured and advocated.

All of this is, of course, evidence of that implicit rationalism we have been concerned throughout to identify. Here we see it not in the discussions and debates of the theorists but in the decision-making practices of the politicians and the administrators. All of it, however, is also leading to those effects we earlier suggested were the inevitable results of this kind of approach to curriculum planning. In particular, we must note the effects of this on those pupils who are already disadvantaged by their social or ethnic background. For a major current concern is with the under-achievement of a significant proportion of the school population. It is time this was recognized as the inevitable consequence of a system of education planned and predicated on these particular values — moral, social, political and aesthetic.

For there could be no better example of the results of an education system planned according to the values of the dominant ideology within society. If you begin your curriculum planning with a meritocratic view of education and of society, its results will be a meritocratic system of education and a meritocratic social order. The *status quo* will be maintained and education for a large proportion of the population will continue to be the sham it has always been.

It is this that is the focus of the current conflict between the politicians and the administrators (including, unfortunately, Her Majesty's Inspectorate) on the one hand, and the teachers on the other. This conflict is often characterized — by both sides — as centring on salaries and conditions of service. There is, however, a more fundamental feature to it and that is the struggle for control of the curriculum. It is this that is at the root of the tension over forms of curriculum evaluation and teacher appraisal and accountability. At one level this can be seen as a concern about security of tenure and career prospects; at a deeper level, however, it reflects a concern for the quality and the kinds of educational experience schools are able to offer their pupils.

For, as we shall see in more detail in Chapter 9, some procedures for evaluation, appraisal and accountability are highly *dirigiste* in their effects on curriculum planning, and, furthermore, it is clear that in many cases they are intended to be so. They bring in, often quite deliberately, as the most cursory glance at most of the recent official documents on curriculum will reveal, precisely those attitudes, approaches and values we have been suggesting are counter-productive to the promotion of education in the full sense, of the development of critical awareness in pupils and, in particular, of the development of powers of control over their environment in all pupils. They reveal to a high degree all those features we have seen the sociologists identifying and inveighing against.

The teachers themselves, on the other hand, are much more concerned in general with the development of their pupils along these lines, are aware of the need to adapt their curricula to meet this kind of need, to attempt to satisfy what they see to be the needs of their pupils rather than the demands of their political masters. It is precisely this that they were heavily criticized for by James Callaghan in his Ruskin speech.

This is the crux of the current conflict over procedures for appraisal, evaluation and accountability. It is essentially a political struggle. The increased professionalization of the teaching force, through, for example, the establishment of some kind of General Teaching Council, on the model of the British Medical Association, would do much to resolve the problem, but it could only do so by swinging the balance of power in the direction of the teachers. It must, therefore, be seen as a very remote possibility in the current political climate.

There would seem to be two major explanations for the situation which has just been described and for those general political points which were made earlier. The first is that assumption of certainty over values which we have suggested must lead to some form of dogmatism. Whether this is a result of an acceptance of that carefully argued rationalist epistemology we explored earlier, of the uncritical adoption of its conclusions or of a more cynical attempt to impose one's own values regardless of their status, the effects will be the same — a form of education designed to promote 'academic excellence', concerned with 'academic standards', framed in terms of traditional school subjects, defined in terms of its content and thus alienating to large numbers of pupils — especially those whose social and/or ethnic origins render them already 'underprivileged' in relation to the school system. If all educational prescriptions are ideological and none has any greater claim to representing 'the truth' than the others, then the worst kind of prescription is that which does not recognize this. And a major criticism of rationalist epistemologies is that they do not permit such recognition.

The second kind of explanation of what is being described here derives from this but is worthy of somewhat fuller discussion. We have seen that, even when we recognize a plurality of value systems, indeed precisely because we recognize them, we are forced to see education as a battleground for these systems, for competing ideologies. For these values, these ideologies, are seen as inhering in, as expressed through, the content of the curriculum. Education is seen as the transmission of knowledge and thus of the values implicit in that knowledge.

It is for this reason that it is being claimed here that the only acceptable theory of education in a democratic society is one that emphasizes the processes of individual development which it should be concerned to promote rather than the bodies of subject-knowledge, along with the values implicit in these, which it might be expected to transmit. For a solution to at least some of the problems just delineated may be to see education not as the transmission of knowledge and of values but as the kind of developmental process designed to promote those qualities of mind which it was suggested earlier constitute what it means to be educated, as the kind of process we saw in Chapter 3 was advocated by John Dewey as the only form of education fitted to a democratic community.

Thus it has been suggested that we should view, and plan, education in terms not of transmission but rather of transaction, that we should accept the notion of curriculum negotiation and acknowledge the right of the recipient to exercise some say in the planning of his or her educational experiences. If one accepts the value and the legitimacy of working-class culture, for example, or of the culture of ethnic minorities, one must accept as a corollary of that the need to frame a curriculum predicated on the major features of those cultures rather than offering a curriculum based on what, while it might be felt or claimed to be the dominant culture of society, is in fact the culture of the dominant element in society. Thus the curriculum must be developed from the knowledge and the values the pupil brings into the school and not based on the 'educational knowledge' of the teacher (Keddie 1971), of the syllabus the teacher is expected to work to, nor on the superior wisdom of our political masters.

If we can get beyond the idea that education is the transmission of knowledge and values, we may perhaps begin to see that what the perspective of the 'new sociology' can offer us is the view that it is the function of education in society to promote diversity rather than to attempt to impose uniformity, to encourage the development of different value and culture systems rather than the reduction of all to one common culture, and even to the more positive view that it is the function of education to protect individuals from the impositions of the dominant sectors of society, to arm them against the many different sources of such imposition which exist in complex modern societies and, in particular, to enable the poor of the world, as Paolo Freire (1972) puts it, to see their own problems in a reflexive perspective and to act on them rather than to be 'dopes' whose curriculum, and thus whose life, is decided for them by others.

A rationalist epistemology, whether tacit and assumed or overt and reasoned, as we saw earlier, cannot offer the kind of theory of education which will make this possible. For it must give priority to the transmission of knowledge and cannot admit of a plurality of values. It was for this reason that it was also argued earlier that only empiricism can offer us the kind of basis upon which to build a theory of education suitable to a fully democratic society.

If one begins one's curriculum planning from this point of view, then the selection of the content of the curriculum will be made not in terms of the rationalist's notion of what is intrinsically valuable, nor in terms of what reflects, and thus acts as a vehicle for the transmission of, the values of the dominant ideology, but in terms of what seems most likely to promote the kinds of development which are or should be the central concern of a system of education in the real sense. These then become the value positions from which the curriculum is generated; these are its central principles. The fact that we cannot be certain over knowledge, truth and value does not mean that we enter a free-for-all, either socially or educationally. A framework can be provided by reference to the notion of the development of the individual as an autonomous human being, and planning decisions can be made by reference to the guidelines and criteria which such a notion can and will generate. In short, if we accept the validity of such a moral and political stance, if we acknowledge that there is at least a *prima facie* obligation to respect other people's rationality — their right to differ in their views and values, that is, not, as rationalism would have it, their obligation to conform to some fixed rationalist system of values — then a good deal will follow from this and we can go a long way towards planning a curriculum with some hope of avoiding some or even all those dangers and pitfalls we have been exploring.

Some of the implications of this kind of approach to the planning of the curriculum we will explore in greater detail in Part Two. Before we do so, however, it is important that we bring another factor to bear on the debate, one which becomes of great significance if we adopt the stance which has just been advocated — the perspective of developmental psychology. For to adopt that stance is to commit oneself to a concern not primarily for the content of pupils' learning, and certainly not for its quantity, but rather for the quality of the learning that education can and should promote, not for the knowledge which pupils assimilate but rather for the nature and quality of the growth and development which results from the educational experiences which they are given.

We have argued the merits of this approach to education and curriculum planning on philosophical grounds, in terms of the concepts of education, of democracy, of knowledge, of values, and on sociological grounds, in terms of the social relations existing within societies and the importance of the social context in which knowledge is generated. It will now be seen that this view has also the strong support of recent work in the field of developmental psychology, which has stressed the important distinction between learning and intellectual development, and thus between the forms of education and curriculum directed at the promotion of each.

The perspective of developmental psychology

If rationalism was supported by positivist versions of sociology, with their parallel searches for sociological 'truths', it has also been supported and reinforced by behaviourist and quantitative approaches to the study of human psychology. These too are attempts at seeking 'truths', but they also adopt a view of man as a passive creature, of learning as a modification of behaviour, of the study of human learning and behaviour as not qualitatively different from the study of animal behaviour and learning. Furthermore, as for example in the work of Neville Bennett and his associates (1976, 1984), they work from a taken-for-granted view of knowledge, education and curriculum which is essentially that of the rationalist, and this is a major reason why they appear to be the only form of educational research which attracts the attention and the interest of the politicians and the administrators. In general they complement rationalist epistemology by attempting a 'scientific' study of human learning, one which is felt to generate psychological 'knowledge', and by offering this 'knowledge' as a supplement to what rationalist philosophers have been prescribing for education. Thus as recently as 1975, Denis Lawton (1973, 1975) could offer a curriculum planning model in which the role of psychology is to advise merely on questions of methodology, the question of aims and content having been satisfactorily dealt with by the philosopher in terms of 'cultural universals' (op.cit., p.85) and the sociologist in terms of 'cultural variables' (ibid.).

This is probably as accurate a model as any of the rationalist approach to curriculum planning. It does of course partake of all those difficulties we have already identified as inherent in this kind of approach. What is more of relevance and consequence here, however, is that, while no doubt offering a reasonable description of the contribution of traditional forms of psychology to educational planning, it fails to recognize the quite different kind of contribution of recent work in developmental psychology, or to appreciate that this approach to the study of educational psychology is as different from the quantitative approach of the behaviourist as the 'new directions' in sociology of education are from positivism. For recent work in developmental psychology has offered us perspectives on education which go far beyond methodology by exploring not only how learning takes place and thus how it might be promoted, but, far more importantly from the point of view of educational planning, the qualitative differences between forms of learning, in particular between that of the child and that of the adult, and between that of human beings and that of animals.

This new approach to the study of human development and learning has thus complemented both the 'new directions' in sociology and the revolt against rationalism in philosophy to point us towards a more satisfactory view of education and of curriculum, and more productive forms of educational and curriculum planning.

In doing so, it has joined in the general criticism of the kind of approach to education to which rationalism leads. Margaret Donaldson (1978, p.81), for example, is overtly critical of the transmission view of education when she says, 'when we set such store by disembedded modes of thought we make the pursuit of education in our society a difficult enterprise for the human mind — one which many minds refuse at an early stage.' And Friedlander (1965, p.28), as long ago as 1965, criticized the view of the learner as 'simply a receptacle for a set of conclusions that have been arrived at by someone else'. Its theme is thus fundamental to the case being developed in this book, and we must take time here to consider some of its main features.

Perhaps too much emphasis has been placed on the claims of Piaget and others concerning the stages through which intellectual or cognitive development proceeds. It is this that has led people like Denis Lawton to see the role of psychology, and even of developmental psychology, as no more than to help us plan the means by which we can educate children, in this case by advising us on what children can or cannot cope with at various ages and stages in their growth. More recent work in this field, such as that of Jerome Bruner (1966), Margaret Donaldson (1978) and Eliot Eisner (1982), has cast some doubt on the wisdom of interpreting this as rigidly as some have been wont to do, has suggested that children are not so limited as has been thought in their ability to reason deductively and has pointed towards a rather more sophisticated view of the general claim that the child's thinking is qualitatively different from that of the mature adult. It has done this by proposing that it is possible to discern several different modes of representation, several different ways of interpreting and communicating experience, and that, while these may be viewed hierarchically, all of them can be present in the ways children view and interpret their world and all of them can and do persist in the ways in which adults handle their experience. Nevertheless, the notion of different modes of representation and the consequent need to look at children's reaction to experience from this perspective is an important one, not least in that it directs our attention away from the content of their learning and towards the processes of their intellectual development. As Jerome Bruner has said (1966, p.72), 'a theory of instruction seeks to take account of the fact that a curriculum reflects not only the nature of knowledge but also the nature of the knower and of the knowledge-getting process.'

This, then, is a second important distinction which developmental psychology encourages us to make — the distinction between cognitive or intellectual development and mere learning. It is a distinction designed to draw our attention to those questions about the nature and the quality of learning to which we referred earlier. For it stresses that learning in the behaviourist sense of the term can go on, can be brought about with great efficiency, can result in the kinds of behaviour changes as revealed by the kinds of performance the behaviourist is looking for, without intellectual growth or development of any kind having occurred. It is the same kind of point that A.N. Whitehead was making long ago when he advised us in education to beware of 'inert ideas', 'that is to say, ideas that are merely received into the mind without being utilised, or tested, or thrown into fresh combinations' (1932, pp.1-2), what he describes a little later as 'the passive reception of disconnected ideas, not illumined with any spark of vitality' (op.cit., pp.2-3).

Cognitive development, in the full sense that developmental psychology wishes to give it, is brought about only by active forms of learning, and this is the third crucial point we need to note here. Again, this is a notion which is much misunderstood, especially by its critics. Its main thrust, however, is that intellectual growth proceeds not from the passive assimilation of other people's knowledge but from a positive interaction with one's own environment, what Dewey would call genuine experience, which results in significant changes in one's perceptions and one's understanding.

It is not the acquisition of that reified knowledge the sociologists have drawn our attention to; it is the generation of what is significant knowledge to the individual through the reconstruction of experience, through 'making sense' of experience. Nor can one justify any longer, if one ever could, the offering of that kind of reified knowledge on the grounds that it 'sharpens the mind for later use'. The mind is sharpened, honed, developed (whatever imagery is preferred) by being used, not in advance of being used. To quote A.N. Whitehead again, 'the mind is never passive; it is a perpetual activity, delicate, receptive, responsive to stimulus' (op.cit., p.9). The mind must, therefore, be active in its own development. Children, as Seymour Papert (1980) tells us, are builders of their own intellectual structures. We must look to what some have called 'metacognition', the need for the individual to be conscious of his/her own thinking, since the concept of 'active learning' entails that consciousness and intellectual growth be closely linked. If education is to forward this kind of development, it can only do so by promoting genuinely active forms of learning. Again, therefore, the pointer is towards the processes of education rather than its content.

Lastly, we must note that recent work in this field has come to acknowledge that to view this process as one of cognitive or intellectual development only is to take an unduly restricted view of human development and of the role of education within it; it is to fail to acknowledge what Margaret Donaldson (1978) calls the 'human sense' aspect of development. Piaget and Inhelder (1971) had recognized affective factors as integral to intellectual growth, had acknowledged the inseparability and irreducibility of the cognitive and the affective; and this in itself takes us significantly beyond that rationalist perspective which, as we have seen, is rooted in and to the cognitive alone. Recent work, however, has gone much further down this road by stressing the significance of other dimensions of human development. In particular, the social context has come to be emphasized, the context of personal relationships in learning, since these appear to form the matrix in which intellectual growth takes place. Thus, although the claim is that intellectual development is an individual matter, this must not be interpreted as a demand for individualized learning. Individualized learning is the device of the behaviourist and his teaching machines. Intellectual development, while being an individual matter, requires a properly constructed social context, not least because it can only itself proceed satisfactorily if it advances in harness with the simultaneous development of the individual on several other fronts. Again, therefore, this view takes us significantly beyond the confines of a rationalist epistemology, and invites us to take full cognizance of the implications for educational planning of that democratic context which Dewey was at pains to emphasize.

What emerges here, then, is a view of education not as the acquisition of knowledge, and certainly not as the imposition of values, but as the promotion of certain forms of human development, defined not in value terms but in terms of the growth of certain kinds of competence, a heightening of awareness, a raising of levels of consciousness, which will assist the individual towards interpreting the world in his/her own way, negotiating his/her own meanings, creating his/her own values, and, in general, determining his/her own destiny. In short, it is a view of education as a series of processes — towards understanding, towards autonomy, towards critical awareness — rather than as the acquisition of knowledge or the imposition of values. It is not unlike, and certainly not incompatible with, Dewey's notion of education as growth which we explored earlier. And it reinforces the case for adopting that view of education which it has been suggested emerges from the philosophical and sociological considerations which have been offered. For all point us towards a view of education as a process by which pupils may develop to their full potential as autonomous individuals, may acquire the capacity to make their own judgements and choices and decide on their own values, and may thus achieve the maximum degree of control over their own lives and destinies.

Summary and conclusions

This chapter was designed to form a bridge between the discussion of knowledge offered in Part One and that of various aspects of curriculum planning which will be undertaken in Part Two. It began with an attempt to provide an analysis of the concept of education, or at least to set out the concept of education upon which the arguments in this book are constructed and which the book is concerned to argue is the only concept of education which is compatible with the ideals of democratic living. In doing so, it suggested that this view of education is to be found even in the work of the rationalists and in the current pronouncements of the politicians on education, and that it represented a serious inconsistency in their views.

The chapter next attempted to summarize that discussion in Part One of the major epistemological theories, and to point up their implications for theories of values and thus for education. Three main resultant educational perspectives were identified. The first of these derived from a rationalist epistemology and offered certainty of knowledge, assurance about values and thus complete confidence in the framing of educational prescriptions. We saw further how this leads inevitably to a view of education which places the major stress on the knowledge content to be assimilated and thus adopts a model of education as transmission.

The second educational perspective identified was that of John Dewey, which was fully outlined in Chapter 3. The emphasis here is on the tentative and hypothetical nature of knowledge and of values, and thus on education as a process not of acquiring knowledge so much as of developing it, not of assimilating values but of generating them. Thus the emphasis is not on the content of education so much as its processes, the concern is not so much with *what* is learnt as with *how* it is learnt, and the development and growth of the educand become the prime concern. All of this we saw to be predicated on a somewhat simplistic view of man and society as developing and evolving in harmony, and in particular a view of values as universally agreed and accepted, even if tentative.

The third perspective we identified was that of the 'new directions' in the sociology of education. While sharing many of the fundamental assumptions about knowledge that derive from the empiricist tradition and thus being in tune with Dewey on many fronts, this view differed mainly in its unwillingness to accept this last notion of universal agreement over values and its contrary assertion of the fact and the legitimacy of value pluralism. This led to a view of education as in reality the imposition of the values of the dominant, controlling group on the rest of society and to the suggestion that its main focus ought to be on the encouragement of diversity, the promotion of different culture and value systems, and even to a view of education as centrally concerned to arm and protect the weaker members of society against the attempts of the stronger more dominant groups to suppress and control them.

This led us to note the important political dimensions of this debate and to recognize that, since education is a political activity, it is not enough to discuss it merely in terms of epistemology. We must recognize that different epistemological theories lead to different views of society, to different political stances as well as to different theories of education, and that all these must be seen as closely interlinked. We must also recognize the superior attractions of those views of education which acknowledge this and adopt, as a consequence, an open and tentative rather than a dogmatic and prescriptive view of educational values.

In an attempt to resolve the dilemma this uncertainty over values seems to present for educational planning, we suggested that education should be viewed not as the transmission of knowledge and values but as a process of growth and development and we then turned to a different source of advice on educational practice, those theories of instruction and of development which have emerged from the work of the developmental psychologists. We saw that work in this field, especially in recent times, has also led to a challenging of the assumptions made and the positions taken on the basis of rationalism, especially its failure to make qualitative distinctions between kinds of learning, its general tendency towards the promotion of passive forms of learning, its consequent inability to distinguish learning from genuine intellectual growth, and its inadequacy in dimensions of development other than the cognitive. We noted that this line of research has reinforced that of the new wave of sociologists, and, indeed, the empiricist/pragmatist philosophy of people such as John Dewey, in supporting a rejection of rationalism and objectivism as a basis for educational planning, and promoting a view of education as a series of developmental processes rather than as bodies of knowledge-content to be assimilated.

It is to a fuller exploration of this notion of education as process that we turn in Part Two. For, in the light of the considerations set out in Part One and summarized in this chapter, Part Two will attempt four things. First, it will attempt to demonstrate that these considerations are central to many major aspects of the current educational and curriculum debate. Second, it will aim to show how they are relevant to that debate. Thirdly, it will hope to show that a failure to appreciate both of these points has bedevilled many recent discussions of education and is the source of much current misunderstanding and confusion. And finally, it will endeavour to reveal the inadequacies of the rationalist perspective, whether implicit or explicit, in providing a sound base for curriculum planning in the kind of democratic and pluralist society for which current educational provision must be made.

PART TWO
CURRICULUM PLANNING

CHAPTER 5

CURRICULUM PLANNING — EDUCATION AS DEVELOPMENT

Books are not made to be believed, but to be subjected to inquiry. When we consider a book, we must not ask ourselves what it says, but what it means.
(Umberto Eco, *The Name of the Rose*)

In Part One an attempt has been made to outline briefly the main points of dispute between rival theories of knowledge, the intention being not so much to explore these exhaustively, since the discussion has perforce had to be somewhat superficial, but to draw attention to the issues at stake and to emphasize that questions about the status of knowledge and of values are problematic, that no single conclusive answer to them has been produced and that it is unlikely that any such answer ever will be achieved or, indeed, that it is even worth while seeking after such, not least because one of those theories — and that, we claimed, the most convincing and compelling — offers as its answer a view of knowledge and values as ever-changing and never constant.

In Part Two we turn to an exploration of some educational issues for which this debate about knowledge is significant, some aspects of the current educational scene which can only adequately be considered in the context of a recognition of the problematic nature of knowledge and values. Most of these issues, as was suggested in the Introduction, have been bedevilled by a failure to acknowledge this or to recognize the assumptions about knowledge and about values which they implicitly make, or by too ready an acceptance of the rationalist stance and a tendency to view everything from that perspective, whether this is appropriate or not. This will emerge as we now explore some of these issues.

The issues which are most significant in this respect are inevitably those which hinge on the role of knowledge-content in education. This is a question which has recently come to the fore in the United Kingdom, largely through an increased intervention of central government in educational planning, and it is a good example of the kind of issue we have just referred to in which the questions are raised not as part of the process of advocating and justifying certain kinds of educational prescription but by default, through the failure to recognize the problematic and, indeed, ideological aspects of those prescriptions.

We must consider, then, some of the implicit assumptions of those who are currently pressing their views upon us, particularly through their advocacy of a common core curriculum, with its associated notions of curriculum balance and of cultural transmission. In doing so, we will see not only that these views adopt uncritically a rationalist stance, but also that they are in direct conflict with other educational ideals to which their supporters claim to be equally committed — ideals such as those of individual development and educational equality.

First, however, we must consider a question which may be logically prior to those just mentioned and which may also be of more direct and immediate relevance to the individual school and the individual teacher — that of the most suitable approaches to adopt to educational or curricular planning. For here again one often finds the tacit assumption being made that such planning must begin from considerations of subject-content or, perhaps more often, the related assumption that it must start from statements of 'aims and objectives'; and it is the contention here that these assumptions are essentially those of the rationalist, that they are firmly rooted in a view of knowledge and rationality which only a rationalist epistemology can justify and that, as a consequence, it has to be recognized that they must be justified rather than taken as read, and that the adoption of an alternative epistemology points one in the direction of quite different approaches to curriculum planning, approaches whose difference is to be seen mainly in the subsidiary role given to subject-content.

There are at least three different starting-points for curriculum planning, three planning models, three kinds of initial concern, three different bases from which to begin — concern with the transmission and the acquisition of certain kinds of knowledge, concern with certain end-states to be reached and concern with certain forms of development to be promoted. In planning a curriculum at any level, whether at that of the individual teacher or that of centralized national planning, it is important to be clear which approach is being adopted and, more importantly, why that approach is favoured. It is the contention of this book, of course, that neither of these questions is usually faced and that to face the second of them necessitates raising and exploring those questions of knowledge which are its central concern. It is a further contention that the adoption, whether conscious or not, of a rationalist view of knowledge leads to an emphasis on the knowledge which is to be transmitted and to planning in terms of subject-content or in terms of 'aims and objectives' or in terms of an amalgam of both. For the central concern is with the knowledge to be acquired and/or the forms of rationality to be attained. A final contention is that these are unsatisfactory bases for truly educational planning and that an empiricist/pragmatist approach, leading us to plan our curricula in terms of certain processes of development, offers a more appropriate form of educational planning.

Some of the reasons for making that claim were explained in Part One and will emerge again from the discussions which follow. The difficulties raised by the subject-based and product-oriented approaches can best be seen from an examination of what is entailed by the adoption of a process-based approach to planning, and are probably best left to emerge in the course of such an examination, as is the essential connection of these approaches with a rationalist view of knowledge. It is, therefore, on the implications of planning in terms of processes which this chapter will concentrate, not least because this approach is least well understood and documented, while the others have been fully described and advocated in many other places.

We now turn, therefore, to a detailed consideration of the notion of curriculum as process rather than as content or product, in order to show its relevance and, indeed, its superiority as a source of solutions to much existing confusion in educational theory and practice. It would seem to make good sense to undertake such a consideration by looking at an area of education where some attempt has been made both to explicate this idea of curriculum as process and to put it into practice — the English Primary school.

The Primary curriculum

Recent evidence, notably that of the HMI survey of Primary schools (DES 1978) and that produced by the ORACLE team (Galton et al. 1980; Galton and Simon 1980), has suggested that the reality of teachers' practice in our Primary schools does not reflect this kind of approach to the curriculum as clearly or as emphatically as was once thought. It is the contention here that, if true, this is most readily explained by that same epistemological confusion we have suggested is behind many other areas of confused debate.

However, there is an important difference here. For, whereas, in the other areas we shall consider, the problem is that a rationalist epistemology is assumed but is not always recognized nor its incompatibility with some of the claims being made appreciated, here a whole philosophy has been built on an empiricist/pragmatist theory of knowledge and the full force and consequences of that have not been properly recognized. The theory itself has been muddled because it has failed to appreciate the implications of its own philosophical base and thus to make this explicit; subsequent criticisms of the theory have been mounted from a rationalist perspective without the inherent contradictions of that being recognized; and, as a result, practice has continued to be confused as teachers have tried to achieve an uneasy and — certainly at the theoretical level — impossible compromise between a commitment to individual development and a concern, often thrust upon them from outside, for the teaching of subjects and, especially, of the so-called 'basic skills'.

The current manifestation of this is the present pressure towards increased subject specialist teaching in Primary schools. The advocacy of this is usually associated with expressions of the greatest respect for the 'traditional merits' of the Primary schools' approach to education. The failure to see that the two are incompatible is an example of precisely that theoretical and epistemological muddle this book is concerned to identify. However, the important point to note is that here the muddle has resulted from the failure to recognize that the epistemology which underpins the theoretical position which Primary teachers have been encouraged over the years to adopt — by their training, by the literature and by government reports — is fundamentally empiricist and thus quite different from that which underscores the subject-based approaches favoured by most Secondary schools — and, indeed, by Further and Higher Education.

This confusion, arising from conflicting pressures and expectations, has been observable in the Primary sector of education from its inception. Blyth (1965), for example, has drawn attention to three different strands of influence on the Primary curriculum — the 'elementary', the 'preparatory' and the 'developmental'. The case to be made here is that the conflict is at least in part due to a failure to appreciate fully what is entailed in the commitment to the developmental philosophy which clearly runs through the major reports on this sector. It is hoped that this will become apparent, along with some of its important consequences, if we look more closely at that developmental philosophy as it has evolved in Primary education in England and Wales over many years.

The development of the Primary curriculum

Philosophical influences

From the very outset, from the advent of Primary schools in England and Wales in response to the recommendations of the Hadow Reports (Board of Education 1926, 1931), the underpinning philosophy of the Primary curriculum has been that philosophy which has unfortunately been dubbed 'progressive'. The philosophy is 'progressive' in more senses than one, but to call it such has inevitably been to invite suspicion in what is well known as a highly conservative profession and, indeed, in an area of human activity in which most people are inclined to look askance at any kind of innovation. The use of the term 'progressive' here, however, should not be taken as implying that this is a philosophy which is dramatically new or upstart. For it was first articulated by Jean-Jacques Rousseau in the eighteenth century and there is evidence of educational innovations along these lines even earlier than that (Stewart and McCann 1967/8).

It is Rousseau, however, who offers us the first major statement of this view of education and it is well worth looking briefly at that statement so that we may see its major features.

The theme is stated in the opening sentence of his *Émile*. 'God makes all things good; man meddles with them and they become evil.' It is unfortunate that this doctrine of the innate goodness of children is stated so forcibly at the outset, since this is an aspect of his theory which has received — perhaps rightly — much criticism. It is not crucial, however, to what Rousseau wishes to say about education nor to the theory of education which developed from this, the crux of which is that, whether children are born good or not, they have a right to develop as individuals and to be protected from the imposition of the views and values of the adult world upon them. In short, stripped of the unnecessary, superfluous and largely theological trappings of the debate over original sin, this theory states what we have seen the 'new directions' in the sociology of education asserting more recently, that knowledge is control, that 'educational knowledge' enshrines the values of the dominant group in society and that pupils ought to be offered a form of education which will help them to develop as individuals and not as cyphers.

Rousseau is led to this view by his dissatisfaction with existing approaches to education, exemplifying, as they did — and do — that view of Plato which we discussed in Part One, the view which sees education purely in terms of intellectual growth, which is thus concerned almost totally with its content rather than its processes and which is also an instrumental view, concerning itself with the end product of education, what Rousseau called the 'man-in-the-making', rather than with the child who is the subject of that process. Rousseau complains that educationists 'are always looking for the man in the child, without considering what he is before he becomes a man'. He wants us to view the child as an individual and to tailor our educational provision to his or her individual needs. This means in turn that we must not impose on him or her what we think is important; we must let the child learn, grow, develop through experience. 'Give your scholar no verbal lessons; he should be taught by experience alone.' 'Put the problems before him and let him solve them himself. Let him know nothing because you have told him, but because he has learnt it for himself. Let him not be taught science, let him discover it.' Education, for Rousseau, 'is a question of guidance rather than instruction'.

There are two related features of this view which are highly germane to the central theme of this book. The first is its essential individualism — a characteristic feature of that movement called the 'Enlightenment' of which Rousseau was a part. This is a view, then, which cannot generate a theory of education as the transmission to all pupils of certain universally agreed truths or parcels of knowledge-content. It is a fundamental error, therefore, and reflects a gross misunderstanding to criticize this view on the grounds that 'children cannot acquire all the knowledge they need to have by these discovery or enquiry methods'.

Secondly, this individualism stems from an empiricist epistemology. Rousseau is joining with John Locke in his claim that 'everything that comes into the mind enters through the gates of sense', that 'man's first reason is a reason of sense experience', and identifying himself with the development of that view which we saw in Part One was undertaken by David Hume, with whom, incidentally, Rousseau lived for a time during his exile to England. Again, therefore, it makes no sense to criticize this view from a rationalist perspective, to argue again, for example, that it may not or does not lead to the acquisition of certain necessary bodies of knowledge. For that is fundamentally what this doctrine is opposed to, based as it is on that questioning and tentative theory of knowledge which we saw David Hume proclaiming and which we also saw is the starting point, and indeed the main conclusion, of an empiricist epistemology.

Thus, if we accept that it is this so-called 'progressive' theory of education which underpins the rhetoric, if not always the practice, of the Primary school, we must acknowledge that from the outset it has adopted an empiricist base. And we must accept as a corollary of that the need to evaluate it in its own, distinctive, non-rationalist terms.

There is contained, then, in the work of Rousseau, albeit in a less than well worked out form (perhaps this too set a pattern for subsequent work in this field), all the major ingredients of that view of education which was spawned by empiricism. Little of substance is added to it by the well-known figures of the nineteenth century. Pestalozzi, Herbart, Froebel and Montessori all emphasized certain aspects of it and some of them also developed the practice of it, but they added little or nothing which is of philosophical significance. That was to be left to John Dewey.

We looked in great detail at the work of John Dewey in Chapter 3 and we noted there that his developed version of empiricism and the theory of education which he built on it has had a great effect on the growth of that theory of education we are claiming underpins the Primary curriculum. His work was in many ways a culmination of the work of the ninteenth century educationists and its epistemological base in empiricism is made quite explicit. As we saw there, the stress again is on the tentative and transitory nature of human knowledge, there is now the added dimension given by the nineteenth century concept of evolution, there is a corresponding pragmatic view of truth, there is the same opposition to the idea of education as the imposition of the values of the adult world on the next generation, there is the emphasis on experience as the only route to real learning, there is the idea of education as growth, as development, and there is the view of the teacher's role as a form of guidance, assisting with that process of development.

This, then, is the clearest and possibly the most important statement of this view of education. Many attempts have been made to implement it, interestingly enough most of them in the private sector of education, by people such as J.H. Badley at Bedales School, A.S. Neill at Summerhill, Susan Isaacs at Malting House and Kurt Hahn, first at Salem School and later at Gordonstoun. These are the people who have been seen as the pioneer practitioners of educational 'progressivism'. Until recently, as we shall shortly see, the English Primary school has been encouraged, in far less advantageous circumstances, to pursue the same kind of philosophy.

First, however, we must note another source of influence on the development of this doctrine, another, rather different, but very important, strand in its weaving — the impact of developmental psychology.

The influence of developmental psychology

Rousseau had also flagged for us the importance of an understanding of the psychology of the child. It is an inevitable corollary of his philosophical stance. For if we are to tailor our educational provision to the needs of the child, if our educational provision is in some way to reflect the nature of childhood, then clearly we need to know all we can know about child nature. 'We know nothing of childhood; and with our mistaken notions the further we advance the further we go astray. The wisest writers devote themselves to what a man ought to know, without asking what a child is capable of learning.' Thus Rousseau stressed the need for the study of developmental psychology. Herbart too had emphasized the importance of psychology to the study of education, claiming that 'a large part of the enormous gaps in our pedagogical knowledge results from a lack of psychology'. One is inclined to wonder if either of them would have been happy with the kinds of psychology educationists have often been presented with in more recent times, much of which has reflected that rationalism, and a highly simplistic version of it at that, which this approach to education expressly rejects. For much of it, as we saw in Chapter 4 in the brief reference to behaviourism, has been concerned to help us to devise the most efficient means by which children can be helped to acquire that knowledge which the — rationalist — philosophers have determined they should acquire. Indeed, we also saw earlier that this is the role which some, such as Denis Lawton (1973, 1975), have been content to assign to psychology in educational planning.

However, as we also saw in Chapter 4, another kind of psychology has emerged more recently, one which seems to fit more closely with what both Rousseau and Herbart were expressing a need for and one which has, quite rightly, been seen therefore as complementing the theoretical view of education they were wishing to promote. For the work of the developmental psychologists has been concerned to explore not merely the ways in which children learn — and especially not the ways in which animals learn on the assumption that there is no significant difference — but with the ways in which children develop. Thus, again as we saw in Chapter 4, attention was first given to the process of cognitive growth and, more recently, much has been learnt about the growth of competence in the child, about the need for negotiation of meaning, about the child's sensitivity, from a very early age, to the context of his or her development, including, especially, the social context, and, in short, about forms of development which transcend mere learning.

Thus a first major feature of this work is the claim that a child's thinking is qualitatively different from that of an adult — precisely what Rousseau had claimed, although now given some 'scientific' support — and thus that any form of education to be effective must take full cognizance of this, so that a productive theory of education and of curriculum must begin from a consideration of the child and not of the bodies of subject-content to be transmitted.

A second major feature of this approach to the study of educational psychology is the distinction it draws between learning and cognitive development and its consequent emphasis on the active nature of learning. The child develops intellectually by structuring and restructuring his or her perceptions of the environment and by active forms of inter-relationship with that environment. Intellectual development is qualitatively quite a different process from mere learning. Intellectual development is not a passive process of being filled with knowledge; it is an active process which, in early infancy, will take the form of physical or motor activity, but which, as the child develops, will become less overt, although none the less active for that reason. This notion of learning as an active process is clearly linked very closely with those views of learning as experience which Rousseau expressed and which Dewey developed. Thus the idea, expressed theoretically, that true learning comes from the experience of genuine interaction with one's environment, now has again the 'scientific' backing of studies in developmental psychology.

One can thus see why those who have embraced the kind of 'progressive' educational ideology we described earlier were quick to seize upon the work of the development psychologists as offering a 'scientific' justification of their ideology. Thus this work became a second and highly influential factor in the development of this kind of view of education and of the curriculum in the context of the English Primary school. From the 1930s on, not only were student-teachers offered the ideology of 'progressivism', they were also provided with the supporting 'evidence' of developmental psychology, so that teachers entering the Primary schools, particularly at the Nursery and Infant levels, have at least begun their careers thoroughly imbued with this doctrine. To say that they have been thoroughly imbued with it is not of course to say that they have been expert practitioners of it. For we have already noted the muddle with which it was beset, and we have referred to the evidence of studies such as that of the ORACLE team (Galton et al. 1980; Galton and Simon 1980) that the rhetoric of 'progressivism' is not often to be found matched by any reality.

Nevertheless, this doctrine received more than merely an airing in the Training Colleges of the time. It became the official doctrine of Primary education by being enshrined in the two major government reports on Primary education — those of the Hadow Committee in 1931 and the Plowden Committee in 1967. Until recently, therefore, there has been good reason to see this view as the official doctrine of Primary education, and we must look briefly at what these reports set out to support, before we speculate on why their recommendations seem to have had minimal impact and, indeed, are now being rejected.

The official view

The report of the Hadow Committee on *Primary Education* which was published in 1931 stated quite explicitly its support for some profound changes in the provision of mass education. Its immediate predecessor, the Hadow Report on *The Education of the Adolescent*, published in 1926, had created the Primary school by recommending the 'decapitation' of the existing all-age Elementary schools in order to provide Secondary education for all. This new report, however, looking at Primary education itself, marked a shift not merely in organization but in philosophy, from an Elementary to a Primary school philosophy, from a philosophy which saw the education of the young child as a preparation for something that was to come later to one which insisted on viewing it as a process in its own right. It thus clearly reflects that major shift of emphasis which we are claiming is the central feature of the 'progressive' view of education.

It explains that the education of young children had hitherto been concerned almost solely 'to secure that children acquired a minimum standard of proficiency in reading, writing and arithmetic, subjects in which their attainments were annually assessed by quantitative standards' (op.cit., p.xvi) — precisely, one is tempted to say, the kind of curriculum current government policy would favour, and is indeed advocating, a return to. It goes on to say, however, that today education 'handles the curriculum not merely as consisting of lessons to be mastered, but as providing fields of new and interesting experience to be explored; it appeals less to passive obedience and more to sympathy, social spirit and imagination of the children, relies less on mass instruction and more on the encouragement of individual and group work, and treats the school, in short, not as the antithesis of life, but as its complement and commentary' (ibid.).

It goes on to argue that, in the context of this kind of approach to education, the curriculum must be based on the experience of the pupils, that in this way 'knowledge will be acquired in the process, not, indeed, without effort, but by an effort whose value will be enhanced by the fact that its purpose and significance can be appreciated, at least in part, by the children themselves' (ibid.) and that to facilitate this we must adopt methods 'which take as the starting point of the work of the primary school the experience, the curiosity, and the awakening powers and interests of the children themselves' (ibid.).

The report's acknowledgement of the force and the significance of the work of the developmental psychologists is clear from the stress which is placed on the need to relate educational provision to the developmental stage of the individual since 'life is a process of growth in which there are successive stages, each with its own specific character and needs' (op.cit., p.92). And its commitment to that educational doctrine we are attempting to describe here is summed up in its most often quoted words — 'applying these considerations to the problem before us, we see that the curriculum is to be thought of in terms of activity and experience rather than of knowledge to be acquired and facts to be stored.' (op.cit., p.93)

It is all there — the commitment to education as growth and development rather than the acquisition of knowledge, the conviction that this can be achieved only through experience and active forms of learning, the view of curriculum as process rather than as subject-content, and the acceptance of the need to fit the curriculum to the child rather than the child to the curriculum. The advocacy of a 'progressive' educational ideology, and thus of the empiricist epistemology upon which that must be based, is plain. And this official support for such a view did much to reinforce that process to which we referred earlier by which it was disseminated to successive generations of teachers.

It was to be subsequently reasserted and reaffirmed by the Plowden Committee's report, *Children and Their Primary Schools*, in 1967. The report itself offers a summary of its philosophy of education (pp. 187-8):

A school is not merely a teaching shop, it must transmit values and attitudes. It is a community in which children learn to live first and foremost as children and not as future adults. In family life children learn to live with people of all ages. The school sets out deliberately to devise the right environment for children, to allow them to be themselves and to develop in the way and at the pace appropriate to them. It tries to equalise opportunities and to compensate for handicaps. It lays special stress on individual discovery, on first hand experience and opportunities for creative work. It insists that knowledge does not fall into neatly separate compartments and that work and play are not opposite but complementary. A child brought up in such an atmosphere at all stages of his education has some hope of becoming a balanced and mature adult and of being able to live in, to contribute to, and to look critically at the society of which he forms a part. Not all schools correspond to this picture, but it does represent a general and quickening trend.

Again all the main features of the 'progressive' ideology can be seen in that passage — the concern to treat the child as a child, the attention to developmental stages, the emphasis on education as experience and on learning by discovery, the view of curriculum as process, and the awareness that education should not seek to impose values but to encourage the child 'to look critically at the society of which he forms a part'.

We thus have a view of education which is derived from a long and highly respectable philosophical tradition, which is reinforced by the work of some quite influential figures in the field of developmental psychology and which has received the official backing of two major government reports. Yet it is plain from recent evidence, such as that of the HMI survey of Primary schools (DES 1978) and of the ORACLE team (Galton et al. 1980; Galton and Simon 1980), to which reference has already been made, that the Plowden Report was mistaken in identifying this as 'a general and quickening trend', that 'progressivism' is not as widespread in Primary schools as was once believed. It is interesting to speculate why this is so.

It is the concern of this book to argue that the most plausible explanation is to be found in a failure, on the part both of its supporters and its critics, to recognize the crucial significance of the empiricist epistemology which is its base. Thus its supporters have been less than convincing in their advocacy of it and, indeed, have often been, as the quotation from the Plowden Report offered just now reveals very clearly, highly confused in their statements of it. And its critics, consequently, have had a very easy task in demolishing it, since they have set about doing this from the, quite inappropriate, perspective of their own rationalist epistemology, and no-one has seen the anomaly clearly enough to point out to them the illogicality of their stance. Both aspects of this problem we must now explore in greater detail.

The epistemological muddle

It is clear that the Plowden Report was in many ways its own worst advocate. For, although its heart was clearly in what supporters of the doctrine outlined above would regard as the right place, its head remained in the clouds. Although it expressed compellingly the ideals of the 'progressive' doctrine, it failed to offer any kind of substantial theoretical underpinning for them. And consequently, although its rhetoric was inspirational, it offered little in the way of practical guidance to teachers who might be convinced by that rhetoric, so that they were left still floundering in their attempts to translate it into action. Fundamentally, although deeply committed to this approach to education, it failed totally to see all that that entailed.

As we suggested just now, the confusion is apparent in the summary of its philosophy we have quoted. For that summary begins by telling us that the school 'must transmit values and attitudes' and ends by stressing that the child must be able 'to look critically at the society of which he forms a part'. The lack of coherence is clear, and fundamentally it arises from a confusion of the rationalist and the empiricist perspectives, a failure to recognize that either these are values whose transmission to children can be justified as the rationalist would claim, or the child must be helped to develop his or her own values as the empiricist position requires. One cannot have this particular cake and eat it.

The attitude to the curriculum which the report evinces, even allowing for the fact that it was written almost twenty years ago, is naive to say the least. In particular, it reveals a view of curriculum as subject-content which is quite incompatible with the view of curriculum as process which, it is being argued here, is endemic to this particular educational philosophy. To press the view of education as growth and development and then to discuss the curriculum in terms of the subjects of which it does or should consist is to miss the point completely and to fail to recognize that the first position, requiring us, as the report seems at times to recognize, to begin our curriculum planning from a consideration of the child, cannot be reconciled with a view of the curriculum which suggests that its planning should begin from statements of its necessary and essential content. Again this reflects the same epistemological misunderstanding. The place of subject-content in education needs to be explored fully, especially in the context of a supposedly 'child-centred' approach to curriculum planning. The Plowden Report not only failed to undertake this kind of exploration, it also failed to see that it was logically required by the other positions it had adopted.

It is not surprising, therefore, that it quickly became easy meat for the critics. It was not, however, its inconsistencies which were castigated. These were recognized no more readily by the critics than they had been by the authors of the report. The report had gone sufficiently far down the road towards those rationalist assumptions we are suggesting its fundamental philosophy invalidated for it to be evaluated, criticized and even in some respects demolished by attacks mounted from that very rationalist perspective it should have made clear it had rejected. Nor did such attacks come only from political sources, as, for example, the contributors to the Black Papers (Cox and Dyson 1969a, 1969b); they came too from the 'philosophers of education'.

Thus Primary education was castigated as being 'strong on method but weak on aims', as emphasizing methods and ignoring objectives (Hirst 1969). To which the response should not have been 'Mea culpa', but 'Yes. That is precisely the point and the strength of this approach to education.' For, as we have seen, its essence is that it is concerned with the child here and now and with the growth and development of that child, and not with some preconceived end-product of education. It is concerned with education as a process and not as a means to some predetermined end. It is precisely its emphasis on methods, or rather processes, which gives it its distinctive character and constitutes its strength.

Similarly, it was criticized as not certain to ensure that each child would acquire all the knowledge deemed to be necessary. Enquiry learning, it was argued, might lead anywhere and certainly could not guarantee full coverage. Learning by discovery, as was mentioned earlier, was criticized (Dearden 1967; Peters 1969a) as a method most unlikely to ensure that everything necessary was learned, instead of being seen as a means of ensuring that that which was learnt was fully learnt, or, rather, that the educational process might transcend mere learning in an attempt to attain that real form of intellectual development we saw the Hadow Report offering as its justification of this approach.

Such methods, it was further argued, would not ensure that pupils were initiated into all of those seven forms of knowledge posited by Paul Hirst (1965), so that much effort was put by people such as Robert Dearden

(1976) into attempting to show how this requirement could be reconciled with the demands of the developmental approaches to the Primary curriculum. It was an attempt to mix oil and water. For, again, these criticisms were mounted from a rationalist perspective and thus made all kinds of unwarranted assumptions. Coverage of essential knowledge is not of fundamental concern to anyone who lacks the conviction of the rationalist that he or she knows what essential knowledge is. Initiation into all seven forms of knowledge or understanding is of little significance to anyone who does not share the rationalist's confidence that seven such forms exist. And enquiry learning and/or learning by discovery are not methods by which prepackaged knowledge is to be acquired; they are processes by which development is promoted, and that active form of learning we attempted to define earlier is fostered as a means of ensuring such development. They are notions which represent a different philosophy from that of traditional approaches and not merely differences of methodology.

Some of the notions central to this view, such as those of 'growth', 'interests' and 'needs', have also been heavily criticized (Dearden 1967, 1968, 1976), mainly on the grounds that these are all value terms and that they thus do not offer us a firm basis for educational planning but expose children to the vagaries of the value systems of their teachers. It has even been argued that this is a kind of 'pedagogical megalomania' which leads to a form of manipulation and social control every bit as serious as those attempts to impose predetermined bodies of knowledge-content. The contrast intended of course is with the objectivity of the values implicit in the educational planning of the rationalist, who, having convinced himself or herself of the objectivity of a rationalist system of values, has no difficulty in persuading him or herself of the objectivity of the educational prescriptions which follow from that system.

Again, the inappropriateness of the perspective from which such criticisms have been mounted is clear. And one is tempted to ask whether the value systems of those committed to a hesitant and tentative view of human knowledge and values are really likely to be more harmful to the child's development than those of people who are assured of their own rightness. Education, by its very definition, requires that we make judgements of value. The question is not whether it is undertaken from a value position or is in some sense planned 'scientifically' or objectively; it is which value position it is to be undertaken from. All educational prescriptions, as we saw in Chapter 4, are ideological. And a theory which recognizes this is likely to be far less harmful than one that does not. Certainly, its fundamental differences must be recognized.

Nor does the problem stop here. For it goes far beyond the mere making of criticisms of Primary school theory and practice and can be seen in the underpinning assumptions of some quite influential pieces of 'research' into the work of Primary schools. The work of Neville Bennett and his teams (1976, 1984), for example, says much that is critical of Primary schools and has had a considerable impact on the way in which their work has been viewed and evaluated both within and outside the teaching profession. Yet it lacks any kind of underlying theory of education or of curriculum, such views as it evinces on these being mere unquestioned, unexamined and unstated assumptions, all of them of a rationalist kind. It is thus typical of that behaviourist approach to educational psychology which has concerned itself only with questions of means to ends which themselves remain unchallenged and undebated, and which it was suggested earlier has very serious limitations as a contribution to the development of any kind of valid educational theory. It is purely descriptive and neither shows nor can seriously pretend to any understanding of what it purports to describe. This kind of approach not only represents a serious weakness in the research (if that were all, we might merely ignore it), its effects have also been to inhibit and hold back the development of that view of education and curriculum it fails itself to comprehend (Kelly 1981).

To offer these kinds of criticism, then, of the Primary curriculum, or, worse, to mount influential research projects on the same mistaken assumptions, is to miss the point entirely; it is to fail to recognize the significance of its underlying theory; it is, in particular, to ignore, and even to reveal complete ignorance of, its quite different epistemological base; and it is thus to attempt to criticize and evaluate it in terms which are quite inappropriate. As was suggested in our Introduction, it is comparable to attempting to criticize poetry by the rules of prose.

Nor is this kind of muddle only to be found in the work of those whose intention it is to be critical of the Primary school's approach to education. It is still to be found in some attempts to offer teachers positive advice on their practice. For the confusions which it has been claimed are to be seen in the Plowden Report are replicated in more recent attempts to outline a philosophy and prescribe approaches to teaching in the Primary school (Kelly 1985), such as the Schools Council's *Primary Practice* (1983) and the Inner London Education Authority's 'Thomas Report' (1985).

The problem stems essentially from a failure to appreciate fully what is entailed by the notion of education as process and, in particular, to recognize and accept what this means for the role of subject-content in curriculum planning. For this is the focus of the problem, the rationalist viewing knowledge as in some sense 'out there', 'God-given', certain and thus demanding to be transmitted, the empiricist seeing it as tentative, as uncertain, as evolving, as a human product, and thus seeing education as a process of development rather than of knowledge acquisition, and curriculum planning as to be undertaken from a concern with that process or those processes of development rather than with statements of the knowledge to be acquired or the end-products to be attained.

This is the crux of the epistemological problem in relation to curriculum planning and we must now devote some time to exploring it.

Processes and content

It was suggested earlier that a major weakness of the Plowden Report was its failure to explicate or even to explore the appropriate role for subject-content in a curriculum framed in terms of educational processes. This is one reason why the curriculum of the Primary school, and, in many ways, that at all levels of education, reflects an uneasy compromise between what is thought to be necessary knowledge and those things which are felt to have value for the development of the pupil. The notion of education for personal development has been widely employed at all levels, including that of Higher Education, but what it really implies and what it might mean for the subject which is assumed to be the vehicle for such development has seldom been fully worked out. One notes again the rationalist assumption that value in some mystical way inheres in certain kinds of subject.

Thus, if one asks why certain subjects or certain bodies of subject matter are to be found on the curriculum of most schools and/or in the recommendations of official publications on the curriculum, the answers one comes up with are interesting and varied, but they seldom bear much relationship to education in the full sense.

Some subjects and some kinds of subject matter are clearly on the curriculum for instrumental or utilitarian reasons. They are felt to be necessary to the economic health of society, to conduce to greater industrial efficiency, and thus even to enhance pupils' career prospects. These are thus the subjects which at times of economic stringency continue to be given a large share of the budgetary cake — subjects like mathematics, science, Craft Design and Technology, and, more recently, Computer Studies. There is nothing intrinsically reprehensible in this. Schooling must take account of the economic needs of society and the career prospects of pupils. One might question the advocacy of these subjects when it reaches the stage, as it has at present in the United Kingdom, where the emphasis on these subjects is leading to a devaluing of other kinds of knowledge, especially in that area designated as the Humanities, and a reduction in the financial support offered to them — not least because of the implications of this for the quality of life in a society which places so much stress on the material aspects of living (Powell 1985). And one might also regret the implications that this kind of justification often has for the manner in which these subjects are taught, since this frequently results in the loss of those additional educational advantages the study of such subjects can have. But the essential point here is that the prime justification is economic, utilitarian, instrumental; it is not as we have seen, therefore, an educational justification (although, of course, it is often to be found dressed up as such). The concern is with the usefulness of the subject, not its contribution to the development of those studying it, nor even with any notion of its intrinsic worth or cultural value. Such arguments, then, will not help us in our search for an answer to the question of the appropriate role for subject-content in a curriculum designed to promote certain educational processes.

The second kind of reason one finds for the existence of some subjects on the curriculum is even less helpful. For recent work in the social history of the curriculum, such as that of Ivor Goodson (1981, 1983, 1985 a & b; Goodson & Ball 1984), as we saw in Chapter 4, has revealed very clearly that some subjects have a place on the curriculum primarily because people who have a vested interest in the study and the teaching of them, such as those employed to teach them in schools and universities, have worked very hard, at a political level, to establish and maintain them there. That they later come to be included in some philosopher's list of intrinsically worthwhile activities or essential forms of knowledge or understanding is a pure bonus, and reflects the power of tradition over reason even in some versions of rationalist philosophy. Thus by such devices as the setting up of subject associations, the drawing up of national syllabuses and, in particular, the establishment of public examinations, a subject such as geography has brought itself, or its teachers have brought it, to the point where its right to inclusion in most people's list of core curriculum subjects is likely to go largely unchallenged. Again, therefore, we look in vain for an educational justification, or any real discussion of the contribution of the subject to the processes of development.

Attempts at an educational justification for the inclusion of certain subjects in the curriculum begin and end with the kinds of claim about knowledge which are made by rationalism, with notions such as those of intrinsic value and of subject hierarchies. The main difficulties with justifications of this kind are, first, that they are fundamentally rationalist and thus carry no weight with anyone who does not accept that view of knowledge, and, second, that they create more problems than they solve when it comes to educational practice. For, while some agreement may be granted to the general proposition that education should consist of intrinsically worthwhile activities, little agreement is possible or likely over the question of which activities satisfy the criterion of intrinsic value and even over that of which of those that do should be selected for inclusion in the curriculum.

A third, and serious, problem with this approach to educational planning is that there is nothing within it which will obviate — except by accident — the kind of inert learning which Alfred North Whitehead (1932) warned us of long ago. For the concern is with the knowledge to be transmitted and thus with the acquisition of it by pupils, which is why there has always been a strong link between this view of the curriculum and behaviourist psychology with its claims to advising us on the most efficient methods of ensuring such acquisition. There is nothing in this view or in the model of planning it has spawned which concerns itself, or can concern itself, in any way with the manner in which pupils are to acquire such knowledge or achieve such learning. If we are concerned with this aspect of education — and it is difficult to see how any concern for education could ignore it — then the impact of the knowledge on the pupil is what is crucial; it is what he or she makes of it that matters; in short, it is its contribution to his or her development which is of central importance. There is thus, as we have already seen, a fundamental contradiction in the work of those theorists who argue for a curriculum framed in terms of certain bodies of worthwhile knowledge while at the same time professing a concern about the manner and form of the pupils' learning. For that manner and form will be determined to a large degree by the pupil's response to what is offered, so that it is that response which becomes the crucial element in curriculum planning and the focus of that planning must be the processes of development.

The logic of the notion of education as concerned with learning which is active rather than inert pushes us, then, towards a form of educational planning which begins not from the subject or discipline but from the development of the child, so that it is best expressed not in terms of subjects or disciplines but in terms of developmental processes, areas of experience, the 'eight adjectives' of *Curriculum 11-16* (DES 1977) or any other phrase or concept which alerts us to the need to give first priority to the impact of the study on the pupil, its contribution to his or her growth and development, and not to the subjects or disciplines themselves. Fundamentally, as was suggested in Chapter 4, this is really the main thrust of Paul Hirst's claim (1965) that education requires the initiation of the pupil into all the forms of rationality, knowledge or understanding. One may disagree with his characterization of knowledge, but one must recognize that essentially he is recommending that education should concern itself with the — albeit intellectual only — development of the child.

The central question for curriculum planning, therefore, becomes not what content should the curriculum include but what developmental processes should it be concerned to promote. The second question then becomes what kinds of subject-content, and what kinds of method and approach to the teaching of that subject-content, will help to promote those processes. To express it differently, the first criterion of choice of subject-content in curriculum planning becomes not a consideration of the subject's utility, nor of any intrinsic value it may be claimed that it possesses, but its potential effects on the educational development of the pupil. On this analysis the educational justification of any subject, discipline or piece of knowledge-content presented to pupils can only be found in its impact on them, its contribution to their growth and development, and not in its own intrinsic value, whatever that might be, nor in any mystical or metaphysical properties it may be claimed it is possessed of. Content, as Charity James (1968) said, is an element in planning not a ground-plan.

This is the thrust of that theory of education which is built on an empiricist/pragmatist epistemology. Its implications for the role and the place of subjects in the curriculum is far-reaching and quite central, even though this has so seldom been appreciated. It also has important implications for the manner in which we set about promoting learning; indeed, one of its merits is that it encourages, even requires, us to ask questions about that which go far beyond those of mere methodology.

To say this is not of course to say that the curriculum will not, or even that it should not, contain subject-content selected by teachers or others on the grounds that it is regarded as worthwhile. No-one would be, or should be, a teacher who has not come to a love of some areas of knowledge and/or experience, a preference for some kinds of activity over others, and much of the value of educational experiences would evaporate if teachers did not capitalize on this and endeavour to share that love and those preferences with their pupils. It is, however, to say that that love and those preferences are not sufficient justification in themselves; they must be matched by an awareness of the need to demonstrate the contribution of what is being offered to the development of pupils. It is to say too that there is no justification in offering pupils such knowledge and such experiences, along with the values implicit in them, in a manner which is designed or likely to discourage them from questioning for themselves the worth of what is being offered or its implicit values. There is a real sense in which it is only when one's pupils reject — after careful consideration and for good reasons — what one has offered them that one can really be sure one has succeeded in educating them. Finally, it is also to say that education is an individual matter, that the development of countless numbers of individual human beings cannot be planned as some kind of exercise in mass production nor can it be undertaken by remote control. (It is not surprising that the imagery of the factory floor immediately suggests itself here.) The subject-content we offer will in part be selected by reference to what we ourselves are familiar with and have come to admire and respect, but the central and overriding criterion must be our professional perception of how that content can contribute to the developmental needs of each individual pupil.

And let us not at this point get ourselves bogged down in quibbling arguments over the concept of 'needs'. Most of that debate, in any case, as we have seen, is rooted in that rationalist epistemology which this view of curriculum has rejected. Teachers are not mere teaching machines. They are, or should be, prepared by their initial courses, even if they do not all have access to subsequent in-service tuition, to make educational judgements, to take decisions concerning the appropriate forms of educational provision for their pupils, and that can only be done on the basis of some assessment of educational need. It is logically impossible to set about educating anyone without making some judgement of what that entails. As we saw just now, any theory of education requires the making of judgements of value. The crux of this view of education and curriculum is that teachers should be encouraged, helped and prepared to make such judgements by reference to the developmental needs of their pupils and not out of concern for the demands of their subject, and that, furthermore, they should do this with full acknowledgement not only that these are judgements of value but also of all that that implies, and, in particular, that the idea of some value-free assessment of children's needs is a nonsense. It is this that reveals the major inadequacies of many of the recent official pronouncements and indeed current government policies on teacher education. For the characterization of the teacher's role which is displayed there has only two facets — subject content and methodology. The view of education as transmission and thus of the teacher's sole problem as being a concern with the methods of such transmission is plain. Such a characterization evinces a disturbing failure to understand or to appreciate what teachers actually do and are required to do.

The view of education and of curriculum, then, which emerges once one recognizes the inadequacies of the rationalist base, or at least its incompatibility with the empiricist/pragmatist tradition, requires us to see education in terms of developmental processes and to regard subject-content as a consideration which is secondary to them. There have been in recent times some examples of attempts to implement this approach — and not all of them are to be found in the Primary sector of schooling. The whole Integrated Studies movement of the late 1960s and early 1970s, imperfect as much of it was, may be seen as a series of attempts to plan education by reference to the developmental needs of pupils, and it is interesting to note that an integrated, undifferentiated view of knowledge was one of the first consequences of making such attempts. It is also worth noting that this movement was hampered in its own development primarily by the opposition of rationalist attempts to preserve the 'purity' of the disciplines and to maintain the content-based approach to the curriculum. One can also see developments in Craft Design and Technology, indeed the creation of that subject from those 'handicraft' subjects from which it grew, as an example of the same kind of philosophy, a result of attempts to ask what the subject has to offer which will promote educational development — particularly creditable, perhaps, in a subject which might have relied more readily than most on utilitarian and vocational forms of justification of a kind which it is still being encouraged to embrace — at the risk of losing much of its hard-won educational validity.

Other more specific examples include those well-known projects, the Schools Council's Humanities Curriculum Project (HCP) (Schools Council 1970) and Bruner's Man: A Course of Study (MACOS)(Bruner 1966). The potential of the latter as a vehicle in itself and as a starting point for a process-based approach to the curriculum of the Secondary school has been well brought out by Gwyn Edwards (1983) in his account of his own work with the project's materials at Meopham School. Another example is the Schools Council's project, Learning through Science, the underlying principles of which have been well set out by its director, Roy Richards (1983). Indeed, the very title of this project makes our point for us. For it is what children may learn *through* a subject rather than what they must learn *of* it that now becomes crucial.

In turn this implies that the questions we should be asking about school subjects are not those of rationalism, What subjects ought to have a place on the curriculum as of right? or What particular subject content should we be aiming to transmit to pupils?, and certainly not those of the politician or the economist, What economic value or usefulness has the teaching of this subject? or What is its vocational potential?, but the very different questions of What forms of development can subject x promote? and thus How can we justify its inclusion in the curriculum in *educational* terms? It is not the kinds of knowledge we offer that is the crucial concern in curriculum planning but the kinds of engagement with knowledge which we promote.

It is this kind of question that people such as Eliot Eisner (1979) and Mary Newbold and Maurice Rubens (1983) in the Inner London Education Authority have been tackling in relation to the contribution of art to children's development. It is these questions that Roy Richards was asking about science in the Learning through Science project. And these are the underlying questions of projects such as the Humanities Curriculum Project and Man: A Course of Study in relation to the Humanities.

The best examples of this approach to the curriculum in practice, however, are undoubtedly to be found in the English Primary school, and perhaps particularly in Infant schools and departments. For this is the kind of approach to curriculum planning and to teaching which, as we saw earlier, teachers in the Primary sector have long been encouraged to adopt. Its implications, however, as we also suggested earlier, have never been fully spelled out to them or appreciated. Current pressures for increased subject specialism in Primary schools must accelerate the movement away from that approach and must set back the development of a theory of education which we have seen has a long history and tradition dating at least from the time of Rousseau. Such contrary pressures might be acceptable if one was convinced that they were a result of a careful consideration of the issues and, indeed, of a full appreciation and proper understanding of them. They clearly stem, however, from those muddled rationalist assumptions this chapter has been concerned to identify and, what is perhaps worse, a utilitarian view of schooling which must ultimately act to the detriment of education, however one defines it.

That same utilitarianism is also apparent in the current fashion of planning education in terms of its end-products, its 'aims and objectives', and we must conclude our discussion of curriculum planning by looking briefly at that.

Product-oriented planning

The view of education as the acquisition of certain kinds of knowledge is often to be found associated with the view of education as product-oriented and thus as something to be planned from initial statements of its 'aims and objectives'. The difficulties of this view of planning have been fully debated elsewhere (Blenkin and Kelly 1981; Kelly 1982) and it is not the intention to rehearse them all here. Several points must be briefly made, however, since they are germane to our present debate.

First, a product-oriented form of planning begins from a concern with what education is *for* rather than with what it *is*. Thus its focus is on what we earlier referred to as 'the man(or woman)-in-the-making'. It is this that links it firmly to rationalism. And it is this which makes it quite incompatible with that view of education which we have seen derives from an alternative epistemology. For that view, as we saw, is primarily concerned with what children are rather than with what they must be turned into; it sees education not as a process of moulding but as a process of guided growth and development.

Secondly, we must note the uncritical acceptance of the 'aims and objectives' model by so many people at so many levels within education. Among the plethora of recent official pronouncements on the curriculum emanating from both local and central governments in the United Kingdom, it is difficult to find a single document which does not urge teachers to begin their planning with a statement of their 'aims and objectives', even when these same documents are also advocating a concern with the processes of education, the incoherence and inconsistency of confusing these two stances remaining unrecognized. Sometimes, as in the document *English from 5 to 16* (DES 1984a), the difficulties of this approach are acknowledged, but there is no consequent questioning of its suitability or consideration of the adoption of an alternative model which might be more appropriate.

The unsuitability of this approach to the planning of large areas of the English curriculum, which the difficulties remarked upon by this document alert us to, reveals a further problem. For this is clearly an approach which is quite unsuitable for large areas of the curriculum generally, where the prespecification of learning outcomes is totally inappropriate. Areas such as personal, social, moral and emotional development, for example, which we will look at more closely in Chapter 8, clearly cannot be planned in terms of such learning outcomes, in terms of behaviour changes towards achieving which we can adopt the methods advocated by behavioural psychology. Yet, if development is our concern, these are aspects of development we can hardly ignore. The inability of rationalist approaches to education to provide any basis for appropriate forms of planning in these areas of the curriculum will be the major concern of Chapter 8.

Finally, we must note that we have here a classic example of the rationalist's main technique. As we saw in Part One, what rationalism is fundamentally concerned to do is to derive prescriptions — moral or educational — from definitions, from analyses of meaning, from exploration of essences. This is the modern manifestation of essentialism. Thus Paul Hirst argues (1969) that since rationality is characterized by intentionality, by being goal-directed, education, if it is to rank as a rational activity, must also be goal-directed so that educational planning must begin with a statement of its objectives.

There are two errors in this. The first is the procedure of deriving prescriptions from this kind of source, of seeing conceptual analysis not merely as a tool of conceptual clarification but as a basis for imperatives. This, as we saw in Part One, is a salient feature and a fundamental error of rationalism. The second error, however, is to assume that one can make this kind of deduction from a consideration of merely one aspect of rationality. For, even if the procedure were valid, one could argue as well that rationality is characterized at least as much by a concern with principles as by a concern with intentions, and that it thus would lead as well to a view of educational planning as requiring a statement of procedural principles as to one demanding a declaration of goals. Indeed, this was a central feature of Kantian moral philosophy, since the concern there was with duty rather than consequences as the only acceptable guiding force of moral action. A moral action, for Kant, was an action performed for its own sake and not for any extrinsic purpose. This too is the force of that concern with things which are 'ends-in-themselves' which is also characteristic of rationalism and which is reflected in Richard Peters' preference for activities whose value is intrinsic rather than extrinsic.

There is thus an inherent inconsistency in a theory of education which advises us to plan education in terms of intrinsically worthwhile activities and at the same time in terms of its goals. This is thus another of those muddles in 'philosophy of education' which we have commented on from time to time. There is no doubt that teaching is an intentional and goal-oriented activity, as Peters (1967a), Scheffler (1967) and others have claimed, but there are no grounds for assuming that its intentions or its goals must be framed in terms of subject-content or of end-products. They can be framed as well in terms of the processes of development education is concerned to promote.

Summary and conclusions

This chapter has been concerned to challenge the appropriateness and the effectiveness of knowledge-content as a starting point for curriculum planning, and also the associated approach to planning through statements of 'aims and objectives'. It attempted to do this by examining an alternative approach to curriculum planning, that which starts from a consideration of developmental processes, and to do this in what continues to be its most concrete manifestation — the curriculum of the English Primary school.

The chapter began by endeavouring to show that, in spite of apparent inadequacies of practice, a distinctive philosophy of education has emerged in the Primary sector of education in the United Kingdom, a philosophy which owes most to the educational thinking first of Rousseau, then that of some major figures of the nineteenth century and finally that of John Dewey, which owes a good deal too to the work of developmental psychologists such as Jean Piaget and Jerome Bruner, and more recently those such as Margaret Donaldson and Eliot Eisner who have built on and modified that earlier work, and which received official blessing from the Hadow (1931) and Plowden (1967) Committees. An attempt was also made to demonstrate that the bedrock of this philosophy is an empiricist/ pragmatist epistemology, even though this has not always been appreciated even by its advocates.

Indeed, it was suggested next that it is the failure to appreciate this that has led to the kinds of theoretical muddle (and consequent practical inadequacies) which the chapter went on to list. It was claimed that the Plowden Report's statement of it lacked theoretical or philosophical conviction, primarily because it was itself unclear about its theoretical base, that much of the criticism that was offered of the Plowden doctrine, and, indeed some quite influential research projects, were mounted from the quite inappropriate perspective of a number of rationalist assumptions about knowledge and about values, and that, in particular, the whole debate foundered on the failure by both parties to recognize the implications of an empiricist epistemology for the view of the role of knowledge-content in educational planning.

An attempt was finally made to explore some of those implications. It was argued that values are endemic to education and to the making of educational judgements. It was suggested, however, that this view of education requires us to seek those values in the concept of education as a process of development and not in its subject-content. Subject-content will inevitably be chosen in the light of the teacher's own preferences or even in the light of whatever agreement appears to exist in society concerning the merits of certain kinds of knowledge and certain aspects of culture. If education is seen in terms of its processes, however, such preferences, such apparent agreement will not and cannot be the first criterion of choice. That first criterion must be the contribution likely to be made to promoting the development of the pupil.

The prime concern of the rationalist must be with knowledge, and especially that knowledge which he or she is convinced has some intrinsic, universal and overriding value. The prime concern of an empiricist philosophy of education must be with the development of the individual, since it is only by starting from there that allowance can be made for the tentative nature of knowledge and values, that the continued evolution of both to which empiricism commits us can be promoted and that the ossification and the reification of knowledge can be prevented.

It is this concern not merely with development but with individual development that we must turn to next. For, if our intention is to promote learning which is real rather than inert, which is active rather than passive, which is conducive to growth and development rather than to the mere acquisition of knowledge, then it would seem inevitable that this must be recognized as an individual process. If this is so, it will clearly have wide-reaching implications for the kind of universal planning of educational provision which is a major current preoccupation in the United Kingdom. It is to this, then, that we turn in Chapter 6.

CHAPTER 6

CURRICULUM BALANCE AND CENTRAL CURRICULUM PLANNING — EDUCATION AS INDIVIDUAL DEVELOPMENT

A general State education is a mere contrivance for moulding people to be exactly like one another.
(John Stuart Mill, *On Liberty*)

Nowhere is the dogmatism and the unwarranted confidence of the educational 'experts' so apparent as in the debate about the desirability of establishing a common core curriculum in the schools of the United Kingdom. For every kind of confidence is evinced not only about the idea itself but also about the precise composition of such a common core. Yet the wide range of disagreement between these 'experts' on what that composition should be is the clearest possible evidence of the futility of the exercise of seeking certain answers in this field, and of the claim which this book is making that all such pronouncements are fundamentally ideological, that they are made from the perspective of a particular value position, and that any claims they make to objective support or validity are misguided and spurious.

For recently resurrected phrases like the 'essential' curriculum, the 'effective' curriculum and especially the 'balanced' curriculum, along with the debate about the desirability of establishing a common curriculum, are all, at least in part, restatements of an idea that goes back at least to the time of Plato, that a proper education necessitates some kind of balanced initiation into certain readily identifiable kinds of knowledge. Thus they all make certain assumptions about the nature and status of human knowledge and those assumptions are essentially rationalist. It is not being argued here that they must make these assumptions, merely that they do and that, because they do, these notions have been far less helpful to educational planning than they might have been if the assumptions had been recognized and challenged. For, when they are recognized and challenged, not only are the terms seen to take on rather different meanings, much of the dogmatism also goes out of the statements and a clearer view of the essential questions becomes possible.

For those terms have been coined as part of a campaign to achieve two purposes. The first of these is to persuade us that the curriculum must be viewed and planned as a whole. Thus they are associated also with expressions like 'the whole curriculum' and 'the total curriculum'. The second purpose is to encourage the search to identify some basic principles of curriculum construction, some fundamental considerations to guide us towards a consistency and coherence of curriculum planning. With neither of these goals would most of us wish to quarrel.

In almost all cases, however, they have been used to suggest that two further assumptions can legitimately be made and it is here that their uncritical adoption of a rationalist epistemology becomes apparent. For they are inclined also to assume that there can be a successful outcome to such a search in the discovery of some objective criteria for educational planning. This is a good example of the way in which the overcommitment to rationalism has encouraged what Bill Reid (1978) has called a futile search for a single theory of curriculum development. And they have further assumed that the focus of attention for that search should be the subjects or subject-content of which the curriculum is to consist. Thus concern about curriculum balance arises when it seems that the curriculum contains too much that is scientific or too much that is in the area of the Humanities or too much that seems to be overtly vocational and utilitarian. And the solutions proposed to this kind of concern invariably involve the introduction of other 'balancing' subjects into the programme. We are told, for example (DES 1985, p.44), that 'a balanced curriculum should ensure that each area of learning and experience and each element of learning is given appropriate attention in relation to the others and to the curriculum as a whole.'

It is the contention here that this represents an oversimplified view of curriculum balance and, further, that this oversimplification is due entirely to certain epistemological assumptions of a rationalist kind. It is also the claim that, once this is recognized and those assumptions are challenged, not only does the familiar inconsistency of this stance become apparent but also a clearer view of what might constitute a central core and of what might be seen as a balanced provision becomes possible, with consequent effects on educational practice. For the notions of a common curriculum and of curriculum balance make better theoretical and practical sense when seen from the perspective of educational processes than from that of curriculum subjects or bodies of knowledge, from the perspective of the educand rather than from that of the content of his or her educational programme. The only intelligible concept of curriculum balance is one defined in terms of the experiences of the pupil rather than the presumed properties of the forms of knowledge to be transmitted, so that the very idea of 'balance' implies that view of education as a process of development which we discussed in Chapter 5, and attempts to translate that into subject terms represent again a fundamental misunderstanding and inconsistency.

This chapter, then, sets out not to define or describe 'the balanced curriculum'. That, it will be argued, is a quite inappropriate thing to do. Rather its concern will be to explore the concept, to pick out the concerns it encapsulates, to identify the problems it raises, and the difficulties and pitfalls it creates, and, in general, to offer clarification rather than prescription. It will also be argued in particular that much of the confusion currently surrounding this notion is due to certain rationalist assumptions upon which its use is invariably based, and that it is thus a prime example of an area of educational theory whose clarification must begin from a challenge to those assumptions.

The most interesting arguments offered in this field are those purporting to be based on some notion of curriculum balance and it is on that notion that we will concentrate our gaze in this chapter. It will be useful, however, if we first consider some of the arguments put forward in support of a common curriculum or of a common core to the curriculum, not least in order that we may identify their essential rationalism and thus remind ourselves of some of the difficulties inherent in that stance.

A common core curriculum

There are at least three kinds of argument one finds adduced in support of proposals to institute a common curriculum or a common core to the curriculum for all pupils in England and Wales. The first of these is the economic argument which takes as its first premise the need of a modern industrial society for large (although clearly reducing in size) numbers of people with the scientific and technological knowledge and understanding to ensure continued technological development and a concomitant economic growth.

This is the kind of argument which we hear increasingly from politicians and their aides; it is part of the case which was put by James Callaghan, as Prime Minister, in his speech at Ruskin College in 1976 which began, or at least made public, the current process of increased political intervention in the school curriculum; and it is the argument which is used to justify the differential allocation of resources to science and arts subjects at all levels of educational provision. It is not, however, an argument which can or should concern us here. For as we have already seen on several occasions it is not an *educational* argument, certainly it is not one to which issues concerning the nature and status of human knowledge are relevant, in spite of the attempts of some to dress it up as such or to run together and confuse what are essentially utilitarian or instrumental considerations with those of an intrinsic kind. It reflects that view of the educational system which the Crowther Report (CACE 1959) described as a national investment, and it does not embrace that other dimension the same report identified — education as the right of every child. Its fundamental concern is with the needs of society, as it envisages them. We must, of course, acknowledge its existence and we must not appear to subscribe to any view which assumes that education can be completely divorced from politics, or from economic necessities, but we must learn to distinguish it from other kinds of argument and we must also recognize that it is not part of our present discussion whose concern is with claims concerning the *educational* validity and justification of certain forms of curriculum, as we defined that in Chapter 4.

The second kind of argument is that which is mounted on the basis of a commitment to some view of equality, both social and educational. Equality, it is claimed, can only be achieved if every child has access to the same educational opportunities, and this is usually interpreted as implying access to the same curricular provision. There are a number of interesting features to this form of argument, not least the assumptions about knowledge and values which are implicit in the claims it makes about the kinds of knowledge and the forms of culture to which everyone should be given equal access. These assumptions are clearly a prime example of what this book is endeavouring to identify and they will be given full attention in Chapter 7.

The kind of argument which we must concentrate on here, however, is that which presses for a common core to the curriculum on the grounds that certain kinds of knowledge are superior to other kinds and thus have a prior right to inclusion in the curriculum of all pupils, not because of their utilitarian value nor because of their contribution to the attainment of social and educational equality, but because of their intrinsic merits. Clearly, such a case can only be mounted from the perspective of a rationalist epistemology and a brief review of some of the arguments paraded in support of this kind of claim will quickly confirm that.

Such a review could, of course, begin with Plato and continue with almost all the 'Great Educators' of the Western world, including especially those making their pronouncements from the vantage point of the Christian church, but it would hardly be brief. It may be enough, therefore, to refer to several influential assertions of more recent times.

Two main kinds of argument have been to the forefront of the recent debate. The first, that which was a major feature of the work of Richard Peters, is the argument that claims intrinsic merits for certain kinds of knowledge, that they are, for example, disinterested pursuits, that 'they can be, and to a large extent are, pursued for the sake of values intrinsic to them rather than for the sake of extrinsic ends' (Peters, 1965, p.160), that 'their cognitive concerns and far-ranging cognitive content give them a value denied to other more circumscribed activities which leads us to call them serious pursuits' (ibid.), 'they are "serious" and cannot be considered merely as if they were particularly delectable pastimes, because they consist largely in the explanation, assessment and illumination of the different facets of life' (ibid.). To this one might add John White's claim that there are 'Category 1' activities, which must be compulsory components of a common curriculum, because 'no understanding of X is logically possible without engaging in X' (1973, p.27). This is a slightly different kind of argument but it is of course based on the same kind of assumption that an understanding of X is worth achieving; it is thus a second stage of the same argument which Richard Peters offers.

These lines of argument are, of course, rooted in rationalism. Indeed, we saw in Part One that Richard Peters explicitly produces a Kantian-style 'transcendental' argument in support of them, and John White's only answer to the question of why anyone should bother to engage in activities whose distinguishing characteristic (even if we accept this) is that that is the only way to understand them has to be framed in terms of a similar view of their intrinsic superiority. They are lines of argument which lead, therefore, as we have seen, to subject hierarchies, to an emphasis on the cognitive content of educational activities or studies, to those claims to certainty and objectivism which we have seen challenged both by empiricist/pragmatist schools of philosophy and by the 'new directions' in the sociology of education.

What is more interesting, however, is their dependence on arguments derived from a concern with education as development, an inconsistency which was highlighted in Chapter 4. For they are at their most convincing when they are attempting to justify these subjects, areas of knowledge or activities in terms of their contribution to the growth and development of the individual. Thus Richard Peters, in the passage from which several quotations have just been offered, goes on to justify the same activities on the grounds that 'they . . . insensibly change a man's view of the world' (op.cit., p.160) and that 'a person who has pursued them systematically develops conceptual schemes and forms of appraisal which transform everything else that he does' (ibid.). Thus it is not the activities themselves which are the concern; it is their effect on those who study them. One can also interpret Plato's theory of education in the same way, since for him too it is not anything inherent in the subjects he advocates which attracts him, it is the kinds of development they promote in the student. If one relates this to the points made about the role of developmental processes in curriculum planning in Chapter 5, a strong case begins to emerge for a move away from a concern with subject content rather than the opposite.

One might also appeal, as again was suggested in Chapter 4, to the emphasis placed on the growth of autonomy and on the parallel development of powers of critical awareness by all the advocates of this kind of hierarchical view of subject-knowledge. Again, these are aspects of the development of individuals rather than features of the knowledge itself; they are functions of how the knowledge is received and not of anything inherent in it. They are thus forms of development which are likely to be inhibited rather than promoted by too great an emphasis on the intrinsic value of the knowledge or the subjects selected to achieve these forms of development. Again, then, we see that there is an important and quite fundamental inconsistency in such theories.

The second kind of philosophical argument which has been adduced in support of the institution of a common core curriculum is equally interesting, and in the same way. This is the line which has developed from that analysis of knowledge offered by Paul Hirst (1965), who has suggested not only that education is the development of rationality but that, since he sees rationality as having several different forms, education must be the initiation of pupils into all of them. We have noted before that this is a typical — and erroneous — piece of rationalist or essentialist reasoning, since from an analysis of the concept of rationality certain prescriptions are — quite improperly — deduced. We must also note the complete lack of evidence for the existence of these different forms of rationality. What is more interesting for us here, however, is that again, as was suggested in Chapter 4, the fundamental concern is not with the forms of knowledge or of rationality themselves, but with the development it is claimed they promote in the individual. Thus, again, the concern is not with education as transmission, although that term is used quite often, but with education as development of a certain kind. The fact that the focus is on cognitive development alone we will pick up in Chapter 8.

A second point of interest is that this kind of analysis of rationality into several forms is the current version of a view of knowledge which has been around for a long time. It can certainly be seen in Plato's educational theory and, as Paul Hirst (1965) reminds us, it is the basis of the *trivium* and the *quadrivium* of the medieval curriculum. Furthermore, it has attracted a good deal of — often uncritical — support in recent times, and has been taken for granted too readily by a number of other advocates of a common core curriculum. Thus not only have writers such as John White used this kind of analysis to reinforce their case, but also writers such as Denis Lawton (1973, 1975) and Robert Dearden (1968, 1976), without facing the fundamental questions about the status of knowledge which this raises, have been concerned to argue the case for dividing knowledge into discrete parcels, and have based their demands for a common core to the curriculum on the need to include all of these parcels in every individual's educational Xmas stocking.

Clearly a further underlying claim here is that the curriculum should be 'balanced' and, since there is a good deal more to that concept than most have appreciated, and since too an examination of it will reveal much that is of relevance to our general argument, we will turn now to a detailed exploration of what might be meant by 'curriculum balance'.

Curriculum balance

The intention is to begin by looking at the background to the development of this idea of a balanced curriculum or a balanced education and to attempt to identify the assumptions behind it. Next, some recent developments will be described, most of them tending towards the erosion of those assumptions. Then some major problems of definition will be outlined. And, finally, an attempt will be made to draw some conclusions from the discussion, conclusions which will endeavour to show that much of the difficulty surrounding both the theory and practice of education in this area is due to the unquestioned rationalism that has continued to permeate all the claims which have been made under this heading.

The background

Some notion like that of balance has been around in education theory from the very beginning. For Plato, a key concept in education, as in all else, was that of 'harmony'. Harmony required an appropriate balancing of intellectual and physical pursuits in his early system of education, of 'music' and 'gymnastic'. This was a more sophisticated notion than that merely of *mens sana in corpore sano*, a phrase which has sometimes, quite inaccurately, been used to characterize it, since it suggested not just the proper upbringing of the mind and the body but their proper upbringing in unison. An educational diet consisting of properly balanced elements of both would be justified primarily by its effects on the development of the 'soul' of the individual. Imbalance would lead either to the effete artist or to the brutalized athlete. A proper balance was needed for true educational success. Similarly, his higher system of education was planned to ensure a proper harmony between the three elements of the human 'soul' — the appetites, the 'spirit' and the intellect. Thus balance was a key notion from the start of thinking about education in Western Europe and there is no doubting the continued influence of Plato on that thinking.

Balance was an important consideration for Aristotle too. He, however, introduced a factor which is more important than has often been recognized and which we will need to return to later. For, in his discussion of the so-called 'golden mean' of morality, he suggested that this had to be seen in its context and in relation to the individual concerned. His analogy is interesting. For he suggests that just as individuals differ in relation to their dietary needs — an ordinary man's balanced diet, to use his example, being very different from that of the wrestler, Milo — so they will differ in respect of what might be right behaviour. We might add that they will differ too in relation to a balanced educational diet. It is perhaps because this introduces an element of relativism which is quite unacceptable to rationalism that it was not taken up. It becomes, however, an important consideration in educational planning, as we shall see, once that rationalism is challenged, and it is the focus of our concern in this chapter.

It was Quintilian who introduced the idea of a broad balance of subjects in the curriculum. To some extent, his *De Institutione Oratoria* can be seen as a broad restatement of the educational ideals of Plato, adapted to the changed context of his time — the education of the orator rather than that of the philosopher. His work does, however, introduce for us another dimension of balance, of which we shall later see the importance. For Quintilian's prime motivation is the desire to show that an education in rhetoric need not be the arid, vocational, instrumental, utilitarian affair it could often be seen to be in his day. Properly planned, it could offer that balanced educational diet which would lead to the education of the whole man, the sage, even the good man.

It was the discovery of the text of Quintilian's *Institutes* in 1416 which sparked off a series of works reaffirming his educational doctrines. Thus the work of Humanists, such as Elyot and Erasmus, can be seen largely as a restatement of Quintilian's views, and thus by derivation those of Plato. Their proposed curriculum consisted of the *trivium* (grammar, rhetoric and logic or dialectic) and the *quadrivium* (music, arithmetic, geometry and astronomy). The ideal personality to be developed is now that of the courtier or the governor, rather than the orator or the philosopher, but the ingredients are essentially the same and the notion of a proper balance continues to be fundamental.

Thus the theoretical base was set for the development of educational practice along these lines and, particularly when one adds to this the influence of the Christian church on both the theory and, through its many endowments, the practice of education, it is not surprising to discover that educational thinking and practice has reflected these principles and assumptions well into the present century. We have already seen that this is the basis for Paul Hirst's advocacy of a curriculum consisting of the seven forms of knowledge, understanding and rationality.

Certainly, these were the basic assumptions of the public school tradition in the United Kingdom. And, since that was taken as the model, they came to be built into the state system too in the United Kingdom, and, indeed, throughout Western Europe where a similar tradition has held sway (Nicholas 1983). For the early grammar schools adopted the curriculum of the public school, as indeed had the universities. Thus, this was the curriculum which became formalized in the public examinations system. And, of particular interest, the universities' matriculation requirements, reflected in the 'subject-grouping' system of the School Certificate examinations, embodied that continuing notion of a balanced educational diet, often described as 'a broad, general education'.

Some important assumptions of this view could perhaps with profit be picked out at this point. The first thing to notice, of course, is the fundamental rationalism of this position. That rationalism leads it to make clear assumptions about the intrinsic superiority of certain kinds of knowledge and their consequent right, on objective and non-utilitarian grounds, to inclusion in a properly balanced educational curriculum. From this follow a hierarchical view of knowledge, a dogmatic view of what kinds of knowledge are educationally valuable and a consequent devaluing of any kind of 'practical' activity or study on the grounds that anything practical must be utilitarian, instrumental and perhaps even vocational. Where it is conceded that such activities or kinds of study might be necessary — for other, non-educational reasons — every effort is made to counterbalance them with a proper diet of intrinsically worthwhile knowledge. There is also a devaluing of the role of the emotions in human development, a concern to repress rather than to educate them, or to reduce them to some kind of cognitive perspective rather than to acknowledge that to a large extent they are non-cognitive. But that is another story, which we shall pick up in Chapter 8.

These were the major assumptions underlying the curriculum in the age of 'drift' (Hoyle 1969 a, b), before the advent of the era of planned curriculum development. They still persist as unchallenged assumptions in much that is currently said and written about education, but the advent of curriculum planning, and the societal changes which have prompted it, have introduced a number of considerations which have resulted in the erosion of much that lies behind this kind of thinking, and we must now trace some of these developments if we are to move towards clarifying the issues.

Recent developments

At the practical level, the process of erosion can be taken as having begun with the advent of the General Certificate of Education examinations to replace the School Certificate examinations in 1951. For whereas a major feature of the latter had been groupings of subjects to ensure a balance, the Certificate being awarded only to those candidates with an approved combination of subject passes, the former was from the outset a 'single subject' examination, permitting the taking — and passing — of a single subject or any number of subjects in any combinations. This, in turn, has led to the largely piecemeal planning of Secondary school curricula, which has gone on mainly within individual subjects. This has also been associated with the development of the 'options' system, providing a smorgasbord of subjects from which pupils choose the requisite number at 14+ as they embark on their final run-up to the first public examinations, a system which has been notable often for the absence of any restriction on choices other than time-tabling practicality. Thus, the recent DES survey of Secondary schools (DES 1979) expressed a good deal of concern about the lack of 'balance' in the programmes selected by many pupils at thi, stage in their careers and it is interesting to note that their findings have led to a reiteration of demands for curriculum balance.

A second stage in this process of erosion at the practical level might be seen in the modifications which have been made to university entrance requirements. There is no doubt that the emphasis now is on depth of study in areas of specialization rather than a breadth or balance of educational experience. The reaction of the universities to the proposals to redesign VIth form examinations in order to restore this kind of balance is indicative of a shift of concern at that level from breadth to specialization and thus to some erosion of the notion of a balanced education.

A further factor has been the introduction of those 'practical, realistic and vocational' elements into the curriculum which were advocated by the Newsom Report (CACE 1963, para 317). These developments, prompted by the commitment of the 1944 Education Act to education for all according to age, aptitude and ability, led to the appearance of the notion of 'relevance' in curriculum planning and a corresponding desire to offer a curriculum whose relevance would be recognized by those pupils who, whether from age, aptitude or ability, or, more likely, from social and/or cultural background, were finding little relevance in the balanced curriculum devised for the public and grammar schools. It was with the courses devised, often at the prompting of the Schools Council, in preparation for the raising of the school leaving age in 1972, that the practical and the vocational began to gain ground. And that process has gained further momentum with the recent involvement of the Department of Industry in curriculum planning in the Secondary school through initiatives like those of the Manpower Services Commission (MSC) and the Technical and Vocational Education Initiative (TVEI). For these developments either represent a denial of a balanced curriculum to large sections of our young people or they represent a challenge to the notion of curriculum balance. That some people view them in the former light is clear from the concomitant re-emergence of demands for a common core to the curriculum which may help to offset this imbalance. Either way, this is an issue which needs to be clarified and some examination of underlying epistemological theories is essential for any such clarification.

The commitment to the provision of education for all has resulted in an erosion of the assumptions underlying the notion of curriculum balance at a deeper theoretical level too. For it has led to an acceptance of cultural diversity and of cultural and value pluralism and this represents a major threat to the traditional view of knowledge upon which most pronouncements on curriculum balance have been based. This is a problem we shall explore more fully in Chapter 7, but we must note its general implications here. If working-class culture is different from rather than inferior to the culture embodied in the traditional school curriculum, if the cultural heritage of ethnic minorities is different from rather than inferior to that of the society of which they are now a significant part, then it is no longer possible to justify building a curriculum on that traditional basis or in relation to that larger society, nor is it possible to define curriculum balance in terms which exclude all elements of those other cultures. To do so is not to provide access to an objective, God-given, superior form of knowledge for all but, as we saw in Chapter 4, to impose on them the ideology of the dominant group in society (Young 1971). To attempt to develop suitable curricula for those pupils from 'working class' backgrounds or those from ethnic minorities is either to offer them something inferior and thus deny them educational equality (an issue we shall take up in Chapter 8) or it is to challenge the subject hierarchies of traditional approaches to knowledge and education, it is to reject the view of knowledge on which they have been based, it is to question the notion of curriculum balance they have given rise to. In short, it is to deny that rationalist view of knowledge that has held sway for so long, and this we must appreciate if we are to clarify our theory and our practice in this area.

This becomes completely apparent once we begin to explore the problems of defining curriculum balance.

Problems of definition

The first thing that needs to be noted about the concept of 'balance' is that its connotations of scientific exactitude are spurious. It is a very good example of the inability of many theorists, and practitioners too, in education to live with the uncertain, shifting, ever-changing notions of educational values and their predilection for a false form of certainty. It is thus comparable with all those attempts to study education scientifically and especially to make scientific measurements of educational progress. This attitude is also of course reflected in that commitment to rationalism which it is our main concern to challenge.

The term 'balance' when used in a scientific context is quite precise. In physics it might refer to the relation between forces exerted around a fulcrum, the ratio of weight, force and distance. In mathematics it refers to the exact equivalences of, for example, the two sides of an equation. In such contexts, balance is something precise, quantifiable, measurable, objective.

Unless we can accept the rationalist's view of all knowledge as objective and all spheres of human experience as the potential objects of such objective knowledge, we must accept that the use of the term in educational contexts is figurative. It is an import from elsewhere. It is a metaphor and, like all metaphors, it is only partly valid. It is not necessary to see it as an inappropriate metaphor but it is crucial to recognize the limitations of its appropriateness and the important differences of its meaning in this context.

The most important of these differences is that in the educational context its meaning is judicial rather than scientific, as the Schools Council's Working Paper No. 55 pointed out (1975b). And, as in the judicial case, it is concerned with judgement rather than with measurement, in spite of the symbolic scales of justice which embellish the roof of the Old Bailey. This in turn implies that its meaning is relative, that it lacks the objectivity it has in its scientific uses. It is not value-neutral. Like all else in education, it is a term which is value-laden. And what that suggests is, first, that different people will have different ideas about what constitutes a balanced education. Secondly, it suggests that a major factor in these differences of view will be the perspective from which they are taken, especially whether from the vantage point of society or that of the individual. And, thirdly, it implies that we must recognize that, as we suggested earlier when considering Aristotle's view of 'the golden mean', the precise definition of a balanced education will also vary according to the circumstances of the individual receiving it, that, as with the administration of balanced legal judgements, the provision of a balanced educational diet must be determined in such a way as to meet the idiosyncrasies of each individual case. Central planning of a balanced curriculum is likely to be no more effective than the taking of decisions centrally concerning the administration of justice to individual offenders in the law-courts. It is only if we are relying on the spurious objectivity of the scientific use of the term that we can make global pronouncements in this area.

The assumption of scientific exactitude, then, is one major error which is made in most discussions of curriculum balance. There is at least one other unwarranted assumption which must also be noted. For it is often assumed that a balanced curriculum will lead to and is a *sine qua non* of the development of the balanced person. There are in fact several assumptions implicit in this one. To begin with, it is worth noting that, if this is the justification offered for curriculum balance, then the concern is with development and not with the transmission of knowledge (indeed, it does seem as though this is the only interpretation which can make any sense of the notion), so that again we see that conflict and inconsistency within the rationalist perspective which we have noted before. Then there is the assumption that we all know what a balanced person is. Plato certainly had no doubts that he did. Yet not all of us would quite so readily accept his view. There is also the assumption that a certain kind of curriculum must inevitably lead to the emergence of this kind of person. This is another example of the assumption we have already commented on in rationalist theories of education that exposure to 'worthwhile knowledge' must automatically lead to the kind of educational development which is desired. This is further evidence too that 'balance' is another of those 'hurrah' words with which education theory abounds. And this must raise the question of whether it is anything else, whether the concept has any kind of usefulness in educational planning.

The same question emerges when one goes on to recognize the different dimensions of balance from which one can or might view educational provision. It is generally assumed — and again the unquestioned rationalism is apparent — that a balanced curriculum is to be judged by reference to the range of subjects which it embraces. This was certainly the assumption of the HMI survey of Secondary education (DES 1979) to which reference was made earlier; for the examples given there of imbalance in the curriculum are all framed in terms of over-concentration on a narrow range of subjects.

> The loss of some subjects reduced the range of opportunities, whether for employment or for continued education, open to these pupils at the end of their fifth year. The loss of other subjects removed opportunities to enlarge experience and understanding in ways potentially valuable for the future of their lives as adults and citizens (op.cit., p.41).

There is of course point and validity to this criticism. What is important here is that it suggests a view of balance in education as definable purely in terms of content and even of subject areas. It thus reflects that notion of balance between the physical and the intellectual which we saw earlier underpinned Plato's view of a balanced or harmonious education, and, in particular, as the details of the examples given in the HMI survey reveal, that traditional view of the need to balance the arts and the sciences in education, which has led to some very unsatisfactory practices, especially in VIth form curricula, and which was given its most coherent and, indeed, classical statement in C.P. Snow's disquisition on the two cultures (1959, 1969).

Indeed, this view has been endemic to many more recent discussions of educational provision. It is there in John White's desire to balance the theoretical and the practical (1973). It is there in Paul Hirst's claim (1965) that education must concern itself with the development of, and access to, his seven putative forms of understanding or rationality. It has thus been very much to the forefront in all those many debates about curriculum integration, since if you put subjects together or offer pupils some kind of integrated experience you have no way of assessing whether they are receiving enough of each subject to constitute a balanced education. Yet even as committed an exponent of interdisciplinary study as Charity James (1968) felt it necessary to advocate a balance not only between subjects but also between subject study and interdisciplinary study. Denis Lawton (1973, 1975) has subsequently even gone so far as to add interdisciplinary study as a kind of new and different 'form of knowledge' to Hirst's disciplines (albeit reduced from seven to five). It is perhaps this point more than any other that raises questions about the validity of this concept. It also raises questions about the validity of the rationalist perspective in education.

For a moment's consideration will reveal that even within the views just listed, in spite of the fact that they are ostensibly similar, there exist several quite distinct views of curriculum balance and that these views will be seen to be in conflict with each other as soon as one attempts to plan a curriculum by reference to them. It is to attempt the impossible to balance within the same curriculum arts and science, theoretical studies and practical studies, disciplinary study and interdisciplinary studies, and at the same time Hirst's seven forms of understanding. It is worth noting in connection with the latter, if only to confuse and compound the matter even further, that quite cogent claims have been made for the need to achieve some kind of balance within as well as between these forms. Eliot Eisner, for example, argues that within the aesthetic form 'the expressive content of the visual arts cannot be duplicated in music, the expressive content of music cannot be duplicated in poetry' (1979, p.114). It will be clear then not only that the notion of balance in education is far from being a scientific one, but also that it is difficult even to conceive of it in its judicial sense. The balance the educational planner needs is not that of the scientist or mathematician, nor even that of the judge. It is that of the juggler.

Yet there is much more to come. So far we have only noted the many different dimensions which can be identified when one considers attempts to define educational balance in terms of subject content. More balls must be thrown into the air when one begins to juggle with other possible definitions and dimensions.

First, there is the claim that we must balance breadth of study and depth of study, general education with specialization. In fact, the idea of a balanced curriculum is often contrasted with that of specialization and offered as a counterbalance to it. This is a notion beloved of universities, many of whose degree programmes are framed in terms of a balance of the two. It is this kind of consideration which, for much the same reasons and from much the same pressures, lies behind much of the recent and current debate over public examinations, especially in the VIth form, and over the 16-19 curriculum. The assumption is that breadth of study can offer something which depth cannot give — not only between subjects but also within each of them. That something which is assumed is balance, and it is further taken for granted that specialized study cannot be balanced. Yet, as Keith Thompson pointed out sometime ago (1972, p.80),

> Pleas for the education of the whole man, it may be said, are pleas for the postponement of specialization or for avoidance of undue specialization. But until what point should specialization be postponed and what constitutes *undue* specialization? Many utterances in this area are almost empty of meaning.

Lack of meaning in this area is one point. Another, much more germane to our present debate, is that we have here a new and different dimension of balance. Furthermore, the concern here is not always merely with breadth as study of a range of subjects and depth as study of one or two; it is also and equally with breadth and depth within subjects; and that is another new and further complicating dimension.

Add to this the need that some would argue to balance not just the cognitive and the affective dimensions of education (a claim which might be seen in subject terms) but, more specifically, the intellectual and the emotional development of the pupil, that balance of reason and feeling, of the head and the heart, which many see as a serious lack of weakness in traditional, rationalist, theories of curriculum. Throw in too personal, social and moral education and consider the problem of balancing the claims of these against other kinds of demands.

Add too the need to balance vocational and liberal aspects of schooling — the utilitarian and the intrinsic. This has long been a major consideration in the educational debate, at least since the time of Quintilian, and it continues to be so, as is made quite explicit in some recent documents which have called for a better balancing of these emphases in schooling. Again the HMI Secondary survey (DES 1979) is a good example of this. For it draws attention to the fact that for some Secondary schools an important principle of planning the choice of options for Years 4 and 5 is the need to balance subjects 'thought to have vocational importance or significance for higher education' (p.2a) with 'a subject or subjects from a different, otherwise absent, area of the curriculum' (ibid.). The same principle is apparent in more recent definitions of the 'entitlement curriculum' (DES 1984b) and in the current debate over the 16-19 curriculum and in particular the arrangements for examining at 17+. This does of course raise the question of whether (and if not, why not) a subject cannot be both useful and educational, both vocational and liberal, and it thus invites us again to question those traditional rationalist assumptions handed down from Plato. It also, however, and more relevantly to our purpose here, introduces another definition and dimension of curriculum balance.

A final and further dimension is introduced by those who wish to define balance in terms of the experiences of the pupils. This is the thrust of the claim of the Schools Council's Working Paper No. 70 (1981) that we should seek for a balance of our curriculum aims. It is also the essence of the '6 Cs' of the Royal Society of Arts 'Education for Capability' programme, the '6 Cs' in question being 'comprehend', 'cultivated', 'competent', 'cope', 'create' and 'commune'. And it is the force of the famous 'eight adjectives' of the HMI discussion document, *Curriculum 11-16* (DES 1977), those eight adjectives being 'aesthetic/creative', 'ethical', 'linguistic', 'mathematical', 'physical', 'scientific', 'social/political' and 'spiritual'.

It is with this kind of definition that we realize how complex and tangled an issue this is. For, although it is usually assumed — not least by HMI themselves, even in the same document — that those eight adjectives correspond to certain subject areas of the curriculum, this is not self-evidently the case. For one can readily think of many subjects which would want to claim that they can and do offer experiences in several of these areas. Teachers of English, for example, would have good cause to be aggrieved if it were not recognized that, when they are doing their job properly, they are offering pupils experience of an aesthetic/creative, ethical, linguistic, social/political and spiritual kind. This is surely the thrust of that other claim made by Her Majesty's Inspectorate (DES 1985, p.44) that 'balance also needs to be preserved within each area by the avoidance, for example, of an undue emphasis on the mechanical aspects of language'. The corollary of this is not, however, recognized, that the availability of this range of experiences within one subject might well be seen to obviate the need to include others in the curriculum and to insist on the exposure of all pupils to them; certainly it weakens the argument for their inclusion merely to satisfy some notion of 'balance'. Thus balance seen in these terms might result in the demise of many subjects and thus a narrowing of the curriculum as defined in terms of the subjects to be included within it.

The question remains, then, whether 'balance' is in any way a useful concept to the curriculum planner. It is far from being a scientific concept. It is riddled with unquestioned assumptions of many different kinds. These assumptions are often in conflict, revealing that there are as many theories of what might constitute curriculum balance as there are views of education. And there is conflict over this issue even among those who share a view of curriculum as content and of curriculum planning as essentially beginning from a subject base. And so we must recognize, as the Schools Council's Working Paper 53 pointed out (1975a, p.18), that the curriculum 'is a reconciliation of diverse and often conflicting claims and the balance which is achieved between them can never be a perfect or definitive one.'

Further complicating dimensions

The possibility of many different dimensions and interpretations of balance in education is, then, a major source of the confusion which besets our thinking and thus our practice. There are at least three further complicating factors, however, which we must note.

The first of these is the notion of educational equality or of education for all. The need to provide a full education for everyone is one of the major arguments put forward for the establishment of a common core curriculum as we noted earlier, and it would seem to follow from that that if a balanced curriculum is necessary for educational development then the notion of educational equality requires that all should have it. Again Working Paper 53 makes this point for us (1975a, p.51): 'If the concept of a balanced education has inherent merit, then the advantages it offers should be available to all pupils.' There is support for this too in the recent DES publication, *The School Curriculum* (1981, p.12), which asserts that

'There is an overwhelming case for providing all pupils between 11 and 16 with curricula of a broadly common character designed so as to ensure a balanced education during this period.'

Yet a moment's consideration will reveal the inherent contradiction and/or the practical impossibility of implementing any policy framed on these lines. Previous attempts at providing equality of education have led to the offering of irrelevant experiences to large numbers of pupils, those from working class backgrounds, for example, and, perhaps particularly, those from ethnic minorities. They have led to the stark segregation of pupils through selective procedures and grouping devices such as streaming — the only way to teach everybody Latin or French or even to provide them with the same diets in mathematics and English. They have led in turn to the establishment of differentiated curricula — high-status knowledge for the able and privileged, low-status knowledge for the rest. And, finally, they have led to grossly unbalanced forms of curriculum for virtually everyone — lots of practical and relevant studies for the less able, as recommended by the Newsom Report (CACE 1963), handicraft, social studies, moral education and so on, with little that is theoretical or 'academic' to balance this; and lots of academic courses for the intellectually able with little or no time allotted to practical work of any kind or to moral and social education. The truth of this is clear from the history of our failure in the UK to achieve anything worthy of the name of mass education or of the name of comprehensive education, in spite of the 1944 Education Act, Circular 10/65 and the rest. It is already becoming abundantly clear that the same factors are hindering the achievement of anything like an appropriate form of education for the many pupils in our schools who hail from ethnic and cultural minorities. These are points we will return to in Chapter 7.

Another point must be noted which further emphasizes the inadequacy of the notion of balance to help with these problems. If we provide the early leaver with a curriculum which is balanced according to these criteria, then one thing he or she will not have experienced is the opportunity to specialize. That is the privilege of the VIth former or the student in Further or Higher education. Yet if a balanced curriculum is to encompass also balance of study in breadth and depth, a pupil who has not proceeded with education beyond 16+ will, by this principle, be denied this, and thus denied that real understanding of any subject which those of us who have been privileged to take our studies further know can only come from depth of study, and with it that form of personal development which is at the heart of these demands for a balanced provision.

It will be clear then that the notion of balance, although prominent in many arguments for a form of education which offers true equality, does not help at all with the achievement of such equality — any more, in fact, than the idea of a common curriculum does. It will also be clear that balance cannot be achieved by way of establishing a common core to the curriculum. For reasons we will pick up shortly, the two notions may well be incompatible.

The second additional complicating factor we must note follows on from what has just been said about the denial of depth of study to the early leaver. A major reason why this occurs is that the assumption is constantly made that balance must be ever-present in a balanced curriculum, that at all stages a pupil's educational diet must contain all forms of nourishment. To quote Working Paper 53 again, 'there is a need for a balance of curriculum content at any particular stage of a pupil's schooling' (op.cit., p.47). The broadly common base which the HMI Survey of Secondary Schools (DES 1979) found in most schools up to the end of the third year reflected the kind of balance which they felt was largely satisfactory; it was the disappearance of this from the programme of some pupils in the 4th and 5th years that disturbed them, as we indicated earlier. The assumption which is clearly being made here is that balance must be ever-present.

Yet it might make more sense to consider the balance of all eleven years of compulsory schooling, to ensure that, if we feel we can identify all of the elements which go to make up such balance, all of those elements are to be found somewhere in the experience of each pupil, not that they must all be there at all stages. There have been suggestions recently of a kind that go some way towards this, for example that 'balance need not be sought over a single week or even a single month since in some cases it may be profitable to concentrate in depth on certain activities; but it should be sought over a period of, say, a term or a year' (DES 1985, p.44). Thus some degree of specialization would become possible as and when it seemed to be appropriate, and pupils would be permitted to pursue some study in depth provided that 'balancing' experiences were offered, and enjoyed, at other times. This is a practice whose advantages many teachers in the Primary sector are well aware of. If we are really committed to the idea of a balanced education, it is one we ought not to ignore.

The third point to be made in this discussion of further complicating factors follows on from this. It has already been suggested that some subjects might in themselves claim to be offering a balanced curriculum, a wide spread of experiences. The example was given earlier of the claim of English teachers to be providing many different kinds of experience to pupils. One might also instance what, as we saw in Chapter 5, has been said about the many different contributions which art can make to children's development (Eisner 1979; Newbold and Rubens 1983). Newbold and Rubens, for example, claim that art offers the experiences of communicating, investigating, exploring, discovering, analysing, expressing, decorating, illustrating, reading, recording, recognizing — a wide range of experiences which, if true, certainly would seem to add up to some kind of balance within the one subject.

The converse, however, is also true and must be noted here. For, just as it might be claimed that some subjects offer a range of experiences, so it must be said that many subjects, while differing in their subject matter and thus ostensibly perhaps complementing each other, and while even appearing to offer access to those different forms of understanding which Paul Hirst (1965) posits, are in reality offering the same experiences as each other. This is perhaps particularly a function not of the subjects themselves but of the approaches teachers adopt to the teaching of them.

Again it is worth noting the findings of the HMI survey of Secondary schools (DES 1979). For they concluded that the approaches adopted by teachers often led to a similarity of experience for pupils of such a kind as to provide no balance at all and this point was re-echoed in the Schools Council's Working Paper 70 (1981). It is difficult to argue that pupils are enjoying a balanced education when in all of the six, seven or eight different subjects they are studying the methods by which they are encouraged to learn are the same — listening to teacher, answering his/her questions, reading a text book, copying notes from the board, writing brief essays and so on. Yet this is manifestly the experience of many pupils in Secondary schools. There is no acknowledgement of different forms of understanding, different techniques for acquiring or extending knowledge, none of the things that might make sense of the notion of balance — merely a range of subjects whose subject matter is different. It is again a good example of the aridity of educational experience which the rationalist emphasis on knowledge can encourage and lead to.

We must recognize, therefore, that 'the true balancing agent lies not in the subject content but in the methods and approaches of the teacher and his interaction with the pupils' (Petter 1970, p.43), and that 'the way in which something is taught affects profoundly the form that it assumes in the consciousness and behaviour of learners' (Schools Council 1975a, p.16).

Curriculum balance and the problem of knowledge

The issues raised in the last section point us inexorably towards an interpretation of balance which does not begin from considerations of the knowledge-content of the curriculum but from a concern for the experiences of the pupil. They thus point us in our search for educational balance away from a rationalist epistemology and, indeed, reinforce the claim that it is a too ready acceptance of and adherence to that kind of epistemological stance which is at the root of much of the confusion in this area — a confusion in theory which inevitably results in a corresponding confusion of practice.

It is not forms of knowledge, of rationality or even of understanding which are crucial in education; it is modes of experiencing. And it is not forms of knowledge, rationality or understanding which need to be balanced; again it is the modes of experience. The balance we should be seeking is not a balance of subject-content but a balance of experiences for the pupil. This, indeed, must be the base for all notions of curriculum balance, since the only coherent reasons for demanding it must be those which derive from a concern with the totality of the pupil's experience. The notion of somehow balancing the knowledge-content itself has no meaning.

There are at least two aspects of this which need to be explored a little more fully. The first of these is that this view of balance leads us to acknowledge that balance must be seen and assessed at the level of the individual pupil. A balanced education, like a balanced diet, must be planned and prescribed for each individual; it cannot be the subject of universal legislation. As we saw earlier, the proper diet for Milo, the wrestler, is far too rich and heavy for most ordinary people. One would rightly lose confidence very quickly in a doctor or a dietitian who had one prescription for every patient or client. This is one reason why many people are currently losing confidence in those politicians and administrators who are claiming to direct present-day curriculum development. Indeed, at the time of writing, there is one shoe manufacturer whose television advertisement reveals more awareness of the individuality of children's feet than most current political pronouncements on the curriculum reveal of the individuality of their minds or personalities. Education is at least as personal and individual a matter as health or diet. It is a rationalist preoccupation with the knowledge-content of education that leads some people to lose sight of that. This is why it is only this individualized interpretation of a balanced curriculum that will enable us to offer an education which is both balanced and adapted to the needs of different pupils — especially as we shall see in Chapter 7, those from diverse cultural and ethnic backgrounds. And this is why it was suggested earlier that the idea of a balanced education and that of a common core curriculum, although often to be found associated with each other, are incompatible — at least when the latter is interpreted, as it usually is, in subject terms. Education should not be seen, or used, as a device for inhibiting individuality and promoting conformity.

This brings us to the second point which needs to be made. It is not necessary to interpret the idea of a common core to the curriculum as implying that this must be a common core of subjects. A debate has raged for well over a decade between subjects and integrated studies, whether the curriculum should be planned in an integrated, undifferentiated way or whether subject boundaries should be maintained. This debate has been misdirected, or at least it has not gone deep enough. For the real issue is whether educational planning should begin with considerations of the knowledge-content to be transmitted, however it is organized, or with the experiences to be offered to pupils. The crucial debate is between subjects and processes, between educational provision planned primarily in terms of its content and that planned in terms of the development of pupils. To provide a balanced education is to offer a range of experiences and not merely to transmit selected parts of a range of different subjects. This in essence, as has been suggested on several occasions, is the real thrust of Paul Hirst's claim (1965) that we should initiate pupils into a range of different forms of understanding. The crucial difference, however, as we have seen, is whether we interpret this from the point of view of the forms of understanding themselves or from that of the development and experience of the individual pupil who is being initiated into them.

The notion of balance when seen in terms of a balance of processes helps us to make much more sense of our educational provision than when it is defined in terms of subjects. It permits individualization; it can accommodate ethnic and cultural differences; it allows for both breadth and depth of study; it can cope with the notion of balance within subject areas as well as between them; and it allows us to tailor educational provision to the perceived needs of our pupils rather than to the assumed demands of subjects. What it cannot do, therefore, is to support the idea of central prescriptions of curriculum content. The only things which can be centrally prescribed are the processes which must underpin the educational development of all pupils, the principles upon which everyone's education must be built.

It is towards this kind of view of balance and, indeed, this kind of approach to centralized planning that some of the more sophisticated ideas of balance which we noted earlier seemed to be directing us. The 'eight adjectives' of *Curriculum 11-16* (DES 1977) outline a range of processes or educational principles which few would wish to quarrel with as a definition of a balanced education. The '6 Cs' of the RSA's 'Education for Capability' initiative also point us in the same kind of direction.

Things begin to go wrong when our interpretation of what this means for educational planning lacks sophistication, or when its level of sophistication does not match that of these first premises. In particular (and this brings us back to the central thrust of this book), problems begin to emerge when we slip back into those rationalist forms of thinking which require us to translate these principles and processes into subjects, disciplines and, in general, knowledge-content. The two approaches are philosophically incompatible since, as we have seen, they derive from quite different epistemological traditions. To try to have our cake and eat it must always lead us into incoherence. If our concern is that pupils should have experiences of certain kinds (and this, it has been suggested, is the only coherent interpretation we can place on the notion of curriculum balance), if we approach our educational planning in these terms, in particular if we see educational balance as a rounded integration of experiences, we must acknowledge that the sources of these experiences may, indeed must, vary enormously from pupil to pupil and that the role of subject-content in education is not as the prime determinant of educational planning but as a subsidiary factor, that through which pupils' development is promoted rather than that which in itself somehow constitutes that development. Such a view is quite incompatible with that rationalist epistemology which has dominated and confused our thinking about education, and thus consequentially our practice of it, for too long. It is also a view that offers us more hope of achieving not only a balanced education but also an 'equal' education for all pupils.

It is perhaps worth adding that this does not imply the provision of totally idiosyncratic curricula for every pupil. The claim that educational provision should be individual is not a demand that it be individualistic. The notion of individualized education has come to be associated with behaviourist psychology and, in particular, with its use and advocacy of teaching machines. We can be quite happy to leave it there. What is being claimed here is not that each child should be encouraged or even permitted to go off down a totally individualistic road. It is that our educational planning should attempt to take full account of the individual development of each pupil. Given the opportunity to pursue individual interests, most children choose to do so in groups anyway. And the importance of the social dimension of learning has been stressed as a result of recent work in developmental psychology, as we saw in Chapters 4 and 5, and this ought not to be ignored. Individual provision, then, does not imply idiosyncratic provision. It suggests that we take full account of the individual character, personality, situation and background of each pupil in determining the kind of provision which will help him or her towards the full achievement of that which we have elsewhere defined as education in the full sense. As the Plowden Report stressed (CACE 1967, p.25) 'Individual differences between children of the same age are so great that any class, however homogeneous it seems, must always be treated as a body of children needing individual and different attention'. What is individual is the activity of learning not necessarily the content, so that 'personalization' might be a more accurate and helpful term than 'individualization'.

It is the contention of this chapter that it is to this conclusion that any coherent notion of curriculum balance must lead us and it is this which is inhibited by the associated claims for a common core curriculum defined in rationalist terms by reference to its subject-content.

Summary and conclusions

It has been the intention of this chapter to identify and reveal some of the many confusions which attend the notion of curriculum balance, too often assumed to be non-problematic. In particular, it has been the concern, in line with the general message of this book, to demonstrate that many of the confusions, and much consequent unsatisfactory practice, are attributable to a too-ready acceptance of that rationalist epistemology it is our concern to challenge. It is only to some extent, however, that the problems arise from the adoption of that stance. More often the confusion arises from the fact that many, while groping towards something different, have failed to recognize how totally different that towards which they are groping is, and thus have tended to slip back into those rationalist assumptions which are theoretically quite incompatible with the other positions they have adopted.

The confusions which were identified in general derived from the number and range of the possible interpretations of balance in education and in particular from the dominance within this number and range of interpretations of the notion of a need to balance the subject-content of education. This, it was suggested, reflects a rationalist epistemology and raises again the two points this book is concerned to make about this epistemological position, namely, first, that it is not God-given and thus unchallengeable, in fact its validity and its suitability for educational planning need to be explored and questioned much more closely than hitherto, and, second, that it is incompatible with that other, equally valid, epistemological position which underpins other, quite different, views of education.

In particular, it was apparent again in this debate that the issue rests between curriculum as content and curriculum as process. It became clear that the second of these views offer us a much more satisfactory interpretation of curriculum balance than the first, one that permits interpretation and individualization or personalization of curriculum provision while retaining the central and most important principle inherent in the notion of balance, the need to plan the curriculum of every pupil as a whole and not as a series of discrete and largely unrelated experiences.

The claim that education must be planned in terms of its processes rather than its content raises important issues concerning the role of subject matter, of knowledge, in education, which we attempted to explore in the previous chapter. The examination of the notion of a common core curriculum and, particularly, the associated idea of curriculum balance, which this chapter has undertaken, has reinforced much that was said there. It has also added a further factor, the need for a concern with education as an individual and personal matter, something that cannot be achieved by the techniques of mass production or by remote control.

To suggest that education should not be seen primarily as the transmission of knowledge is also to raise questions about how far it should be seen as cultural transmission, as the means by which a society maintains its cultural traditions, and in particular how this kind of concern can be reconciled with that desire to achieve educational equality which we have seen is another strand in the argument for common curricular provision. It is to these questions that we turn in the next chapter where it will be seen that these issues too crucially hinge on that epistemological debate which is our constant preoccupation.

CHAPTER 7

CULTURE AND THE CURRICULUM
— THE PROBLEM OF KNOWLEDGE
AND EQUALITY

He is a barbarian, and thinks that the customs of his tribe and island are the
laws of nature.

(George Bernard Shaw, *Caesar and Cleopatra*)

A major difficulty for the notion of curriculum balance was seen to be, in
the discussions of that concept which the last chapter undertook, the
difficulty of reconciling an interpretation of it in terms of subject content
with an acceptance of cultural pluralism. It is to an examination of culture
and the curriculum that this present chapter turns.

Like all the chapters in Part Two of this book, this chapter sets out to
look at this issue both as one of current educational importance in its own
right and as an instance of an area of discussion where the failure to
recognize the problematic nature of knowledge, which Part One
attempted to elucidate, has been a major source of confusion and inimical
to the possibility of any real advancement. In this case, that muddle has
been compounded by a lack of clarity over the meaning of 'culture' which
has been in many discussions superimposed on an existing lack of
awareness of the problem of knowledge.

The link between education and culture is very close. Indeed the very
etymology of the word 'culture' with its horticultural, agricultural and
even biological connotations of controlled growth, of growth which is
deliberately brought about, implies a very close relationship with the
comparable notion of education. Furthermore, it would not be difficult to
argue that the connection is not merely contingent but is also necessary,
that a concept of education which did not embrace some notion of cultural
transmission would be no concept of education at all. For the transmission
of a society's culture is always a major part, and in some cases the whole,

of the educational process. In primitive societies, for example, such as those explored and analysed by Margaret Mead (1928) and Ruth Benedict (1946), systems of education, albeit not formally organized in the manner we have become used to in so-called 'advanced' societies, have as their prime, and perhaps their only, function the handing on to the next generation of not only the skills and knowledge but also the values and ways of life of the present generation. Thus do societies renew themselves through each successive generation and thus they maintain the high level of social cohesiveness which is a characteristic of primitive groups.

Inevitably, the issue in several important respects becomes much more complex in the context of 'advanced', more sophisticated societies. In the first place, the provision of education becomes more formalized. Schools are established to take over those responsibilities for providing education which are fulfilled in primitive communities by largely informal means; and certain members of society are given responsibility for this task, so that it ceases to be the direct concern of all adults.

Next, questions about the most suitable form of curriculum for these schools arise and in particular the problem appears of how far their emphasis should be on vocational concerns and how far they should promote something that might be called a liberal education. This in turn raises questions concerning what a liberal education might consist of. The fact that often the liberal education of today is the vocational education of yesterday, that we can best ensure that what we are offering is not vocationally oriented if it has clearly outlived its economic usefulness, is brought out tellingly and amusingly in Harold Benjamin's well-known description of the 'saber-tooth curriculum' (1939, 1971), the curriculum of the mythical society he depicts in which the skills which had been essential to the economy of the past — 'fish-grabbing-with-the-bare-hands', 'woolly-horse-clubbing', and 'saber-tooth-tiger-scaring-with-fire' — having lost their utilitarian value have become the main ingredients of the present-day 'liberal education'. The parallel with some recent and per-haps still current notions of what a liberal education should consist of is not hard to see.

However, whether we take this rather cynical, and perhaps superficial, view or not, there is no doubt that the question of the liberal/vocational division becomes an important one once a society moves beyond a stage that might reasonably be described as primitive.

Another dimension of this, which is essentially a more fully developed version of the same debate, is the question of whether it is sufficient to see education as a process of cultural transmission or whether one ought to regard it, and, indeed, plan it, as a major and positive agency of cultural transformation, whether its concern should be not with cultural maintenance but rather with cultural development, whether, as Raymond Williams (1958) suggests, the task of education is to anticipate cultural change. Merely to hand on existing knowledge and skills is to do nothing positive to promote or even to permit the growth and development of either. And in the field of moral, social and aesthetic values the issue is more clearly stark. For, once accepted, the notion of social development, however that process is defined, commits us to a form of education which will permit of, and indeed facilitate, such development and which, if it is to do so, must go well beyond the idea of cultural transmission. This was the major thrust of Dewey's philosophy, as we saw in Chapter 3.

Thirdly, the issue is further complicated when a society decides to establish some kind of mass education or education for all. For the debate over what kind of education one should be providing for the élite of society, however selected, pales into insignificance alongside that of what we should be providing for all citizens. For this second debate raises sub-questions such as whether we should attempt to offer all the same curriculum or invent, like Plato, different curricula for different ability groups, whether we should be offering a liberal education, however conceived, to some only or to all, whether the curriculum for some pupils should be wholly, or almost wholly, vocational and so on. All of these are questions whose relevance to current educational planning will be immediately apparent.

Finally, the recognition of cultural pluralism, which must follow from the issues we have just identified, as well as from the evidence of cultural differences in modern societies, adds the last complicating ingredient to this mix. Once we acknowledge that advanced societies are not characterized by their social cohesion so much as by their social differences, not by what Émile Durkheim called 'mechanical solidarity', but by what he called 'organic solidarity', unity in difference rather than unity in sameness (Bernstein 1967), once we accept notions such as that of working class culture (Hoggart 1957; Williams 1958, 1961; Thompson 1963), and, especially, once we recognize the major ethnic differences in society, we are forced to the conclusion that to see education as the transmission of a single culture, and to attempt to define what that culture is, is to be engaged in an enterprise which is at best naive and which may, at worst, as our discussion of the politics of knowledge in Chapter 4 revealed, be sinister.

The link between education and culture, then, in an advanced industrial society is important but it is also highly complex. Some of those complexities this chapter will attempt to unravel. It will do this, first, by exploring the meaning of the word 'culture' or, rather, the several different meanings which it can be seen to have. For it is clear that the problems of the relationships of culture and education in advanced societies which have just been identified derive as much from a lack of clarity over definitions as from any other source. In this context, the debate is or should be focused as much on what culture is as on its place in educational provision. Secondly, we will look at the major features of this debate in the context of the establishment of mass education. Thirdly, we will examine this issue in the context of cultural, and, especially, ethnic, pluralism, which heightens the focus even more. For it is here, as we suggested just now, that the problems are seen most starkly. And finally, we will consider it in the light of the problems of knowledge described in Part One since again the intention will be to show that a lack of understanding of this aspect of the issues has contributed perhaps more than any other single factor to our failure to achieve clarity in this field.

What is culture?

The question of what is meant by the term 'culture' is one with which we must both begin and end our discussion. For it is necessary to identify some of the issues implicit in this question in order to understand the problems which the debate over culture and education has raised, but it will also be necessary to return to the matter in the light of our examination of that debate not least because, as we shall see, at the heart of the problem lie those issues of knowledge which are our central concern.

A good many of the problems which beset discussions of education and culture are due to the fact that the word 'culture' is used in several different ways, with several different meanings, and, in particular, to the fact that these meanings are often confused and run together — sometimes even, as we shall see, quite deliberately.

The etymology of the word — from the Latin *cultus* — suggests that its basic meaning is a purely scientific and descriptive one. For the earliest meaning of *cultus* in Latin is 'cultivation' in the sense in which we find it used in 'agriculture', 'horticulture', 'silviculture'. It is only later that one finds its being used in a figurative sense. In this straight descriptive use, then, it refers to the control of natural growth, to the bringing about of certain kinds of growth in nature, to the use of natural forces and processes to produce certain kinds of plant. It is with the same meaning that the biologist uses the term 'culture' to denote those forms of growth which he or she in certain contexts is concerned to bring about. It is important to note that in these uses the term is largely value-neutral, although clearly the implication is that no-one would spend their time cultivating anything unless they felt it was in some way worth while.

It is with its figurative uses that the complications enter the debate. For, developing naturally from the concept of the cultivation of plants, comes that of the cultivation of people, and thus of the 'cultivated person', 'cultivated' in the aesthetic sense, initiated into 'high culture', that which Matthew Arnold in his *Culture and Anarchy* defined as 'the best that has been thought and said'. When 'culture' is given this meaning its connections with education become apparent. What should also be apparent is that in this use it is clearly value-laden. We are no longer speaking of something largely descriptive and scientific; we are making value judgements concerning the aesthetic merits of certain kinds of activity, those which go to make up the 'high culture' of society, those which represent 'the best that has been thought and said', not all aspects of society, not all society's achievements or all society's customs and ways of life, but only those deemed — by someone — to be the best. And the cultured person is not someone who has been brought up anyhow but one whose upbringing reflects a measure of refinement, even of civilization.

There is a third meaning of the word, however, which takes us back to the scientific, descriptive, value-neutral use while retaining the human context. For the word culture is used by sociologists, and particularly by anthropologists, to refer to all aspects of the life of a society — its customs, its ways of life, its beliefs, its attitudes, its mores. It is in this sense that the term is used by people such as Margaret Mead and Ruth Benedict, to whom reference was made earlier, to refer to all aspects of the 'culture' of the societies they studied and attempted to describe — not merely that deemed to be the best, that regarded as the 'high culture', but everything that is to be observed there.

It should be clear that these meanings are quite different, that, if we leave aside the original, biological, agricultural meaning of the term and focus on its use in relation to human society, we still have two quite distinct meanings — one descriptive, scientific, largely value-free, the other prescriptive, judgemental, value-laden. It is the conflation of these two senses of the word that leads to the confusion in our thinking over culture and education and thus those consequentially unavoidable confusions in our practice.

It must be noted, however, that while the conflation is the source of much muddle (exactly how it is will become clear later), it is a procedure which has been explicitly recommended by some as the route to a resolution of the problem of culture and education. Bantock, for example, has claimed that, in the context of education, 'culture' should be seen as having a third meaning. 'In this book the word "culture" is being used in a sense which lies between the two' (Bantock 1968, p.2). Denis Lawton (1975) too quotes Bantock with approval and himself embraces this conflated meaning.

To slide from value-neutral to value-laden meanings has ever been the source of great confusion of debate. It is, logically, an illicit process, even when it is done openly and overtly, the argument from 'is' to 'ought', the Naturalistic Fallacy as philosophers have come to call it, having been exposed as invalid as long ago as the 18th century by David Hume, as we saw in Chapter 1. Its prime effect is to conceal the value element from us, to encourage us to believe that we are dealing with factual, descriptive statements when in fact we are dealing with someone's judgements, and thus to discourage us from questioning those judgements.

This becomes immediately apparent when one reads only a little way further into what both Bantock and Lawton, having opted for this 'third meaning', proceed to argue. For Bantock goes straight on to explain (1968, p.2):

> I do not want to include everything in it because that would involve a number of trivialities; so it is applied selectively to important areas of human thought and action. But in itself it is not intended to imply anything about the value or quality of these activities and thoughts.

The contradiction and the confusion are immediately apparent. For it is not possible to decide what is a 'triviality', to apply a principle 'selectively' nor to choose what are the 'important areas of human thought and action' without implying a great deal about 'the value and quality of these activities and thoughts'. It is clear that, whatever is said to the contrary, a certain system of values is being assumed uncritically and that the issue of values is being treated as non-problematic. Again, therefore, a rationalist epistemology is being taken as read.

The same confusion is apparent in Lawton's argument too. For having quoted, at great length, the above passage from Bantock's book, he then goes on to say himself (1975, p.32):

In some ways this third view of culture (i.e. a partially selective one) is useful for educational discussion since it provides a short cut by eliminating certain aspects of culture, in the anthropological sense, from our educational debate. Again, then, there is no recognition of the fact that one can only be 'partially selective' and 'eliminate certain aspects' according to some criteria of value. And again the conflation of the two uses of the word 'culture' conceals this and discourages the asking of any searching questions about what these criteria might be and what basis they might have.

It is from this kind of base that Lawton is able to proceed to make out a case for a 'common culture curriculum', a curriculum based on a core of knowledge and/or activities selected from and regarded as largely constituting the common culture of society. This is a view of education and curriculum which has found it very difficult to accommodate the historical reality of the division of our own society into at least two cultures — those of the upper and the working classes, the 'high culture' and the 'folk culture', as Bantock terms them — and, in particular, difficult, if not impossible, to make proper allowance for the multicultural or multi-ethnic nature of present-day society.

To both of these issues in turn we must now address ourselves.

Culture and mass education

There is little doubt that the debate over culture and education began with the advent of mass education which was itself to a large extent a result of the Industrial Revolution. Indeed, Raymond Williams claims that 'the idea of culture, and the word itself in its general modern usage, came into English thinking in the period which we commonly describe as the Industrial Revolution' (1958, p.11). He goes on to argue in fact that five new key words entered the language at that time — 'industry', 'democracy', 'class', 'art' and 'culture'. The reason for this and the interrelationships between these concepts are not hard to see.

Prior to this time, education had been largely a privilege of the few, those who could afford to pay for it, and who did not look to it for any kind of vocational training except that which would enable them to play their part in the government of the land. They thus expected of it the kinds of experience Quintilian had suggested were appropriate to the education of the orator, the kinds of learning the Humanists, such as Elyot and Erasmus, had felt were necessary to the education of the courtier or the 'cultured gentleman'. And the emphasis was that of Plato and Aristotle — on contemplation rather than on action, on the theoretical rather than the practical, on liberal rather than vocational pursuits.

The introduction of mass education, of schooling for everyone and not just those who could afford to pay for it, thus brought with it the crucial question of what form such schooling should take — a question which is still far from a satisfactory solution more than a century later.

Raymond Williams (1961) identifies three different kinds of answer to this question to be found in the thinking and theorizing of the nineteenth century. First, there were those he calls the 'industrial trainers' whose view was that schooling for the masses should concentrate on providing them with what they needed to meet the needs of the new, developing industrial processes, a purely vocational form of training. According to Williams, those who pressed this view defined education 'in terms of future adult work, with the parallel clause of teaching the required social character — habits of regularity, "self-discipline", obedience and trained effort' (op.cit., p.162). The aim, then, was industrial efficiency and a 'gentling of the masses'. This is the view which he claims dominated the nineteenth century debate and this would seem to be borne out also by the evidence produced by Peter Gordon and Denis Lawton (1978).

The opposition to this view took two forms and/or came from two sources. First there were those Williams calls the 'old humanists'. These were those whose concept of education was more liberal, humane or 'cultural' than the 'industrial trainers', who felt that 'man's spiritual health depended on a kind of education which was more than a training for some specialized work' (ibid.), who, in short, had a clear concept of 'high culture' and a view of mass education as concerned to make this accessible to everyone.

The second kind of opposition to the purely vocational approach to schooling was that of what Williams calls the 'public educators', those who believed that 'man had a natural human right to be educated, and that any good society depended on governments accepting this principle as their duty' (ibid.). Their view, however, was not just that to be educated implied having been given access to the 'high culture' of society; it went further than that in so far as they were concerned to develop some notion of popular education, a new concept of education fitted to the context of mass education and taken out of the rather narrow perspective of the education of the 'cultured gentleman'.

This analysis may well be over-simplified, as, indeed, Williams himself admits, but it is clear that these three strands can be seen in the educational debate throughout the nineteenth century. Indeed, they may be seen as reflecting those three possible approaches to education and curriculum planning which we identified earlier, although the third is rather less specific than the view which has been advocated here of education as individual development. It is clear too that although the curriculum which emerged was a compromise, nevertheless the emphasis was definitely on the aspect of industrial training, and it is also clear that the debate has continued into the present century, unchanged in all but its level of sophistication — and perhaps not even in that.

It is here that we begin to see the interlinking of this debate with another of Williams' five key words — 'democracy'. For this emerges as another dimension of the same debate; one which has gained emphasis in the present century with the spread of socialism generally, the rise of the Labour Party in the UK and the formal establishment, through, for example, the explicit requirements of the 1944 Education Act, of the idea of education for all 'according to age, aptitude and ability'.

As a result of these developments, there have been important changes in the structure of the school system — notably, first, the provision of Secondary education for all and, then, the requirement that this be made through the establishment of common comprehensive forms of Secondary schooling — but little or no identifiable progress has been made towards a clear notion of what a comprehensive education or a comprehensive curriculum might look like. Raymond Williams claims (1958, p.11) that 'we are arriving . . . at a point where a new general theory of culture might in fact be achieved'. One would like to join him in that optimism. What is certain is that without such a theory no clear notion of comprehensive education or of mass education can or will ever be attained.

Hence the debate, or the debates, continue — one debate over the weighting of the liberal and vocational emphases, another over what a liberal education is, and a third, as we saw in Chapter 4, over whether the provision of any form of 'liberal education' is likely to lead to universal education in any real sense. And again three distinct stances can be identified.

The first of these is what might be called the hard or strong 'high culture' line. This is a view of education as the transmission of 'high culture', as initiation into intrinsically worthwhile activities (Peters 1965, 1966), as the development of rationality in all its putative seven forms (Hirst 1965), as the study of those subjects of which 'no understanding . . . is possible without participation' and which 'open doors to understanding other activities which logically depend on them for their intelligibility' (White 1973, p.61), as the handing on of the common culture of society (Lawton 1975), as access to certain 'cultural universals' (Smith, Stamey and Shores 1971). Fundamentally, this is the rationalist view of culture and the curriculum, specifically recognized and argued as such by some of its proponents, but taken for granted and treated as non-problematic by others.

There is no acknowledgement in these views of the plight of those pupils who, because of their level of intellectual ability, their social class background, their ethnic origin or even their own preferences and predilections, cannot or do not respond to this kind of diet. We noted in Chapter 6 the problem of reconciling the realities of this view with the rhetoric of mass education and equality of educational opportunity, the alienation, for example, which results from the offering to such pupils of an educational programme which makes little or no sense to them in relation to the context in which they pursue their daily lives. And we noted in Chapter 4 the cogent arguments of the new sociology that this approach must inevitably reinforce underprivilege and cannot ever provide a route to universal education.

The second current view of culture and the curriculum at least has the merit of attempting to grasp that particular nettle. For it not only embraces the 'high culture' line; it also goes on to accept the inevitable élitism of this position and to acknowledge that it implies the provision of different kinds of education for different pupils. There are, it is claimed, two kinds of culture, the 'high culture' or 'upper class' culture and the 'folk culture' (Bantock 1968), and this means that we must provide two kinds of education to match these two cultures.

This is the rationale of the Newsom Report's concern with 'Half Our Future', the half (clearly incidentally, an underestimate) which cannot or does not wish to cope with a curriculum framed in terms of the 'high' or 'upper class' culture, with 'academic' pursuits, and which must, therefore, be offered something different, a curriculum framed in terms of the four key words which that report offers us — 'practical, realistic, vocational, choice' (CACE 1963, para.317). The curricular developments which followed from the publication of this report were clearly élitist, divisive and far from egalitarian — an 'academic' curriculum for those who revealed the intellectual ability and the interest to accept and cope with it, and a realistic, practical, vocational curriculum for the rest. These developments are currently receiving further support from the vocational initiatives of the present government through the schemes of the Manpower Services Commission (MSC). This is the twentieth century version of the 'industrial trainers', that dominant factor in the nineteenth century debate, the current measures to achieve industrial efficiency and a 'gentling of the masses'.

The form of education and curriculum which has emerged, then, is meritocratic rather than democratic and, while the rhetoric of the 'public educators' is heard perhaps more often than was once the case, it is the realities of the instrumentalism of the 'industrial trainers' and the élitism of the 'old humanists' which have been most effective in determining the forms of curricular offerings (Williams 1961).

One must acknowledge, however, that this is the logic of an acceptance of the notion of 'high culture'. For if one accepts that there is such a thing, that it can be readily identified and that education consists in providing pupils with access to it, one must also accept that education in the full sense cannot be made available to those pupils who either cannot or will not accept the privilege of such access. This was the logic of Plato's view and of the 'magnificent myth' he devised to ensure universal acceptance of it — that people are born with gold or silver or bronze in their make-up and must be educated — and treated — accordingly.

Hence there has begun an erosion of the notion of 'high culture' and a third view has emerged, a view which rejects the idea of 'high culture', or at least the idea that it is a superior form of culture, which preaches the merits of 'folk' or 'working-class' culture and which suggests that it is only in this direction that a proper theory of mass education, of egalitarian education and of a comprehensive curriculum can be sought or found. It is not difficult to recognize that such a view must begin from a rejection of that rationalist epistemology upon which the notion of 'high culture' is founded and not merely of the élitist forms of education it has generated.

No-one of course is questioning the existence of folk-culture. The issue is what value, if any, is to be placed on it and how, if at all, education should respond to it. Bantock is quite clear on both of these questions. The folk-culture is qualitatively inferior to the 'high culture'; it is 'all too often cheap and tawdry' (1968, p.71); it appeals mainly to the emotions rather than to the intellect. He thus accepts Arnold's dichotomizing of culture and industrialization and is of the view that education should seek not to embrace this culture but to assist people to transcend it. Lawton, inevitably, accepts much the same view, albeit tacitly; it is a *sine qua non* of his 'common culture curriculum'.

In recent times, however, in the United Kingdom there has emerged a quite different view, prompted by the work of Raymond Williams (1955, 1961), of E.P. Thompson (1963) and, perhaps particularly, that of Richard Hoggart (1957). This is a view which argues for the value, and, indeed, the validity of working-class culture. It claims that such culture should not be demeaned or devalued. It argues that it is different but not inferior. It thus demands that education should acknowledge this and respond to such forms of culture positively, by embracing them rather than by rejecting them. In the specific context of education, this view was given an enormous boost in the early 1960s by certain sociological studies, notably that of Brian Jackson and Denis Marsden, whose study of *Education and the Working Class* (1962) revealed many of the difficulties created for bright working-class pupils by the school's total rejection and devaluing of their cultural background and its imposition of a different, and largely alien, form of culture on them, and, in doing so, helped to pave the way for those 'new directions' in the sociology of education which were to come a decade or so later.

Until then, however, the dilemma remained. For in spite of his championing of working-class culture, Richard Hoggart, for example, still sees education as the means by which pupils of working-class origin — and, indeed, adults too — can be given access to the 'high culture'. His concern is not just with the devaluing and the loss of their own culture but with the failure of the school system to provide them with access to Arnold's 'best that has been thought and said'. 'Thus, it seems to me that the changes described in the second half of this book are, so far, tending to cause the working-classes to lose, culturally, much that was valuable and to gain less than their new situation should have allowed' (1957, p.17).

The position taken, then, remained essentially ambivalent. We must not devalue working-class culture; but we must remember that what is really worthwhile is the 'high culture' and we must do all we can to provide access to that. Essentially, this is a liberal view, but it is also one which is firmly rooted in that rationalist epistemology which provides the only source of validity for the notion of 'high culture'.

It had already been challenged by D.H. Lawrence who had condemned the whole idea of schooling for the working classes on the grounds that it destroyed their natural and spontaneous responses to their environment and to the general context of their lives, by imposing on them forms of thinking which derived from academic disciplines rather than from the kinds of experience with which their everyday lives made them familiar. The conclusion of this position is of course that we should not make any educational provision for such people at all, and that conclusion has been recently asserted, as we saw in Chapter 4, by people such as Ivan Illich (1971) and Paolo Freire (1972). It is a restatement in social class terms of Rousseau's concern that education should not be or become an agency for the corruption of man's natural goodness.

A more cogent challenge is that of the 'new directions' in the sociology of education whose concern it is to change the forms of education offered rather than to reject it outright. The strength of this challenge is that it directs itself first at the epistemological position upon which traditional views are based. It questions the very notion of 'high culture' by challenging the view of knowledge and of values upon which that notion is founded. It argues, as we saw in Chapter 4, that knowledge and values are human constructs, they are not God-given but are created by societies and by groups within societies, so that there is no basis for claiming the superiority of any one system over the rest. It goes on to claim, as we also saw in Chapter 4, that to frame a curriculum in terms of 'high culture' is not to provide access to that culture so much as to impose the values implicit in that culture on those who are the recipients of that curriculum, even when they come from different cultural backgrounds. It is for this reason that it claims, as we have seen, that those groups who control the distribution of knowledge in society also effectively control the society.

Its alternative is a form of curriculum based not on the definitions of knowledge of those who have such control but on what is recognized as relevant knowledge by the pupil, not on 'expert' but on 'commonsense' knowledge (Keddie 1971), a curriculum, therefore, which is framed not in terms of access to a, now completely suspect and alien, 'high culture', but in terms of the development of the knowledge, the experience and culture which the pupils' own background has already provided and which they bring to the school with them. That this background will often be 'underprivileged' is acknowledged, but the 'underprivilege' is now to be defined in specific terms and not in terms of a general cultural inferiority or deficit for which education must attempt to compensate.

Thus the notion of 'high culture' is rejected totally and with it that rationalist epistemology which is its foundation. And the resultant adoption of a more tentative, less certain view of knowledge and values, one which reflects that empiricist/pragmatist epistemology which Part One attempted to define, has opened up the way to the development of a view of education which offers some hope of attaining a properly egalitarian and comprehensive curriculum of a kind which Williams' 'public educators' might approve, a genuine form of popular or mass education. It is, however, a curriculum which cannot be defined in terms of its knowledge content or of the transmission of knowledge of any kind — something which the sociologists themselves find it difficult to appreciate. For what is crucial to this kind of education is the response of pupils to what they are offered. Its base, therefore, must be sought in that response, in the processes of education itself, rather than in its, now widely disputed, content.

It was also pointed out in our discussion of these issues in Chapter 4, and it will be as well to stress this again here, that to make this kind of point is not to commit ourselves to a totally relativist stance, to an acceptance that all is equally valuable and that qualitative distinctions cannot now be made. It was suggested there, and again in Chapters 5 and 6, and the point is now reiterated, that, at least within the context of education, an analysis of, or a statement of, the processes we are concerned to promote will provide us with a perfectly adequate basis for the selection of content and for the making of qualitative distinctions. The point now is that those distinctions will be made not in terms of some claims, rationalist or other, concerning the inherent superiority of certain activities or bodies of knowledge, nor in terms of economic or vocational utility, but in terms of the extent to which what is selected is likely to promote in pupils those powers and capacities, that growth and development on all fronts, which we have claimed that education consists of — the development of understanding, of critical awareness, of autonomy and, above all, of the power to exercise some measure of control over one's environment and thus one's destiny.

Denis Lawton's reaction to this problem of diversity of provision is to attempt to preserve his 'common culture curriculum' by arguing that it should consist only of 'classless knowledge' (1975, p.49). If there were, or ever could be, such a thing as 'classless knowledge', this would be the ideal solution to the social class problem. But it certainly does not solve the knowledge problem implicit in the debate we have just rehearsed, since it merely reintroduces the rationalist notion of knowledge which transcends individual human perceptions and values, and thus misses the whole point of the debate. It does, however, draw our attention to the naivety of seeing the debate in terms of class divisions and thus in terms of two cultures only. For it becomes apparent that this is an impossible solution as soon as one extends the debate to embrace that range of cultural diversity which must be accepted once one recognizes the multi-ethnic, multicultural and pluralist nature of complex modern societies. For the acceptance of cultural differences whose origins are ethnic rather than social adds not just one new dimension to the issue but several, and makes it necessary that the debate be raised to a much higher level of sophistication.

Cultural and ethnic pluralism

If the idea of a common culture is difficult to sustain in the context of the social class divisions in society, it becomes completely untenable, along with the associated notion of 'high culture', once one accepts the existence not just of ethnic but also of cultural pluralism. For the acceptance of cultural pluralism implies a rejection of those absolutes offered us by the rationalist. If it does not, then we are merely paying lip-service to the idea of pluralism, we are accepting the existence of a plurality of cultures but not their equal validity. It is this which has bedevilled both our thinking and our practice in the development of a curriculum suited to a multi-ethnic and multicultural society.

There are at least four possible strategies which can be adopted in the planning of education in and for a multicultural society. The first of these is to begin from that hard 'high culture' line we discussed in relation to the education of the working classes and to see education as primarily concerned to offer access to this 'high culture'. This is the policy of 'assimilation' which was initially adopted in relation to the education of the children of newly arrived 'immigrants' in the United Kingdom in the 1960s. They were to be given access to the culture — assumed already to be unitary — of the society they had chosen to join.

The result of this policy was the same in the case of pupils from minority ethnic groups as we saw it was in that of working-class pupils. There was alienation, disaffection and a rejection by most pupils of both the knowledge and the values implicit in what was offered them. There was massive underachievement, defined in terms of that knowledge and those values (Coard 1971). In short, there were all those problems of achieving equality of educational opportunity for these pupils which we have seen arising from the attempts to provide the same equality for working-class pupils.

There thus arose the notion of compensatory education, and programmes such as the 'Headstart' scheme of pre-school education in the United States and the designation of Educational Priority Areas (EPAs) recommended by the Plowden Report (CACE 1967) in the United Kingdom, forms of education provided, often at great public expense, to compensate these pupils, and those of underprivileged social class origins, with extra resources and thus extra opportunities to overcome the disadvantages of their background and to give them some hope of reasonable success in the educational race.

It soon became clear, however, not only that such an approach would not and could not succeed, but also that it was predicated on some mistaken, not to say arrogant, assumptions about the superiority of white Anglo-Saxon culture, and thus on a rejection of other cultures as inferior. Other cultures were seen as deficient, as deficit systems, from which children must be assisted to escape. This approach raises questions, therefore, about the rationalist epistemology upon which such assumptions were, and are, based, although this has not always been recognized or appreciated, and thus a rethinking and perhaps a rejection of these assumptions become necessary if a more satisfactory alternative strategy is to be developed. A recognition and an acceptance of the multicultural and pluralist dimensions of society demand a complete reappraisal of what curriculum is and a restructuring of our practical curricular provision. The Swann Report (DES 1985b) has identified a need for a major rethinking of what knowledge is appropriate for all pupils in a multicultural society; the question being raised here is whether we should not be going even further than that and asking whether a common provision of knowledge for all pupils is an appropriate target to be aiming for.

The second strategy is a subvariant of this first one. It is that which was adopted in the United States in the face of the vast diversity of cultures which characterized US society certainly in its earliest years (Nicholas 1983). That strategy is to create a single culture from this vast diversity, to use education deliberately to attempt to create a unified culture. The strength of this strategy and one reason why it appears to have succeeded, where the assimilation techniques used in relation to the education of pupils from black minorities have palpably failed, is to be found in the fact that it did not attempt to pick out one culture to be imposed on the rest; it sought a genuine amalgam. It must also be remembered, however, that the cultures it sought to unify, although wide in their geographical origins, were perhaps not so wide in cultural terms, being mostly European and thus deriving ultimately from the same Graeco-Roman traditions, since no attempt was made to include black Americans or indigenous Americans or their cultures in this process. Nevertheless, we have here an attempt, apparently successful, to make one culture out of many, to make a unified society out of a diversity of peoples.

The third strategy which is worthy of note is that adopted by the USSR when faced with a similar problem of providing a common educational diet, determined in detail by central government fiat, for a widely varied nation. It is the strategy of balance and co-existence, the offering of the best of a common Russian culture to all, while at the same time endeavouring to preserve and maintain local cultures (Nicholas 1983). Again, there seems no reason to doubt that this policy has been successful. Again, however, we can see certain features which may have helped considerably towards this success, not least the geographical distinctions which have continued to match the cultural differences. It must be easier to offer a balance of common Russian and, say, Ukrainian culture in schools in the Ukraine populated largely, if not entirely, by children of Ukrainian origin. It becomes much more difficult in a society like that of the United Kingdom where cultural differences of a very wide kind are to be found among children in most schools and in most classrooms across the whole of the country.

Nevertheless, something like this strategy can be seen in those 'integrationist' approaches which some recommend us to adopt as a solution to the problems of establishing a satisfactory multicultural curriculum in the United Kingdom, the attempt to achieve accommodation rather than acculturation or assimilation by striving for a balance between a common core of values and some degree of diversification rather than seeking to impose one system *in toto*. Again it is worth noting that attempts to combine some notion of a common culture with that of local cultures does appear to have succeeded in the USSR. We should note too that again its success must be in large part due to the fact that it has recognized the value and the validity of those local cultures rather than rejecting, demeaning or devaluing them by attempts to compensate for them or to offer escape from them. It is also worth noting that this is a real rather than a tokenistic valuing of them.

The fourth strategy is that towards which again the 'new directions' in the sociology of education points us, that which involves a rejection of rationalism and the acceptance of an empiricist epistemology, that which requires us to recognize and accept the full force of the notion of cultural pluralism. For this strategy derives from an acceptance of Durkheim's categorization of complex modern societies as characterized by a 'mechanical' rather than an 'organic' solidarity, a unity in difference rather than in sameness, a pluralism in the full sense of the term as embracing the notion not merely of difference of value systems but also of their equal validity (Bernstein 1967). It derives too from a complete acknowledgement that no theory of knowledge or of values can offer a firm base from which we can evaluate one form of culture, or one system of values, against another, or a firm base for any notion of a 'high culture' superior to all others. Cultures are different but not inherently superior or inferior to one another. All have their own standards and their own strengths. Again, it must be repeated that this does not create an academic free-for-all within education. The concept of education itself, as it was defined in Chapter 4, offers a base from which educational judgements can be made. The point is that these judgements will be based on the perceived developmental needs of the individual and not on some presumed qualities inherent in the knowledge, the values or the cultures themselves.

This is the force of Labov's claim (1969, 1972) that the language used by certain groups of urban black youths is not in any way inferior to standard English nor, therefore, in any sense incapable of carrying all but the most simple meanings; it is merely syntactically different. This too is the force of Gladwin's paper (1964) describing the navigational skills of the Trukese, whose dead-reckoning, without benefit of any of the navigational aids developed in the European tradition of sail, and without any systematized or articulated theoretical base, is of a very high order. He suggests that we have in this phenomenon an example of 'a contrast between two cognitive strategies' (1973, p.116) and that it is quite unjustifiable to attempt to evaluate between the two or to go any further than recognizing their major differences. A third example would be the fundamental differences between African and European musical forms, differences which resulted in the inability to record black American music by the use of European forms of notation. These differences also reflected major divergencies in linguistic styles and forms, and in turn substantial differences in values, in social attitudes and, indeed, in outlook on life itself. It would be difficult to argue that such differences can legitimately be seen as evidence of inferiority of culture, not least because many of them have subsequently been absorbed by that very European culture which once registered claims to such superiority.

Much the same point is made by some of those who have wished to establish the validity of working-class culture. E.P. Thompson, for example, argues that 'class is a cultural as much as an economic function' (1963, p.13) and Richard Hoggart, especially in his more recent work (1978), has related the work of Labov to some of the criticisms which have been made about the language of the working classes.

The consequence of this is the view that education must accept the potential value of all cultures, that 'educational knowledge' must not be taken as necessarily superior to the 'commonsense knowledge' of the pupils, that to devalue the individual pupil's own culture is to display arrogance rather than judgement, that the grading of pupils in terms of attainment in certain predetermined and clearly defined areas of knowledge-content must be a highly suspect practice and that notions of cultural deprivation and compensatory education need at the very least to be much more closely explored and probably to be rejected altogether — at least in their current usages. In short, this view of what constitutes an appropriate strategy for education in a pluralist and multicultural society requires us to reject that all-pervasive rationalist epistemology, along with the assumptions of an objectivity of values which it generates, and embrace something far more tentative.

In this connection it is interesting to note the development of those African forms of music which were mentioned earlier among the black American population. For, without the aid or hindrance of formal educational provision, which indeed deliberately rejected them even when they were clearly becoming of great interest to white pupils as well as black, these gradually became fused with the European musical tradition in the music of black Americans, and ultimately of all Americans, and a new and vigorous cultural movement developed whose influence has been widespread both musically and geographically. This is a fusion which is now fully recognized in the planning of curricula at the level of both schools and Higher Education.

It must be acknowledged of course that this view in turn brings its difficulties. However much one may question the philosophical and epistemological validity of the idea of cultural superiority, there is no doubt that some notion of this kind is deep-rooted in our thinking nor that there is a dominant culture in any society. Not to give pupils access to this culture, to offer them an education framed in terms only of their own — minority — culture is thus to run the risk of trapping them in that culture, of limiting their opportunities in society by the very fact of attempting to respect and value their cultural origins. We might thus be trapping them in their own culture, as John White (1968) suggested in the criticisms he made of some of the curriculum offerings planned for the education of 'the young school leaver' in the wake of the Newsom Report (CACE 1963) and in response to the raising of the school leaving age which it recommended. As he pointed out, a curriculum devised purely in terms of its relevance to the interests and the cultural backgrounds of these pupils, such as that focused on 'the 97 bus' which was advocated by the Schools Council's Working Paper 11 (1967), would effectively limit the intellectual, and the social, horizons of the pupils to whom it was offered and deny them that broadening of horizons which it might be claimed is central to any notion of education in the full sense. It might thus become, as he suggested, an 'education in obedience' or, as Marten Shipman (1971) called it, 'a curriculum for inequality', perhaps even more effective as such than that very attempt to impose the values of the dominant group within society which the sociologists have complained of. This has been also a major source of criticisms of the attempt to establish 'Black Studies' courses in schools (Dhondy 1978; Fuller 1980), not least because this has been seen as having the effect of denying access to the kind of knowledge which might assist pupils towards the later securing of employment.

It was precisely the divisiveness of this kind of approach which we criticized earlier in our discussion of Bantock's proposal for the establishment of two curricula, which he argues for on the grounds that 'one of the most important [purposes of education] lies in the need to induct children into various of the areas of reality, social and physical, which, will-nilly, they inhabit' (1968, p.72).

Thus we are faced with a dilemma in that to respect any person's culture to the extent of, quite properly, seeing it as the focal point of the educational provision we make for them is to risk seriously limiting their opportunities. For that there is a dominant culture in society cannot be doubted and to be excluded from access to that culture, even as a result of extremes of respect paid to one's own, is to be placed at a serious disadvantage.

The second problem which besets us if we pursue this line is the nagging worry which many of us have that qualitative distinctions can be made between different cultures and, indeed, between different elements within any one culture. After all, part of any culture is its system of values and within that system of values judgements are made, that, for example, a play by Shakespeare is superior to a television soap opera, that a Beethoven symphony is musically more significant than an advertising jingle and so on. If such judgements can be made within each cultural system, then why can they not be made between them? It is precisely this concern which has led many people, such as Richard Hoggart, as we saw earlier, to want some kind of balance, to seek for respect for minority cultures while also providing access to 'the best that has been thought and said'. And it is in part this consideration too which lies behind that concern we just noted over the limitations of a form of curriculum which does not seek to extend the horizons of all pupils in such a way as to open their eyes to these wider experiences.

It is worth dwelling for a moment, then, on the debate concerning cultural and aesthetic values and the basis for asserting qualitative differences between human experiences and activities.

Culture and values

Aesthetic judgements made within individual cultures are largely non-problematic. For they are made within a broadly agreed system of values. Such agreement, however, is not usually very widespread and it is difficult to claim that there is anything objective or universal about these values unless one appeals to those rationalist arguments which we discussed in Part One and which we wish to reject. For, unless one can assume the validity of the kind of transcendental argument outlined there, one is forced to those sociological views of values — moral, social and aesthetic — which we saw are the inevitable concomitant of an empiricist epistemology. One is forced to acknowledge that systems of values have validity only for those who accept them, that values, like knowledge, are 'a product of the informal understandings negotiated among members of an organised intellectual collectivity' (Blum 1971, p.117), that it is only for the rationalist that they are objective or absolute and transcend the subjective attitudes of individuals or groups. Thus they can provide no valid grounds for evaluating between systems of values. There is no such thing as aesthetic knowledge any more than there is any such thing as moral knowledge, and in relation to aesthetic judgements some kind of relativism must be accepted, so that no concept of 'high culture' can be satisfactorily promulgated without the basis of a rationalist epistemology.

It was precisely this problem which we saw in Chapter 3 Dewey was concerned to resolve by attempting to reconcile the empiricist view of knowledge as uncertain, tentative, evolving and open to continuous modification and development with the need for some degree of objectivity and universal acceptance, albeit of a temporary and impermanent nature. We also saw, however, that, convincing as this argument might be in relation to scientific knowledge, it carried far less conviction in the sphere of values — moral, social or aesthetic. For these are matters not of fact, however 'fact' is defined, but of judgement, and judgements will always differ.

There is thus no basis outside a rationalist epistemology for claiming any kind of objectivity in any area of values or of judgements. A rationalist epistemology will provide an underpinning for the concept of 'high culture' but will bring with it all those consequences of acting on such a concept, especially in the field of education, which we noted earlier in this chapter. Other difficulties of such a position will also begin to emerge when we try to unpack this concept of 'high culture' and identify what are its constituent parts. For if this were non-problematic, that whole area we refer to as the Humanities would become equally non-problematic and thus very dull for those who work in that field. It is a field characterized by disagreement over the relative merits of the art, the literature, the music and the other forms of human endeavour studied there. For the rationalist that disagreement can only be explained in terms of a present intellectual inadequacy, which will be resolved as rationality, Hegel's 'Absolute', develops towards the time when all uncertainty will disappear. For the human (as opposed to the rational) being, it is that very uncertainty, the disagreement it generates and the diversity of values it stems from that makes life interesting, and the idea of a time when all will be certain, and when there will be no call upon one to make any kind of judgement, is far from being an attractive prospect. Thus a kind of anti-transcendental argument emerges. The concept of rationality, it has been claimed, can and will lead us to some kind of certainty of knowledge. The concept of humanity seems to entail some notion of individuality, of relativism and of a desirable uncertainty.

This conclusion does, however, leave the educationist in a dilemma. It is a dilemma well exemplified by the work of John Stuart Mill. For his predecessor and mentor, the founder of that philosophy known as 'Utilitarianism', Jeremy Bentham, had clearly recognized the consequences of the empiricist base from which he started. If, as he claimed, utility is the only principle of morals and legislation, then there are no grounds upon which qualitative distinctions can be claimed, so that 'quantity of pleasure being equal, push-pin is as good as poetry'. Mill, who inherited this doctrine, could not reconcile himself to this aspect of it, not least, interestingly enough, because he wished to advocate mass education as access to 'high culture' (West 1965). He thus, in a well-known and often quoted (at least by me) passage of his essay, 'Utilitarianism', claims that 'it is better to be a human being dissatisfied than a pig satisfied; better to be a Socrates dissatisfied than a fool satisfied' (op.cit., Ch. II). The claim is clear. There are certain activities which are qualitatively superior; poetry is, in some objective sense, a superior activity to playing push-pin; and to be fully human one must be apprised of this and encouraged to engage in those activities even if that involves abandoning the life of a satisfied pig and becoming a dissatisfied, ever-questioning Socrates. It is again, albeit in a stark and somewhat primitive form, that argument for worthwhile activities we noted earlier. It is thus of course an argument which is at odds with his fundamental philosophical position. For these arguments, as we have seen, are fundamentally rationalist, while Utilitarianism, as Bentham saw clearly, is founded on an empiricist epistemology. To attempt to graft this kind of rationalist view of values onto it is thus to attempt the impossible and to produce a theory which is at its very roots inconsistent.

What is perhaps more interesting and relevant here, however, is the paucity and the slightness of the arguments he is able to produce to support what is a crucial and far-reaching claim. 'If the fool, or the pig, are of a different opinion, it is because they only know their own side of the argument. The other party to the comparison knows both sides.' One is reminded of Plato's argument for the superiority of philosophy above all other forms of human activity — that this is the view of the philosopher and he is the only one in a position to know. Of more substance is that transcendental form of argument, deriving from Kant, which we explored in Chapter 2, but we also saw there its many difficulties.

The naivety of some aspects of this case will be apparent. So too will be its political dangers. For, no matter how well-meaning the motives of those who would press it, it leads, like rationalism itself, to views of 'high culture', to a mandate for the imposition of the values implicit in this on everyone, to the offering of inferior forms of schooling, as in Plato's scheme, to those who cannot or will not accept it, and to a devaluing of all forms of culture, all kinds of activity which cannot be shown to have merit by the application of these, extremely narrow, criteria, defined in terms of some abstract notion of rationality, which by definition is to be seen in isolation from competing notions such as that of humanity. Again, then, we find rationalism offering certainty, a firm base for our educational planning, but one whose consequences, once fully appreciated, are highly disturbing, while empiricism seems to offer access only to a slough of uncertainty, doubt and even indecision.

Equality, content and processes

Again it would seem that the problem arises from the apparent insistence that the curriculum must be planned, framed and described in terms of its content. We have noted in the previous two chapters many of the difficulties this creates. We have here a further such difficulty. For it is plain that the problems this chapter has been concerned to identify and explore arise primarily from the belief that to plan a curriculum is to list the subjects, the areas of knowledge, the selections from the culture, of which it is to consist. We saw in Chapter 5 that this leads to an emphasis on the content of the curriculum to the detriment of a concern for those forms of development we are suggesting education consists of. Chapter 6 revealed that this same approach also makes it difficult, and perhaps impossible, to tailor our educational provision to the developmental needs of the individual. What this chapter has suggested is that to take this view of the curriculum is to create for oneself some quite insuperable problems over the achievement of educational equality. Indeed, the claim is that the attempt to frame a curriculum in terms of a common content or a selection from the culture of that to which all pupils are felt to have a right to access, even though this is often undertaken with the quite deliberate intention of securing equality of educational opportunity, is in fact, and in practice, at odds with that ideal.

Educational equality cannot be attained via a common curricular provision. To believe it can is to slip into those simplistic interpretations of equality as implying sameness which have long bedevilled discussions not only of educational equality but of social equality too. The Plowden Report (CACE 1967) asserted that equality of educational opportunity does not imply similarity of provision. That is an important point to grasp, but only if one is defining educational provision in terms of the content of the curriculum. On that kind of definition, not only does common provision not lead to equality, it is also a positive barrier to it, as we saw in our discussion of the politics of knowledge in Chapter 4. Define education in academic terms, in terms of those subjects regarded as high on the subject hierarchy, and there will always be those pupils who cannot cope with some or all of these subjects at the necessary level and who will be dubbed 'ineducable'. (Plato at least was honest about this.) As James Hemming has said (1980, p.17) 'The enemy of education is not a genuine regard for the intellect but arrogant intellectual élitism.'

What is more important in the context of this present chapter is that there will also be large numbers of pupils who, whether they can cope with these subjects or not, will not want to cope with them, either because they do not see their point or relevance in their own lives, or because they recognize or sense that they reflect a rejection of their own values, a devaluing of their own culture, whether this be social or ethnic. These pupils will not necessarily be 'ineducable', but they will remain uneducated. Define education in terms of a selection from the common culture of society, and the same will result, simply because there is as yet no common culture, and perhaps there never will be, at anything beyond the minimal level.

A common curriculum, then, defined in terms of its academic knowledge-content or of its cultural content, of the kind a rationalist epistemology points us towards, can never lead to educational equality. Indeed, it must have the effect of compounding inequalities. Plato saw this very clearly as a corollary of rationalism. Nothing which has been said or written since has shown how it can be otherwise. Those writers, therefore, who advocate both a common content to the curriculum, justified in educational rather than utilitarian terms, and educational egalitarianism are guilty of a substantial confusion. Those who advocate that common content precisely in order to achieve equality are even more confused.

Two possible solutions offer themselves. The first is that of Plato, to accept social and educational inequalities, to recognize that there are people of gold, silver and bronze and to tailor our educational provision to that. This we saw earlier is the line taken in more recent times by Bantock (1968), and, as was suggested in Chapter 4, it is the effect, if not the intention, of much current government policy in education in the UK. Apart from the possible moral unacceptablity of that solution, it is also crude and simplistic. No-one would wish to argue with its basic premise that people are different (some of us will perpetually shout 'Vive la difference!'), but few would be prepared to go along with the idea that there are only two or three types of human being, so that we need only two or three types of education (the basic assumption of tripartism). This brings us, then, to the other possible solution.

If the problem arises because of the view of the curriculum as content and because of that rationalist epistemology which presses us towards that view, then an alternative solution is to reject that view as an inadequate base for planning which is educational in the full sense. If we accept the idea that education is a developmental process, in which subject-content plays a contributory but not a prime role, as was suggested in Chapter 5, if one also accepts that a corollary of that position is that this kind of development is an individual matter, as was suggested in Chapter 6, then the attainment of educational equality becomes a realistic proposition only if seen in terms of equality of access to that experience and provision which will promote this kind of individual development, and not in terms of equality of access to certain predetermined bodies of knowledge-content. The content of education may vary; it may vary in such a way as to accommodate those cultural differences and, indeed, those individual differences we have noted; what must not vary, if we are genuinely concerned with equality of educational opportunity, is the right of access to whatever will promote the processes of education, whatever will assist each individual to become an educated person. It is this that we have suggested on several occasions offers us the only basis for making qualitative judgements, especially in relation to curriculum planning.

This is surely what John Stuart Mill was seeking after in his recommendation that we aim to make of everyone a dissatisfied Socrates rather than a satisfied pig. If we interpret that recommendation in terms of certain kinds of knowledge-content, certain kinds of activity deemed to be qualitatively superior, as Mill himself did, we are making rationalist assumptions which are difficult to justify, productive of the problems we listed earlier and impossible to reconcile with other concerns we may have. If we see it as a claim that all are entitled to certain forms of development, which will take them beyond the limitations of the environment into which they were born — whatever form that takes — and which in particular will enable them, as Paolo Freire (1972) suggests, to see the conditions of their lives in a reflexive perspective and to act on them rather than being 'dopes' whose destiny is decided for them by others, then a justification becomes easier to attain. It is a justification, however, which will be framed in terms of developmental processes, in which the selection of knowledge or cultural content will be based on those processes and not on merits claimed for that content itself, and which will entail a rejection of that rationalist epistemology which would give knowledge and cultural values a status higher than this.

We may finally note the extent to which this opens up a richness of possibilities which restriction to a narrower concept of 'high culture' would deny. There is little doubt, for example, that a study of Mogul India can be as educationally productive in every sense as a study of Tudor England, indeed a good deal more productive for pupils from certain kinds of cultural background. There is even less doubt, however, of the educational merits and possibilities of a comparative study of both, since this can add a richness of experience for all pupils which would otherwise be denied. It has also been claimed with some conviction (Miller 1980) that diversity of language can offer equally rich opportunities for teachers. Children who have to operate in two languages seem to be, not surprisingly, far more aware of the nuances of language and far more sensitive to the appropriateness of their speech and the effects it produces on their listeners. Again, therefore, this diversity of background, culture and even language can be seen to offer important educational opportunities to the teacher who is aware of and sympathetic to it, which would be denied to one adopting a narrower view of what might constitute appropriate curricular provision.

Summary and conclusions

This chapter has set out to trace the debate over the relationship of culture and the curriculum. It began by suggesting that some of the muddle with which that debate has been bedevilled has arisen from a confusion of the several meanings the term 'culture' can be seen to have, in particular the conflation of its descriptive, scientific, value-free meaning with that prescriptive, judgemental, value-laden meaning it has in those contexts in which it is being used to denote some form of 'high culture', some collection of supposedly superior activities and achievements.

We went on to explore the implications of this debate for, and its interweaving with, the parallel debate over the most appropriate form for mass education and the kind of curriculum which might be said to lead to equality of educational opportunity, to a fully democratic and comprehensive form of schooling. We noted the problems created by the recognition of the existence of different cultures within society, not only the 'folk' and 'high' cultures, the working-class and the upper-class cultures, but also, and especially, the many ethnically different cultures to be seen in modern pluralist societies. In particular, we noted the problems raised for education by an acceptance of the value and the validity of these cultures.

It became clear that the issue hinges on the notion of 'high culture' and its validity, and we concluded the chapter with an examination of that. It was claimed that the only source of validity for such a notion was to be found in a rationalist epistemology, and that without that the concept lacked any kind of base. It was suggested too that the arguments both for that kind of base and for the notion of a 'high culture' consisting of activities claimed to be qualitatively superior, were very thin, while the case for value pluralism and thus for relativism, like that for the empiricist epistemology which underpins it, carries much more conviction.

The dilemma for educational planning, however, remains. There is no doubt that, valid or not, a high culture exists in society nor that to deny pupils access to that culture because their own cultural origins are different is to put them at an enormous social disadvantage. It is equally clear, on the other hand, that to plan their education in terms of that high culture is to devalue their own and to risk the kind of alienation and even disaffection which has often resulted when pupils have been offered a curriculum whose relevance has escaped them.

It was suggested, therefore, that a solution to this dilemma may be found if we attempt a complete rethinking of our approach to education and curriculum planning and, in particular, if we consider what might follow if we begin that planning not from a concern with the content of the curriculum but from a consideration of the processes of development of which education in the full sense consists. For this dilemma again, like the problems we explored in the previous two chapters, arises from a view of education as the transmission of certain kinds and bodies of knowledge, a view which requires us to debate the issue of what kinds of knowledge we should transmit. Or it arises from the parallel view of education as the imposition of the value systems implicit in such bodies of knowledge; for then again we must ask what value systems we have the right to impose. To view education as a process of individual growth and development, however, is to recognize that the question of what knowledge-content we should offer becomes subsidiary to that of what forms of development we should be promoting, and thus of what kinds of knowledge-content will assist us to promote them, a consideration which in itself opens up rich veins of knowledge and experience for teachers to exploit, and to acknowledge that the concept of education itself requires us to see it expressly not as the imposition of any system of values but as a process of encouraging pupils to explore, to question, to seek understanding, to develop their own value systems and to extend the range of their competency. It is this that constitutes what it means to be both a rational and a human being. And it is in this direction that a solution to the dilemma of culture and the curriculum is to be found.

To advocate this is of course again to advocate a rejection of that rationalist epistemology which must deny the individual the right to his/ her own views and values. By now, however, the need to reject this stance may perhaps be apparent. Certainly, it is to advocate a quite different epistemological base for curriculum planning, and perhaps it is also becoming clear that such a different base may offer us more satisfactory solutions to a number of curriculum problems than those the rationalist perspective has provided.

In particular, it offers us the possibility of viewing education and the curriculum not in terms of its knowledge-content, not in terms of subject-matter, but in terms of growth and development, and, indeed, of development on many fronts. It is to a fuller explication of this that we turn in Chapter 8.

CHAPTER 8

BEYOND THE COGNITIVE — DEVELOPMENT AS MULTI-DIMENSIONAL

How can you put on the blackboard the mysterious internal goal of each creative person?
(Robert Pirsig, *Zen and the Art of Motorcycle Maintenance*)

In the previous three chapters, the attempt has been made to persuade the reader, first, that education can only be planned effectively and productively if it is seen as a number of developmental processes rather than as a collection of knowledge-content, secondly, that this becomes a highly individual matter and not one which can readily be guided or controlled, except in terms of the very broadest of guidelines, from a distance beyond that of the individual school or classroom and the interaction of the individual pupil with his/her own teacher(s), and, thirdly, that it is only when we acknowledge and accept this that we will be able to achieve anything remotely resembling equality of educational opportunity or any viable concept of mass education.

Education has to be seen, planned and evaluated, then, by reference to certain developmental criteria. It is to a consideration of what these criteria might be that we turn in this chapter and, in particular, to a recognition that the education of human beings must be conducted by reference to criteria which go far beyond the merely cognitive. For there is more to the human being than a rational mind in a physical body; the human being is not merely a 'ghost in a machine' (Ryle 1949); and, as William James (1902) once suggested when imagining how the world would look to one who lacked all forms of emotional response, it is 'almost impossible to imagine such a condition of negativity and deadness. There would no longer be any importance, significance, character, expression or perspective'. The development of human beings, therefore, must be seen from several perspectives, must be advanced on several fronts and must be planned and evaluated against a wide range of criteria.

It will also emerge yet again from this discussion that a rationalist or objectivist epistemology is quite unable to help us towards the establishment of wide-ranging criteria of this kind. Rationalists have often expressed difficulty in dealing with the concept of 'the whole man' (i.e. 'the whole person') (Peters 1966), and this is not surprising since by its very essence rationalism's concern is with only a part of man — his or her powers of reason.

It is not the intention here to pursue the question of the forms of cognitive development education should be concerned to promote. These were explored and elaborated in Chapter 4, and it was suggested there — and, indeed, on several subsequent occasions — that there is a fair measure of agreement, if often merely tacit, that education has something to do with assisting people towards the development of understanding, the ability to make sound judgements, the capacity to explore issues, solve problems, even develop new knowledge — all those things which Richard Peters (1965, 1966) once claimed to be part of the concept of education, part of what it means to be educated — cognitive perspective, critical awareness, autonomy and so on — as well as those which, as we saw in Chapter 3, John Dewey stressed were necessary both for the development of one's own knowledge and understanding of the world, one's own ability to solve the problems presented by the environment of one's life, and for the evolution of knowledge on a higher plane.

The intention here, then, is to concentrate on dimensions of development beyond the cognitive. What must first be noted briefly again, however, in relation to cognitive development is the incompatibility of some of these criteria of education with the objectivist stance of the rationalist on the question of the status of knowledge and of values. For, as we have seen, it is difficult to see what autonomy, for example, could mean in the context of an objectivist system of values. We saw in Chapter 2 the logical conclusion Hegel drew from this kind of objectivism, that freedom is some kind of conformity and that the only choice the autonomous individual has is whether to accept what rationality or the 'Absolute' dictates or to reject it. In spite of all the claims which have been made concerning the need for autonomy to be seen not as complete licence to think whatever one likes, regardless of all considerations, and for it to be seen as necessarily based on some kind of understanding and awareness, it is difficult to argue that it means very much if the greater that understanding and awareness the more it points in one direction only. Education, on Plato's analysis, led to his rulers *knowing* what was right;

there was no autonomy there; nor were their powers of judgement needed; they were 'dyed with the laws'; as Socrates is told at the end of that passage in *The Republic* where he completes his outline of the education of his élite, 'you have finished off your ruling men beautifully, Socrates, like a sculptor'. This is inevitable if one's view of autonomy or judgement is rooted in an objectivist view of knowledge and values.

The second aspect of this which we must note is its inability to cope with all forms of development other than the cognitive and that takes us into the main concerns of this discussion.

Affective development

Much has been made in recent discussions of education of the importance of the affective dimension of educational development — the education of the emotions and, related to that, personal, social and moral education. We must also remember that for many people aesthetic education is as much or more a matter of how people come to *feel* about certain objects — novels, poems, plays, paintings, performances and so on — as of what they *know* about them. To say that is not of course to say that the two are not interrelated nor to suggest that knowledge is not an important aspect of appreciation; it is to stress, however, that the affective dimension is there and cannot or should not be ignored.

There are several reasons for making this claim. The first of these is that feeling is integral to large areas of the curriculum and even of the rationalist's common core curriculum. It would be difficult to conceive of an educational programme in art, in dance, in music or in CDT, for example, from which the affective dimension were excluded or even in which it were regarded as something which could be clearly distinguished from the cognitive and treated as separate and distinct. There is no doubt that knowledge is necessary in all of these spheres, nor that its possession will enhance and change one's affective responses and reactions. This is part of that interlinking to which we referred above. But to suggest that they can be planned, evaluated or in any way treated separately, as for example in the domains of Bloom's taxonomy of educational objectives (Bloom 1956; Krathwohl 1964), is to misunderstand completely the nature not only of the activities but also of human development and learning.

The same is true of all those subjects which constitute what are often called the 'Humanities'. Etymology itself would suggest that the concern here is with human interaction and that this is something which goes far beyond logic and rationality. Thus in curriculum subjects such as English, history, large areas of geography and so on, the concern is not merely with acquiring knowledge but with understanding the human feelings involved and evoked and, indeed, with responding emotively oneself to what is being studied or explored. This point can be illustrated particularly well by reference to Bruner's project, Man: A Course of Study (MACOS), which was mentioned in Chapter 5. For a major aspect of that project, or at least a major feature of its implementation, was the emotive response of the pupils to the materials (Jones 1972).

This leads us to a second reason why one wants to stress the importance of acknowledging and accepting this affective dimension to education. For what has just been said about the Humanities points us towards a view of man which is very different from that of those who would reduce all to the cognitive. For, underlying this acceptance of the important role of feeling in education and human development is a view, or a model, of a man as a *human* being, a being whose feelings and emotions are important constituents of his essence, and a being who must be seen as active not only in his/her own education but also in his/her environment. Not to acknowledge the importance of feeling is to see man as passive, as acted on by forces in his environment external to him, or it is to see man as a rational being, whose essence consists solely of his rationality. We will return to this point later, since it is integral to the rationalist view. It is sufficient to note here that, if we take a view of man as a human rather than a merely rational being, as a person rather than a computer, then we are thereby committed to attempting to devise a form of education which will embrace these wider aspects of his being.

A third kind of argument for doing this is that derived from the work of developmental psychology which we looked at briefly in Chapter 4 and have referred to since. For we saw there that, from the very beginning, those working in this field have found it necessary to recognize the complete intertwining of the affective and the cognitive and thus the need to keep the affective dimension in view even when exploring the cognitive development of children. And this is precisely because, unlike behaviourist psychology, which has treated all learning, including animal learning, as if it were the same, developmental psychology has directed its attention specifically to human learning and has thus inevitably found it necessary to go beyond the cognitive. We saw too that more recent work, such as that of Margaret Donaldson (1978) and Eliot Eisner (1982), has taken this much further and has stressed how crucial an awareness of a number of aspects of affective development is. This work has suggested not merely that we should take account of this dimension of development, but that we cannot avoid doing so, or, rather, that, if we attempt to do so, we will fail to ensure adequate development even on the cognitive front.

Rationalist epistemology provides us with no basis for planning on these other fronts, since by its very nature it is rooted in the cognitive. Again, therefore, it proves a less than satisfactory base from which to plan educational provision. That this is so, and, indeed, why it is so, we must now attempt to show.

Rationalism and the affective dimension

We saw in Part One that, from the very beginning, rationalism has seen man as a rational being rather than as a human being. It has seen rationality as man's essence, as that which distinguishes him from other creatures, and, taking the essentialist view that function is derived from essence, it has deduced from this that it is man's function to develop, to use, to activate that rational faculty above all else. We have had cause to notice before the fallacious nature of this reasoning from essence to function, from description (even if and when accurate) to prescription, from 'is' to 'ought'. We must note here, however, its centrality to the rationalist position and, in particular, the view of man and of man's obligations which it leads to. For Aristotle, for example, man's rational faculty is that which he shares with God (who, for him, is 'self-thinking thought'), unlike those other aspects of his being which he shares with the rest of the animal kingdom, so that it is that which he must cultivate and it is that which he must spend as much time as possible using. Thus contemplation is for him the supreme form of human activity, precisely because it transcends human, and certainly animal, existence and gets us closer to the eternal preoccupation of God. We have noted before the attractions of this doctrine for Christian theology and its consequent perpetuation in the Western European philosophical tradition. What we must note now is that it is predicated on a view of man as a thinking being rather than as a feeling being, and not even a view of man as a being in whom thinking and feeling go hand in hand. There is no place for feeling in this doctrine and thus no base for the development of any notion of the education of feeling, of the education of man as an emotive being, of any affective dimension to education or development.

There are only two ways in which this philosophy can cope with the manifest truth that man is possessed of emotions as well as of powers of reasoning, both of which are apparent throughout the literature of rationalism. The first of these is to advocate the suppression of feeling; the second to attempt to reduce as much as possible in that area to the cognitive. We must look at each of these devices in turn.

It will be remembered from Part One that Plato described the soul of man as having three aspects — reason, 'spirit' and the appetites — and that he likened these respectively to a man, a lion and 'a beast with many heads'. It will also be remembered that the only form of 'education' he felt the last of these elements was amenable or susceptible to was 'taming'. Thus we have the first statement of rationalism not only that we must distinguish and treat as separate rationality and feeling, the mind and the appetites, reason and the passions, but also that our only way of dealing with the second of these is by some form of repression. Aristotle too saw what he called 'pleasure' as in conflict with reason, as likely to distract man from following the dictates of reason and from the supreme form of rational activity, contemplation, and thus as something to be kept well under control, and permitted to express itself only under controlled conditions, as, for example, through the safety-valve of *catharsis*.

Thus from the beginning the appetites, the passions, the emotions are treated as a problem, as in conflict with reason, as a serious hindrance to morality, as a feature of human nature not to be welcomed but to be deplored, to be wrestled with, to be overcome or at least tamed in the interests of the development of rationality. Education's only concern with the affective dimension of human experience, then, is to suppress it as a hindrance, an unfortunate encumbrance that man is lumbered with.

The Judaeic tradition reinforces this view, as does the Christian ethic which derived from it. Nor is there anything here to make a subsequent fusion of the Greek and Judaeic traditions difficult. For that same attitude to the human passions is to be seen there. Man's appetites are the domain of Satan who brought about Adam's fall from grace, and they constitute that burden of original sin we are all encumbered with from our entry into the world. This original sin must be overcome by whatever means are necessary and possible; the passions must be suppressed, so that man can develop his powers of reason, his intellectual capacity, what Aquinas called 'the intellectual love of God'.

Thus this dualism, the dichotomy of reason and the passions, has dominated thinking in the Western world. We have seen before that the Christian influence remained strong even after the re-emergence of philosophy at the time of the Renaissance and this dualism is one piece of evidence for this. For it is to be seen even in that developed form of rationalism which Immanuel Kant offered us. We noted in Part One that Kant is at pains to stress that his system of morality is for rational beings rather than human beings, that it is based on an analysis of morality as an abstract concept rather than as a human characteristic, that his concern is with the 'metaphysic of morals' and emphatically not with the human conditions within which moral behaviour is seen to occur. In fact, and inevitably, it leads again to a view of human beings as being unfortunately hindered in their search for a rational morality by those passions, those emotions, those feelings with which their humanity encumbers them. Again, therefore, the solution is found in control and suppression. Morality is a matter of discovering through the use of reason what the right course of action is. Feelings merely serve too often to deflect one's judgement or one's resolve once this rational process has been completed.

It is here that a fundamental contradiction becomes apparent. For it is never appreciated that nothing which could be called a moral existence (nor, indeed, a Christian existence) would be possible without these feelings and inclinations, even if we accept for the moment that they are for the moral will to overcome. The notion of moral feeling is integral to that of moral existence or moral behaviour and it is a fundamental contradiction in Kant's system that it fails either to acknowledge or to allow for this. It is also a fundamental difficulty for rationalism. 'It has to be allowed that morality is commited both to the destruction of the natural passions and to their preservation: to the former because, in any conflict between reason and the inclinations, it is axiomatic that reason ought to triumph, to the latter because moral reason needs the natural passions both as its antithesis and its instrument' (Walsh 1969, p.30). One would add that it is only a rationalist view of morality of which this is true, because it is only rationalism which clings to this dichotomy.

And it is this dichotomy which is at the root of the problem. For it has made it impossible to develop a theory of morality, or, indeed, of human development, in which reason and the passions are treated as interrelated or in which their interrelationship is properly explored. To quote Walsh again, 'The Kantian doctrine which makes practical reason in effect the godlike element in man and writes down the passions as belonging to his animal nature amounts to a form of dualism as objectionable as any to be found in Descartes. The unity of the human being is entirely lost in this account' (op.cit., p.32). Indeed, that dualism is a direct result of the dualism which Descartes inherited from the Greek and Judaeo-Christian traditions and imposed on modern philosophy, the dualism of mind and body, subject and object, consciousness and experienced reality. It leads to a view of rationality as quite detached from other aspects of the human reality, to a stern, unbending attitude to morality, lacking in any kind of human sympathy or understanding, a moral system, and an educational system, for rational beings rather than for human beings. Again, 'the voice of reason in Kant was as remote from the living being as was Jehovah from the ancient Jews' (Walsh 1969, p.38).

It is also worth noting briefly the impact of this approach on the development of Western art. For it is precisely this leaning towards the rational aspects of human existence which Nietzsche was complaining of in his criticism of what he called the Apollonian form of art or culture. By this he meant that there has been a kind of intellectualizing of art which has led to its having a reduced role in human life and development. We saw Plato's treatment of art merely as a device for holding society together, in particular by displaying to advantage those values upon which society was founded. Its role was not to challenge those values nor to encourage the exploration of new values, but merely, as with all his proposals, to maintain the *status quo*. As a result of this, a great deal of art in the Western world over the ages has been devoted to this kind of purpose, particularly that within the orbit and the patronage of the Christian church, to illustrate and to decorate but never to go beyond what is there nor to offer any significant comment of its own.

It was this that Nietzsche was attempting to challenge in the distinction he drew between what he calls the Apollonian and the Dionysian forms of culture. The former's concern is to gloss over the harsh realities of human existence, to decorate them and thus render them acceptable by remaining unrecognized for what they really are. The Dionysian form of culture, on the other hand, endeavours to face existence as it really is, to reveal it in its starkest form and thus to challenge the values implicit in the Apollonian form. Both of these forms can be seen in Western European culture from the earliest times, including that of the ancient Greeks, but the former has been emphasized, he claims, because the latter involves too open an acceptance of the passionate side of human nature. We would add that a further, and related, reason for this is the dominance of that rationalist epistemology which we are concerned here to show can give no proper account of feeling or the passions. It is no coincidence that developments in art along the lines which Nietzsche would describe as Dionysian have been more evident in Western culture since major challenges to rationalism have been mounted. It is the purpose here to extend those challenges into the sphere of education and to indicate some of their implications.

This leads us to a consideration of a second, and related, solution to the problem of man's emotional life offered by rationalism — the attempt to reduce as much of it as possible to the cognitive, to turn all kinds of human experience into some form of knowledge and thus to make it readily accessible to the intellect, to reason, and thus explicable in rationalist terms. Thus, for example, we have seen that for all the rationalist philosophers, from Plato to the present day, morality becomes moral knowledge rather than a matter of moral judgement, so that solving a moral problem becomes analogous to solving a mathematical problem. This is not always made as obvious as in Spinoza's *Ethics* in which an ethical system is set out in Euclidean form, with definitions, hypotheses to be proved, proofs of these hypotheses and conclusions indicated clearly and firmly with a 'QED'. Obvious or not, however, it is always there. It is clearly there in the work of Kant, which was designed to establish a base in rationality for all moral assertions and, indeed, all assertions of value. It is this, as we saw in Part One, which is the purpose and point of Richard Peters' 'transcendental argument'. Elsewhere too (1973a, pp.80—1) he asserts quite explicitly, 'The basic, *and perhaps paradoxical* [my italics] point I wish to make about "emotions" and "motives" is that, although manifestly these terms relate in some way to our feelings, they are also intimately connected with cognition, that is with our ways of understanding situations.' Similarly, John Wilson (1971, p.1) tells us that the education of the emotions must be a matter of helping people 'to become more reasonable in the sphere of the emotions'. Furthermore, one of Paul Hirst's forms of knowledge or understanding is, at least in some statements of them, the moral form (Hirst and Peters 1970).

So too is the aesthetic form and again we have another kind of attempt to reduce this area, in which feeling must play a very large part, to some kind of cognition. 'The claim for a distinctive mode of *objective* [again my italics] aesthetic experience, using forms of symbolic expression not confined to the linguistic, must be taken seriously' (op.cit., p.64). The issue of aesthetic responsiveness, then, is to be explained by seeing aesthetic experience as a form of knowledge, a body of assertions, albeit expressed not always in linguistic but in other symbolic forms, but a body of knowledge nevertheless, not as a matter of feeling or of human passions.

The same point emerges in a very interesting form in what the

Assessment of Performance Unit team has said about aesthetic education. For it quite rightly criticizes many traditional views for treating reason and feeling as quite separate, referring to 'the common misconception that reason is quite distinct from, or even inimical to, feeling' (APU 1983, p.5). It then goes on, however, to claim that 'judgements about the emotional meaning of a work of art are equally open to rational justification by reference to *objective criteria* [my italics]' (ibid.) and that 'the feelings expressed in and evoked by the work are *intrinsic to it* [my italics again], and are assessable by reference to *objective features of it* [my italics]' (ibid).

Thus again, although we have an attempt to avoid the dichotomy of reason and feeling, we end up with all emotive responsiveness turned into an objective, rational process of cognition. One can see the attractions of this from the point of view of procedures of assessment, and we will consider this aspect of rationalism in education more fully in the next chapter. One must conclude again, however, that, on this analysis, which can be seen as essentially that of rationalism and objectivism, little, if any, scope exists for personal response or judgement, little autonomy exists for the individual, and, indeed, one would also suggest that aesthetic response is seen in a rather simplistic form, consisting as it does only of that which can be expressed and justified in rational terms.

It is worth noting also at this point the difficulty the rationalists have experienced in coming to terms with the idea of creativity in education. This has been an important issue in curricular discussions for a long time and it is not the intention to debate it fully here. It must be noted, however, that it is a concept which rationalism again has had great difficulty in accommodating. Nor is this surprising since the very notion implies an invitation to pupils to go beyond the realms of pure cognition and the boundaries of accepted 'educational' knowledge. Thus the questions which have been posed by the rationalists, or by those who have adopted their assumptions about knowledge, have been questions like 'How can children be expected to create new knowledge or anything new?' and 'How can we expect children to create anything which is original and worthwhile?' Again, therefore, the focus has been on the content and the product rather than on the process. 'The criteria of creativity . . . will be the criteria of what is good or bad in the appropriate art' (Dearden 1968, p.149), and 'the development of creative abilities in children will be a matter . . . of aesthetic *education*. There will be a great deal of learning to be done' (ibid.). There are interesting parallels here with the debate over 'enquiry-' or 'discovery-learning' which was mentioned briefly in Chapter 5.

An even more simplistic view can be seen in the attempt of the behavioural psychologists to plan education in the affective domain not only as separable from the cognitive but as reducible to and expressible in the same kinds of behavioural objectives (Bloom et al. 1956; Krathwohl et al. 1964). The case against this form of planning, at least in the area of the Humanities, has been made in many places (Stenhouse 1970, 1975; Pring 1973; Kelly 1980, 1982; Blenkin and Kelly 1981) and it is not the intention to rehearse it here. It may be sufficient merely to note it as another attempt at reducing this dimension of human development and experience so as to include it within clearly defined categories and thus render it manageable. Its effect, of course, is precisely the opposite. For this aspect of human experience continues to run through the fingers of all who try to capture it in this way. Unfortunately, this means it has come close to being lost in educational planning altogether.

The same can be said of the approach to this area of the curriculum at the political level and it is worth noting finally that the implicit and somewhat confused rationalist assumptions which we have seen contribute hugely to the tone of much of the current political interventionism in curriculum planning also, and inevitably, have the effect of creating, or at least aggravating, this kind of impact on the affective aspects of the curriculum. Thus it is not only their instrumental bias, which we noted earlier, that causes them to be less effective in dealing with this area, where the utilitarian value is less easy to identify, it is also the fact that they share the problems implicit in the rationalist view of knowledge, of education and of humanity.

For both of these reasons there has been a clear reduction in the emphasis on and the attention given to the arts in education in recent years (Gulbenkian Foundation 1982). The utilitarian factor is easy to recognize and to understand, but it is worth noting the significance of that other factor, the rationalist tendency to reduce all to cognition. We have already noted this in relation to the work of the Assessment of Performance Unit in the area of aesthetic education. Another example is the statement of the 1977 Green Paper (DES 1977b) of the importance of the arts in education since this is defined as being concerned 'to teach children about human achievement and aspirations in the arts'. There is no mention of these areas of the curriculum as concerned to provide experiences of an affective kind or to promote development on other fronts; the emphasis again is on cognition, on learning rather than feeling, on the head rather than the heart.

To some extent this may be seen as being offset by the inclusion of the 'aesthetic/creative' as one of the 'eight adjectives', the eight 'areas of experience', listed in *Curriculum 11-16* (DES 1977a). But the failure to see the full implications, both epistemological and educational, of that stance has led to subsequent documents paying somewhat scant, and almost always totally unsatisfactory, attention to the arts in education, however defined. Indeed, the greatest threat to the affective dimension of education, and to the role of the arts in education, from current political activity may come more from the fact that these are totally ignored than from any kind of attempt to pervert them. It was precisely this fear which prompted the Gulbenkian enquiry (1982).

Again, therefore, we note that the threat to education as we have defined it comes not only from the theorists but also from those political sources whose impact on the curriculum is currently escalating. And again we can see that this is in part a result of the adoption by the latter of many of the basic tenets of the former.

It is because of this and the unsatisfactory nature of rationalism's handling of questions of emotional experience generally and of emotional development in particular that there has been a reaction against it and an attempt by some to produce theories of knowledge, of morals and, indeed, of education which will take account of man's emotional life and development, his feelings, his passions and the role they play in human existence, not by denying them and advocating their suppression nor by attempting to reduce them to some bogus forms of cognition, but by acknowledging their existence and their importance and trying to recognize that they are intimately and inextricably intertwined with reason and with the intellect. These are theories, of course, which derive from a rejection of rationalism and we must now look, albeit briefly, at what they attempt to offer us.

Alternative approaches to the affective dimension

It has to be admitted at the outset that the alternative approaches have not often been any more successful in solving this problem for us. They have two advantages, however. For most of them begin from a recognition that the problem is not merely one of forms of cognition, and they approach it with the same kind of view of the tentative, hypothetical and uncertain nature of knowledge which they adopt in all spheres of human experience.

We must note briefly first of all Dewey's attempt to reduce values to the cognitive by suggesting that knowledge, albeit on his tentative definition of what knowledge is, can be as readily attained in this field as in any other. We suggested in Chapter 3 that this was the least convincing aspect of his theory. We can see now one of the reasons for this. His attempt to have the best of both worlds, to reconcile the rationalist's claim to objectivity with the empiricist's recognition of the uncertain and continuously evolving nature of human knowledge, has led him to the same kind of reductionism as the rationalist. 'Inquiry, discovery,' he tells us, 'take the same place in morals that they have come to occupy in sciences of nature. Validation, demonstration become experimental, a matter of consequences.' (1948). This is a step in the right direction, since at least it discourages dogmatism, but it does not help us towards a genuine theory of the emotions nor of their role in education.

The other reactions against this aspect of rationalism do not take us a lot further. They do accept the significance of man's emotional responses to the world and they recognize that these are different in kind from acts of cognition, but, in doing this, they accept and perpetuate the dichotomy between reason and feeling we have described. For the most part, they have continued to see reason and the passions as in conflict.

The empiricist reaction, as was seen in Part One, has led to the view that knowledge is not possible in the sphere of values, so that the only theories of morals, for example, they have been able to offer have been emotivist, that is they have recognized the importance of the emotions in moral behaviour but have gone on to claim that moral beliefs and moral behaviour are explicable only in terms of how people feel. They have thus suggested that moral behaviour is to be assessed in terms of social utility, or in terms of maximizing pleasure and minimizing pain, or they have claimed, as we also saw in Part One, that all moral assertions are to be seen merely as expressions of the feelings of those uttering them, that they are not statements of knowledge of any kind, since they are not susceptible to any kind of empirical test of their validity, and that they do not, as a result, form part of any system of rationality, they are in no way subject to the application of reason. Thus the dichotomy between reason and feeling remains, the emphasis being placed this time on feeling as the central concern rather than reason.

Indeed, the role of reason becomes one of total subordination to feeling. Hume tells us that the role of reason is to help with calculations of means only, of the ways in which we can bring about those things our feelings, including of course our social feelings, urge us towards. 'Reason is,' he tells us, as we saw in Chapter 1, 'and ought to be, the slave of the passions' (*Treatise*). Thus the dichotomy and the resultant tension and conflict remain.

The second reaction is that of existentialism. This too, again as we saw in Part One, began as a revolt against rationalism. The central concern here was with the loss of individualism implicit in the rationalist emphasis on universals, on objectivity, and its preoccupation with man as a rational rather than as a human being. Thus the inability of rationalism to offer any kind of adequate theory of the emotions was from the beginning a major driving force behind the emergence of this form of philosophy.

Again, however, the tendency has been to see a rejection of rationalism as entailing a rejection of rationality or reason. So much so that this form of philosophy has often been dubbed irrationalist. It is difficult, and perhaps academically unacceptable, to attempt to generalize about a philosophy whose essence is individualism and which has consequently appeared in many different forms. However, if there is a main thrust, as we saw in Chapter 2, it is the claim that human beings are individuals, that they must make their own choices, assert their own uniqueness without reference to universal rules or standards, simply because adherence to any such universal rules or standards must suggest a loss of individuality.

It must follow from this view that the role of reason in this kind of process is highly problematic. For if reason is not the generation of universals and if rational behaviour is not acting according to these, it is difficult to know what either is. This is the source of Jean Paul Sartre's notion of 'nausea', that feeling a person has when faced with both the awareness of the need to assert individuality by making choices and a consciousness of the lack of any basis upon which these choices can be made. Again we see, therefore, that this solution to the problem has led to a devaluing, even to a rejection, of reason. It must follow that the role of the emotions is enhanced and, certainly in the work of Sartre, the need for a more positive theory of the emotions is acknowledged.

It will be clear, then, that no satisfactory theory has emerged from any of these traditions. Western philosophy, having created a dichotomy between reason and feeling, has failed to offer any solution to this problem except by suggesting that we reject either one or the other. Feeling has been seen either as an unfortunate obstruction to the path of true reason and thus to be suppressed or as the only source of explanation of values or of interpersonal relationships, so that these have been regarded as beyond the reach of reason in any form. It is the contention here, of course, that the second of these approaches has the merit of recognizing the importance of feeling in human existence and of acknowledging that there are no grounds for certainty or dogmatism in areas of this kind. It also supports that individualism we have recommended elsewhere. We are still, however, some way short of solving this problem. Yet it is clearly crucial for education that it be tackled and that some solution be sought, if we are to escape from those rationalist influences which earlier chapters have attempted to show are inhibiting many other areas of educational advance and development. We now turn briefly, therefore, to a consideration of some of the reasons why the achievement of an acceptable theory of the role of feeling in human life and in education is crucial.

Education and feeling

The effects of the rationalist view of feeling, of the emotions, of the human passions, on education have been far-reaching. In general, as we have already suggested, it has led to an emphasis on intellectual development at the expense of other aspects of growth, a process whose implications for individuals are well portrayed in Herman Hesse's *The Prodigy*. There are several aspects of this which it may repay us to look at in slightly greater detail.

First, this has led to the devaluing within education of activities and subjects whose intellectual or academic content — as defined by the rationalist — is not immediately obvious, and to an emphasis on those areas of the curriculum which seem to score highly on this count. In short, it has led to the emergence of the kinds of subject hierarchy with which we are all familiar. For there is a very direct relationship between the degree to which subjects have gained acceptance in the curriculum and their academic or cognitive content. Thus mathematics, science, English, history and so on are now well entrenched in the curriculum, while art, dance, drama and other subjects whose emphasis may appear to be on the affective are still often regarded as optional extras and even only to be provided for pupils who are deemed to lack the capacity to go very far with anything more intellectually demanding.

There are two effects of this which we must note. First, there is the effect this has on those subjects which do not appear to score very highly against purely cognitive criteria. For either they continue to be held in fairly low esteem in curricular terms, or, worse, they attempt to improve their status by developing for themselves some kind of recognizable cognitive content. Indeed, this appears to be the classic pattern by which all or most subjects have established themselves within the curriculum (Goodson 1985a), as we saw in Chapter 4.

If this is done properly and for the right reasons, it is difficult to find fault with it. For the study, and the practice too, of art, of dance, of drama, of handicraft, can clearly be greatly enhanced if it is given the right kind of academic support and backing. Too often, however, this kind of academic injection is administered for the wrong reasons and thus in the wrong form. It is not difficult to find examples of such subjects being given this kind of injection merely to enhance their status or that of their teachers — often in conjunction with the establishment of a public examination — and the net result is that, by playing the rationalist's game, they devalue and put at risk that which they, perhaps uniquely, have to offer to education and development. For they become like other subjects and must by doing so lose whatever distinctive contribution they may have to make to educational development of a wider kind.

The second effect of this hierarchical view of the curriculum is that it can lead to the loss of something which it may be claimed is of great importance to the intellectual activities themselves, namely a proper concern for the place that feeling should have there too. For it is not only necessary to recognize the importance of those areas of the curriculum whose direct contribution to pupils' affective development is plain; it is also vital that we take full account of and give full weight to the affective aspects of those subjects which can too readily be regarded in cognitive terms only. Perhaps the best example of this has been the recent emphasis within Religious Education on the purely cognitive or descriptive aspects of the subject. This, albeit for reasons other than those suggested above, has resulted in a loss of those other distinctive dimensions of the subject. What Ninian Smart (1968) has called the 'parahistorical' aspects of Religious Education have been ignored and the subject has become a kind of sub-branch of history or sociology.

There are three points which must be made briefly in support of this claim that much is lost if we concentrate on the purely cognitive aspects of subjects. The first of these is the evidence of the developmental psychologists, whose work was mentioned in Chapter 4, that affective and cognitive development must be promoted in harness, that to ignore the affective dimension of development is to put cognitive development itself at risk. Eliot Eisner (1982), for example, has claimed that any effective theory of cognitive development must include an affective component, since concept formation depends upon processes which are more than merely intellectual. We noted in Chapter 5 the claims he makes for the potential of art as a vehicle for many forms of learning and development. Others have gone even further and stressed the importance of children's fantasies, and especially their fantasy play, in promoting their development (Jones 1972; Egan 1983).

education at great length here, merely to spell out those factors which support the claim that rationalism cannot provide an adequate basis upon which we can plan this area of the curriculum or this aspect of the development of pupils.

It should perhaps be made clear at the beginning that this is taken as one problem, the concept of personal, social and moral education being treated as a single concept, since, although those three adjectives draw attention to different aspects of the issue, the focus of all is the same — the need for pupils to be assisted towards the ability to make judgements in relation to their own lives and their relationships with those around them.

The first point that must be made here in explaining the significance of our general theme to this area of education is that it reflects a fundamental misunderstanding to treat morality as a matter of moral knowledge and moral education as the transmission of that knowledge. It is simplistic in the extreme to see moral behaviour as a matter of knowledge of Plato's 'Form of Beauty, Truth and Goodness' or of Aristotle's 'right rule' or of any other comparable manifestation of the rationalist's need to reduce everything to the cognitive. There are several reasons for arguing this.

First, as was suggested at the beginning of this chapter and earlier in the book, a commitment to the importance of individual autonomy, which loomed very large, as we saw, in Kant's work and which has played an equally prominent part in the analyses of education which we have been offered by 'philosophers of education' in more recent times, is not compatible with a view of moral knowledge as 'out-there', as 'God-given', as reified, as objective 'truth'. Kant's claim that the autonomous moral being must 'give himself the law which he obeys' has very little substance and, indeed, has a rather hollow ring when he goes on to argue that there can be but one law that he must give himself, since it is a rational and universal principle which must hold for all people, or for all rational beings. Such a view can only lead, as Hegel showed, to the sham of seeing autonomy as the right to come into line with reason, with the 'Absolute', or to stand forever convicted of immorality and irrationality. On this analysis, the individual is free merely to conform, to recognize moral 'truths', and Kant's claim that the autonomous moral being is at the same time the creator of these moral 'truths' or of the moral law has little point or meaning.

The very notion of morality itself would seem to confirm this and to

The second point to be stressed is the danger of failing to recognize the aesthetic aspects of all areas of human knowledge and experience. Mathematics and science are beautiful, or they can be for those who are alert to this possibility. To treat them as purely intellectual or academic activities is to lose a good deal of this kind of potential. It is unfortunate but true that this approach is to be found in the teaching of Humanities subjects too — in music, for example, and in literature, both classical and foreign, and even, most unforgivably, English.

Thirdly, if the study of anything is to contribute to education, on any definition, the individual must come to recognize its value and, indeed, to value it himself or herself; there must be some emotional engagement with the material. In an educational context, therefore, again the learning of a subject in the cognitive sense cannot be distinguished from coming to enjoy it, appreciate it and recognize its worth. To attempt to divorce the two, to treat learning as a purely cognitive activity, and to ignore the necessary emotional involvement which must be part of the process of being educated, is thus to put education itself at risk.

These, then, are further dangers of losing sight of the affective dimension of learning. Yet they are what rationalism leads us to by its failure to produce any adequate theory of the role of the emotions in education.

However one sees this, whatever view one takes of the role of feeling in the study of mathematics or science or any area of the Humanities, it would be difficult to deny its centrality to education in the personal, social and moral sphere. An education here which directs its attention solely to the cognitive or intellectual aspects of morality, as we have seen most rationalist moral theories advocate and as we are suggesting they cannot avoid advocating, must be a caricature. We must turn finally, therefore, to some consideration of the implications of rationalist epistemology for this crucial area of education.

Personal, social and moral education

It is in the context of moral education that we see most clearly the dangers and the inadequacy of the rationalist solution to the affective dimension of education. For both of those approaches which we considered earlier in this chapter, the attempt to reduce everything to the cognitive and the advocacy of the suppression of feeling, can be seen here to be detrimental to the development of any acceptable theory of moral education.

It is not the intention to discuss the issue of personal, social and moral require a wider notion of autonomy than this permits. So too would our day-to-day attitude, which does not usually lead us to appraise moral behaviour in terms of duty, or obedience to some universal law, but rather in terms of the judgement made by the individual in the light of all the relevant circumstances. This after all is also how we expect justice to be administered in our courts of law. Kant was surely right to stress the primacy of the will in morality, and in this he was reflecting the common sense view of morality as chiefly a matter of intention. To say that intention is the major concern in evaluating moral behaviour, however, is not to imply that only one kind of intention can be acceptable, that there is only one object the will can or should be directed towards.

Moral education, then, is not a matter of transmitting 'moral knowledge', of handing on moral precepts, of inculcating moral attitudes. To approach it in this way is to convert it into some form of indoctrination. It is overtly to set about that use of knowledge as control which we have seen the sociologists warning us against. It is for this reason that it has been claimed that moral education should be clearly distinguished from Religious Education (O'Connor 1957; Downey and Kelly 1978), since most forms of religion contain a set of moral values as part of their creed or doctrine, and the teaching of these must run counter to the idea of moral education as the development in the individual of powers of moral reasoning, the ability to think for oneself and reach one's own conclusions on moral issues. To say this is not of course to say that knowledge and understanding are not necessary to the making of moral judgements; it is to say, however, that such knowledge is an aid to the making of such judgements rather than a substitute or an alternative to it, and that the kind of knowledge and understanding needed is not the kind the rationalist is thrusting upon us.

If any further justification of this view is needed, it can be found in the evident fact that on many moral issues, certainly on those which loom largest in the day-to-day experience of the individual — issues, for example, such as those centring on interpersonal relationships, and particularly those of a sexual kind — a whole spectrum of attitudes and values can be seen, and all of them must be recognized as having equal claims to validity. Questions of the rightness or wrongness of sexual relations outside marriage, of the use of contraceptive devices, of abortion, are clearly issues not of 'moral knowledge' but of individual judgement. It is a positive disservice to the young to treat them in any other way. This is an important lesson for the educator to learn. It is not one that rationalism can teach him or her nor, indeed, one that rationalism can in any sense cope with. This is one reason why the rationalist perspective is of little value, and in fact has an inhibiting effect, on the development of a productive theory of moral education.

A second point arises from this and can be quickly dealt with. Morality, like values generally, is not merely an individual matter; it is also a matter of group and ethnic attitudes. We noted in the last chapter the difficulties a rationalist epistemology creates for those of us who wish to take full account of these differences of attitude and, rather than evaluate them against our own views, see them as having their own worth and validity. It is perhaps in the moral sphere that these differences are most marked and also strongest in their impact on individuals. It is in this sphere particularly, then, that we need a philosophical stance which will enable us to cope with them by some device more subtle than mere rejection.

The third point which must be made is one which brings us back to the central concern of this chapter. For again it has to be said that the rationalist approach to morality is one which sees people as rational beings rather than human beings and which cannot, in consequence, cope with the affective or the emotional dimension of moral behaviour or of moral education. It is because of the dominance of that perspective that moral education has hitherto failed to come to grips with the emotional aspects of moral existence or has adopted unsatisfactory means of doing so.

We noted earlier that the only way in which rationalism has been able to cope with the manifest fact of human emotions is by proposing their suppression. We must note here, then, the dangers inherent in this approach to the treatment of the emotions in moral education. The most serious aspect of this is what has been revealed to us by those who have explored the effects of repression on human beings. In broad terms, repression is the result of the introjection of the taboos of others, such as parents and other significant adults, especially in the early years of life, and especially when these taboos are reinforced by the unpleasant experience of punishment. It may also of course be a result of particularly painful experiences which may not be deliberately brought about by personal agencies. This is part of that process by which we develop a conscience, the growth of a self-image, the emergence of what Freud called the superego or ego-ideal; it is the internalization of the guidance we receive in our early, formative years.

It is not, then, necessarily to be totally deplored. Some kind of conscience, self-image, ego-ideal must be developed by everyone. It is, however, a highly delicate process; it must be handled very carefully; and a theory which advocates this as the only method of guiding the emotional development of children is not likely to provide us with the most subtle instrument for this kind of careful process. There are in particular two potential dangers to be recognized in this process, neither of which a policy of suppression can help us to avoid, both of which in fact such a policy is likely to push us closer to.

The first of these is that which arises because what we are dealing with here is a largely unconscious process. What is internalized in this way will affect our attitudes and our behaviour in ways we are not likely to be fully conscious of. The emotions and feelings which are repressed in this way will continue to affect our attitudes and behaviour in unconscious and unrecognized ways. In Freudian theory, the 'Superego' is as much a part of the 'unconscious' as are those desires which constitute what Freud called the 'Id'.

The danger here, then, is that the more we repress the more we render unconscious, and the more we render unconscious the less control we give to the individual over his/her behaviour. If moral education is a matter of assisting people to make judgements concerning their own moral behaviour and that of others and to act on these judgements, it is a conscious process, one which requires a full awareness by the individual of all the factors which need to be taken into account — including his/her own feelings. A policy of suppression, if not handled with extreme delicacy, is thus more likely to inhibit than to promote moral education in the full sense. A rationalist approach, therefore, makes moral education, at least in the sense given to it here, more difficult to achieve.

The second danger arises from the ease with which a lack of delicacy in this process can lead to extreme forms of this loss of full control over one's behaviour. At one level, this is the explanation of the extremely strong feelings some people have on issues others regard as relatively trivial, or the inability to distinguish the important from the trivial — the unreasonable objection to 'strong drink', for example, which one meets in some people, or the views of those young children who once declared that, after killing people, the second worst crime in the world is running in the corridors (Kellmer-Pringle and Edwards 1964). At another, perhaps more serious, level, this is the root problem of the psychopath, whose behaviour is not so much immoral as amoral, not so much antisocial as asocial. It lacks that aspect of conscious choice which we have suggested is essential to moral behaviour in the full sense, primarily because his or her behaviour is prompted by unconscious motives which are the result of the kind of repression we are discussing here. 'He appears to be the very antithesis of the morally developed person' (Wilson, Williams and Sugarman 1967, p.272). This, then, is the extreme danger of a policy of suppression in relation to the emotional dimension of moral development. In its very extremity, it reveals the inadequacy of this kind of policy and of the theoretical base upon which it stands.

These are the positive dangers of this approach to moral education. Perhaps more serious is its negative effect, not only its failure to offer us any positive theory of the role of the emotions in morality or in education, but also its effect of discouraging the search for such a theory. For, if we take a rationalist stance, we are committed to resolving the problem either by a policy of suppression or by reducing it all to some form of cognition. If both of these lines fail, as it is being suggested they clearly have done, we are left with nothing. Our only alternative again is to reject the rationalist stance and search for something which is fundamentally different.

To begin with, we need a theory which will enable us to distinguish between those emotions which perhaps should be suppressed or closely controlled and those which might be encouraged and developed. For it is clear that not all of our emotional reactions or our feelings are reprehensible on anyone's definition. Feelings of benevolence, for example, which, incidentally, played a major part in some early empiricist theories of morals, are, one would imagine, in anyone's book, to be promoted rather than stifled. Yet, to make this kind of distinction, to identify 'good' emotions, it is necessary to have a positive theory of the affective dimensions of human behaviour. This rationalism must deny us. It must also deny us, therefore, what might follow from that, a theory of how those emotions might be developed and, especially, how they might be developed in harness with reason.

For the first step towards such a theory must be to recognize that the distinction between reason and feeling may be a false distinction. Certainly, it is one which has encouraged a mistaken view of the relation of the emotions to the intellect. For, as we have seen, it has become customary to see them as in conflict, as pulling the individual in different directions, with reason offering us the 'right rule' and feeling pulling us, animal-like, towards less satisfactory forms of behaviour.

Yet a moment's reflection will reveal this as a caricature of human experience. Our inclinations do not always pull us away from what our reason suggests to us is the right course of action. Sometimes reason and feeling are in harmony. This, in fact, seemed to worry Kant, since he felt that in such circumstances it was impossible to tell why a certain action was performed, whether (morally) in accordance with reason, or (immorally or amorally) in response to feeling or inclination. To him duty did not seem quite like duty if one actually enjoyed doing it. Nothing reveals the problems we inherit from rationalism more clearly.

Furthermore, it is seldom the case that a moral dilemma takes the form of two possible courses of action, one dictated by reason, the other offered temptingly by our passions. It is never as simple as that; moral choices are much more complex. Even if what reason dictates is plain — and it seldom is — our emotions will always offer a confused and confusing mixture of conscience, desire, pleasure, feeling for others and so on. Unravelling these is not a task for reason alone. Reason and feeling are inseparably connected in any real moral context, and a theory of moral education must recognize this and attempt to handle it. It is yet another example of that impossibility of distinguishing the affective and the cognitive dimensions of education and development which we have constantly stressed.

We need a theory, then, which recognizes and attempts to cater for this interconnection. Rationalism, with its policy of suppression or of reduction to the cognitive, cannot offer us such a theory. Some suppression, as we have seen, is necessary; we need a theory which can help us to decide when and how such suppression is appropriate.

We must recognize too that some reduction to the cognitive is also needed; we must not appear to reject that totally as a solution. What we must reject is the view that this is the only solution. To reject it out of hand would be to perpetuate the very dichotomy we are concerned to destroy; it would be to treat the passions as if they were always irrational, never susceptible to reason, and thus always to be seen as its obverse.

However, although the etymology of a word like 'passion' would suggest that it refers to things we suffer (Peters 1973a) and which are thus not open to reason, other words such as 'emotion' and, perhaps particularly, 'motive' do not have this kind of connotation, rather they suggest that there might be rational passions and that 'although manifestly these terms relate in some way to our feelings, they are also intimately connected with cognition, that is, with our ways of understanding situations' (op.cit., p.81).

Clearly, how we feel about things is to a large extent a product of what we know or understand about them. It is only a knowledge that snakes are poisonous that leads us to a quite rational fear of them, and it is only a knowledge that this particular specimen before us is a non-poisonous grass snake which dispels our fear. Reason may also influence not only how we feel about things but also the way in which we give expression to our feelings, and, indeed, whether we give expression to them at all. The danger comes, however, when we attempt to see moral behaviour in terms of reason only and to solve all problems created by our emotional reactions by reducing them to the cognitive. The relation of feeling and reason in human experience is one of reciprocity rather than conflict. The conflict model is unsatisfactory, as is the attempt to resolve the conflict either by suppressing feeling or by turning it into a form of cognition. Education must take full account of this and moral education in particular must recognize the need for a proper interlinking of affective and cognitive forms of development.

A final point must be made about the importance of recognizing the interlinking of feeling and reason in moral education. Mention was made earlier of Kant's doubts concerning the moral worth of actions which, while they might be in accordance with one's duty, happen also to be in accordance with one's feelings. Doubts may equally be expressed about the converse of this, the kind of behaviour which would have Kant's full approval, that which is in accordance with one's duty but which, because it is not in accordance with one's feelings, may be done in a grudging and, literally, heartless manner. It may be recalled that a basic moral principle of Christianity is that one should 'love thy neighbour'. To require this is to require more than the determined implementation of the dictates of reason. And, for most people, moral behaviour does seem to imply something more than the cold performance of duty, of the kind evinced, for example, by so many characters in the novels of Charles Dickens. And, indeed, it may be argued that there is rather more to the concept of will and its role in moral behaviour than Kant's definition gives it. Moral behaviour may be amoral, as Kant suggests, because it is not a result of the will of the agent but performed rather out of obedience to some authority or out of blind and unthinking habit. This is what Bertrand Russell, in commenting on Plato's theory of morals, described as 'right behaviour with the wrong emotions'. It may be equally unsatisfactory, even equally amoral, to perform actions for the right reasons, according to the dictates of reason, but again with the wrong emotions, or even with no emotions at all. Again we see the problems which emerge when we fail to develop a moral theory in which the emotions have a proper place or, worse, attempt to set up a theory in which they can have no place at all.

We need a moral theory which will encompass both reason and feeling, and we need a theory of moral education which will do the same. For, without that, it will be difficult for us to go beyond the cognitive concerns of schooling and give the attention which is due to the needs of pupils in areas beyond the cognitive, and especially in the area of personal, social and moral development. It will be difficult too, if not impossible, to recognize and allow for that intertwining of the affective and the cognitive we have been concerned throughout this chapter to stress.

There have been recently some interesting attempts to acknowledge the need for moral education to take full account of the emotions. Projects such as that of the Farmington Trust (Wilson et al. 1967), for example, have deliberately pointed us in the direction of seeing morality and moral education as requiring the development of certain kinds of attitude to ourselves and others as well as certain forms of cognition. These are steps in the right direction. They still, however, are inclined to see the two as separate, to base their recommendations on an analysis of moral education into its component parts, and thus to perpetuate that distinction between feeling and reason, between the intellect and the passions, between the cognitive and the affective, between the head and the heart, which it has been suggested is at the root of the problem.

A rationalist epistemology can do little else. It must thus be found to be as wanting in relation to forms of educational development beyond the cognitive as in those other areas we have explored in the earlier chapters of Part Two. If we agree that education, when seen as the growth of competence, must attempt to embrace competence of all kinds, and in particular must extend to competence in the field of interpersonal relations, we must acknowledge the need for a theory which is not in itself rooted to a concern for the cognitive alone. In fact, once we have accepted that education is a matter of development, a matter of processes, any attempt to pursue that line, to build an educational theory on that base, within the context of a rationalist epistemology, is doomed to failure, since it must be beset at every turn by the limitations imposed by the central elements of that philosophical stance.

Summary and conclusions

Earlier chapters in Part Two have set out to reveal the inadequacies of a rationalist epistemology in relation to any view of education as a process of development. This chapter has attempted to add to this by showing its special inadequacies in relation to any notion of education as development in dimensions other than the cognitive.

This was attempted first by arguing for the importance of other dimensions and, indeed, by claiming that they are so closely interwoven with cognitive development itself that no proper theory of education, even as the development of forms of cognition, is possible without an acknowledgement of this. Then it was claimed not only that rationalism offers no base for the development of any genuine theory of education in the affective mode but also that its impact on this aspect of education, and on those subjects and areas of the curriculum in which this dimension is clearly important, has been a detrimental and inhibiting one. In particular, it was claimed that this can be the only result of a theory which is rooted in rationalism and thus can only cope with feeling either by devaluing it as a form of human experience and recommending that we ignore it or repress it, or by turning it into some form of cognition.

Both of these devices we then argued are particularly in evidence, and particularly damaging, in the area of personal, social and moral education, where, it was claimed, the need for a proper theory which recognizes and allows for the interaction of emotion and reason is particularly strong, and where, it was also argued, the effects of rationalism have been especially harmful, not only by offering unacceptable theories of moral education but also by inhibiting the search for a more productive theory. It is thus the adoption of the basic assumptions of rationalism by those currently pressing their curricular prescriptions on teachers in the United Kingdom which makes their offerings in areas such as this even less helpful.

One of the problems here of course is that affective or emotional development is not easy to monitor or measure. Like many of those processes we have discussed in earlier chapters, it does not lend itself to simple forms of evaluation, appraisal or accountability. As in the other areas we have explored, it cannot be defined or planned in terms either of its objectives or its content, so that assessment of success is rendered rather more difficult.

This is one reason, and a powerful one, why there is that tendency to cling to the rationalist outlook which we have noted throughout. It is also the case that, in the current political climate of increased demands for evaluation and accountability, that tendency is likely to increase and the notion of education as development to become even more difficult to attain or to implement. Unless, of course, we can devise forms of evaluation and appraisal fitted to that kind of approach. It is to this question that we turn in our final chapter.

CHAPTER 9

EVALUATION, APPRAISAL AND ACCOUNTABILITY
— THE CURRENT REALITIES

> The teacher, like the artist, the philosopher, and the man of letters, can only perform his work adequately if he feels himself to be an individual directed by an inner creative impulse, not dominated and fettered by an outside authority.
>
> (Bertrand Russell, *Unpopular Essays*)

It might be felt by anyone who has the stamina to have read through to this point that there is a certain amount of idealism in earlier chapters, that it is the moon they have been asking for, that the discussion has been too divorced from current realities. To some extent such a charge must be accepted. It must be said, however, that if educators have not some idealism, or at least some optimism, they are unlikely to educate anyone. For education is essentially an enterprise of optimism. It must also be stressed that the main point of those earlier chapters has been not so much to set out and describe a new version of idealism but to attempt to direct thinking into different channels and to challenge the bland assumptions of much current educational theory and practice. It must also be added that an attempt has been made throughout to direct the criticism offered not only at the theoretical discussions of the 'philosophers of education' but also at the uncritical adoption of their basic tenets by others, and especially by those responsible for the current political directives.

The present chapter, however, is offered as some kind of counterbalance to any such possible idealism. For its concern will be to try to place earlier discussions specifically into the realities of the current educational climate, in particular by considering one of its major features, the concern with evaluation, appraisal and accountability in education. It will be argued that this concern, or rather the manner in which it is presently being translated into practice in many places, brings with it further invitations to rationalism, and thus represents another source of threats to those aspects of education we have highlighted and, indeed, advocated in our earlier chapters — the idea of education as development, as individual development, as development beyond the purely cognitive and as something we are committed to providing for every pupil.

This will have the additional advantage of providing us with an opportunity to conclude the book by summarizing the major issues it has addressed itself to. For an examination of this feature of the current political scene, in addition to placing our discussion in the context of present realities and highlighting another aspect of our general theme, will also in many ways point up and pull together all those features of the rationalist approach to educational planning which earlier chapters have considered. For it is proving to be the forms and the style of evaluation and accountability procedures which govern, more than any other single factor, the form and style of our approach to curriculum planning, so that if those procedures are predicated, as we shall see they often are, whether consciously or by default, on assumptions of a rationalist kind, their effect must be to plunge us back into those difficulties we have attempted to show are endemic to that view of education.

In general terms, as was suggested in Chapter 4, the current political climate of education in the United Kingdom is one of increased political intervention in the work of schools at all levels, and, indeed, in that of Higher Education too. One major dimension of this is that pressure towards the kind of centralized curriculum planning we considered in Chapter 6. A second is the growing movement towards a closer monitoring of the work of schools and, indeed, of individual teachers. It is that we look at now, not least because, as was just suggested, it may well be the crux of the whole problem this book has directed its attention to.

The political context

It is only over the last thirty years that one can detect any serious interest in curriculum planning in the United Kingdom. Prior to that the curriculum which had been established at the very beginning of the century continued in largely unchanged form, except, as we have seen, in some Primary schools and departments. If it developed or changed, it did so in a largely random fashion, responsive more to individual whims and fancies than to any carefully or deliberately worked-out set of principles. Where official interest was expressed in education, it was, with the notable exception of the Hadow Report on Primary education (Board of Education 1931), focused mainly on the organization of schooling, on, for example, the creation of Secondary schools for all and the organization of those Secondary schools.

A change of attitude came in the 1950s and, in particular, with the technological advances of the period after the Second World War and, perhaps more significantly, the 'cold war' which followed it. It has become something of a cliché to associate the appearance of deliberate curriculum planning with the launching by the USSR of the first space satellite, Sputnik I, in 1957. However, there is little room for doubt that that event symbolized the advances the USSR had made in space technology, sent shudders of apprehension through the Western world and encouraged a closer look at the work of schools and universities. In short, it prompted a directing of attention not only towards how we should organize schooling but also to what form of curriculum schools should offer.

It is not the intention here to rehearse the details of this change as it manifested itself both in the United Kingdom and in the United States. Two points must be made, however. The first of these is that, if we are right in explaining the advent of curriculum planning of a deliberate kind by reference to these technological advances and the associated political tensions they induced, we must recognize that the initial impetus was both technological and political. The second point is that, in spite of this, the responsibility for curriculum planning remained largely with the academics and the teachers. In the United States, it was to the universities that the politicians turned for advice on the planning of the curriculum. In the United Kingdom, responsibility was given to the teachers or at least left to them. For, on the one hand, they continued to enjoy a degree of freedom and autonomy in relation to the curriculum of a kind unmatched in any other developed society; and, on the other hand, they achieved control of the body which was created to promote the development of the curriculum, the Schools Council for Curriculum and Examinations — albeit after a struggle with those who would have given control of this new national agency to the politicians. This may be seen as the first major battle in that war between the teaching profession and its political masters which was referred to in Chapter 4.

As a result, the major influences on developments within the curriculum in the United Kingdom during the 1960s and early 1970s were the teachers themselves and those who were in a position to influence their thinking, the theorists who taught them in the institutions of teacher education. This is why the influence of theorists such as Richard Peters was as strong as we have seen it to be. For he, along with those immediately around him and generations of their students, in the terms of ethnographic studies of the curriculum (Goodson 1981, 1983, 1985a,b; Goodson and Ball 1984), defined the newly emerging study of education and of the curriculum, and thus, by implication, the curriculum itself. This task was rendered easier because what these theorists were offering was largely a reaffirmation of the *status quo*, a justification for the existing and traditional curriculum, at least as it was to be found in the Secondary sector of schooling. It was through this work, therefore, as we have seen, that the rationalist influence on our thinking about education was reinforced. It was of course also through the theoretical debate which was thus established that it later came to be challenged.

That theoretical debate, however, was soon to be overtaken by considerations of a more practical kind. There are those who argue (Lawton 1980) that, throughout this period, attempts to re-establish political control of the curriculum were quietly proceeding and that the surfacing of these during the last decade is the culmination of a process which began when the battle for control of the Schools Council ended in victory for the teachers in 1964. Whatever the truth of this, there is no doubt that the last decade has seen not only pressures for increased external control of the curriculum but also the establishment of procedures for achieving this, not only criticisms of schools such as those voiced by James Callaghan, as Prime Minister, in his well-remembered speech at Ruskin College in 1976 and the 'Great Debate' which followed, but also legislation such as the 1980 and 1981 Education Acts, designed to shift the balance of control away from the teachers towards agencies external to the schools. And this process has been accompanied and reinforced by a massive outpouring of publications on the curriculum from official sources — surveys, discussion documents and proposals for change.

There are two main features of this development and of the general tenor of these official publications it has spawned, features which may well be incompatible with each other and which are certainly rather uneasy and uncomfortable bedfellows. The first of these is their utilitarianism or instrumentalism. A major thrust is towards the acquisition by pupils of *useful* skills and knowledge; a major emphasis is on the vocational aspects of schooling; gone is that antipathy towards vocationalism and stress on education as liberal which we have seen was a central feature of the curriculum which was established in the United Kingdom at the beginning of the century. Thus the pressure is away from the teaching of Humanities subjects towards an increased concentration on science and technology, and to this end the allocation of resources has been redirected. Thus, at root, the justification for much of the curriculum is to be found in its intended products, in ends extrinsic to it, and Raymond Williams' 'industrial trainers' are enjoying a growing ascendancy.

This is not always overt, however; often it is concealed behind a facade of claims to or assertions of the intrinsic value of these subjects and activities. This is the second, and largely incompatible, feature of recent developments, and it is here that one can see a reaffirmation of the rationalist perspective on knowledge. The curriculum is seen in terms of its content, assumptions are made about the superiority (not always the superior usefulness) of certain kinds of subject or activity; and the thrust is towards a view of education as the transmission of knowledge rather than as growth or development.

Thus most of the official discussions of the school curriculum have been, and continue to be, conducted in subject terms, as we saw in Chapter 6, on the assumption that knowledge has the kind of status rationalism claims for it and that subjects are a reflection of some properties inherent in knowledge rather than of those sociological and historical factors which have been offered as a more convincing explanation of their presence on the school curriculum. Attempts are now being made, as we saw in Chapters 4 and 5, to extend this kind of subject-based approach within the Primary school too and to discourage, and even debar, the adoption of curriculum models predicated on the notion of education as process or development. There is a basic conviction of the value of certain kinds of subject knowledge and, where that value is not defined in terms of utility, it can only be defined by reference to some notion of the universal and God-given values propounded by rationalism.

Thus current political pressures are reinforcing the view of curriculum which derives from that epistemological stance; and they are ignoring not only the alternative epistemology of empiricism/pragmatism but the support for its associated view of education which we saw in Chapter 4 has come in recent times from work in history, in ethnography, in sociology of education and in developmental psychology. One could accept these developments more readily if they were a result of a deliberate adoption of rationalism; they evince more evidence, however, of complete ignorance of the nuances of this debate. They thus constitute yet another example of what this book is designed to identify and to criticize — those rationalist assumptions, usually unrecognized, unacknowledged and thus unquestioned, which are built into much of our current curriculum planning.

This is one major, and perhaps fundamental, aspect of the general lack of conceptual clarity evinced by the official documentation with which teachers are being bombarded. Not only do the authors of this confuse utility with rationalist notions of the intrinsic value of certain kinds of knowledge, so that they steer an uneasy course between product-based and content-based views of the curriculum, they also confuse these two views by their emphasis on an 'aims and objectives' approach to curriculum planning in all areas. Thus they display that same confusion that we have seen in rationalism itself, especially apparent in the pleas for 'balance' which we explored in Chapter 6, the basic assumption that the educational value of certain subjects is to be found in the kinds of development they promote in the pupil lying cheek by jowl with some contrary metaphysical notion of that value as somehow inherent in the subjects themselves. Thus, as we shall see, the emphasis in recommended procedures for evaluation, appraisal and accountability is often on results (even on examination scores and successes) and the focus of curriculum planning is on subjects. Furthermore, terms are used whose meaning is never defined, and which presumably are regarded as being non-problematic, and even self-evident, yet which, as this book has attempted to show, encapsulate a whole philosophy of knowledge and of education, which intellectual honesty, if nothing else, demands should be made clear and overt and should itself be part of the debate. Thus we hear a good deal about 'relevance' although this term is never defined and we are left with a strong suspicion that the relevance required is economic or vocational rather than educational. And much is also made of 'standards', which are also never defined, but which again one can detect are purely academic standards of a traditional kind.

This in turn alerts us to the problem we identified in Chapter 4 and explored in greater detail in Chapter 7, the claim that this kind of approach is working, and must work, to the disadvantage of that large proportion of the school population, consisting of those who are already disadvantaged because of their social or ethnic origins. This, it has been suggested, is a major barrier to the achievement of that universal educational provision to which the 1944 Education Act committed us. This is another salient feature of the current political scene in the United Kingdom, and its connection with the underlying values of present government policies must be reasserted here and noted as a prime example of what this book has been concerned to identify and challenge.

These political pressures and developments manifest themselves in two main forms. First, there is that movement towards increased centralization of curriculum planning which we discussed in Chapter 6, the advocacy of a common core to the curriculum, a proposal which we saw is essentially rationalist, certainly in the form in which it has hitherto been made. Secondly, there is the associated pressure for increased monitoring of the work of schools through evaluation, appraisal and accountability procedures. This may be seen as a much more subtle form of *dirigisme*. For, while it would not be easy, nor even desirable, to argue against the idea of some kind of check on the work of schools, it is quite clear that in many cases the procedures which are being established for this purpose are controlling the curriculum more effectively than overt and direct attempts to dictate its form and content. Thus, more than the pressures for centralized curriculum planning, the form of many recent and current demands for teacher accountability is reinforcing those rationalist influences on the development of the curriculum we are concerned to challenge.

Evaluation, appraisal and accountability

It should be made clear immediately that it is not the idea of evaluation, appraisal and accountability which is to be criticized. Accountability, as was well appreciated by the ancient Greeks, is an essential element of democracy — an element which is too little in evidence in present-day versions of democracy. And some form of evaluation or appraisal of performance is clearly its base. Thus, in the context of schooling, teachers, along with all others responsible for educational planning and provision, must expect to be required to give an account of their attempts to meet their responsibilities, and some procedures of evaluation and appraisal must be instituted to assess the degree of their success or failure. Furthermore, without some kind of evaluation it is difficult to see what basis might exist for any real development either of the curriculum or of the teachers themselves. For a prerequisite of improvement must be some evaluation of previous performance.

The problem, then, is not the fact of accountability; it is the form it has taken and is taking in many places and the kinds of procedure which have been adopted in attempts to achieve it. For too often these have been unduly simplistic and have been predicated on simplistic views of education and of curriculum. In particular, they have often been based on those views of education as either content-based or product-oriented or both, which we have commented on critically elsewhere. For clearly it is much easier to measure the assimilation of knowledge by pupils or the attainment of performance objectives than it is to evaluate those more subtle forms of developmental process we have discussed in earlier chapters. To concentrate in evaluation procedures on those things which can be most easily measured, however, is to invite schools and teachers to adopt similar emphases in their teaching and curriculum planning. It is thus to press the curriculum towards that emphasis on knowledge-content and prespecified objectives which we have suggested is endemic to the rationalist perspective and which we have argued is an inadequate model of education and curriculum. If it is not in itself rationalist, then (and it is never overtly so), it has the effect of reinforcing rationalism, along with those unhappy consequences of rationalism which earlier chapters have identified.

This is also a form of evaluation which, whatever its use in relation to accountability, is likely to provide no kind of basis for the improvement either of the curriculum or of the teacher, since its emphasis is on measurement of what the evaluator thinks is important and not necessarily therefore of what the curriculum is designed to do or what the teacher is attempting to do. As Donald Frith (1983) has said of the procedures adopted in Croydon, for example, while 'it is presumably hoped that a plan will emerge which will command the understanding and support of most teachers', the reality is that 'in Croydon it seems that the process has been for the elected members to make up their own minds on some sort of absolute grounds what the curriculum should be; to define the required outcomes, all of which must be simply measurable by tests; and then to take suitably punitive action against any school or teacher whose results do not reach certain standards. It is felt that this will make quite clear what the schools *are supposed to be doing* [my italics] so that all parents will know where they are.' This is too often the picture one sees. Nor is it very different from the procedures used in many parts of the United States where 'a condition of funding of major educational programmes . . . is that evaluations are professionally conducted' (Brookfield 1982), conducted by agencies outside the school and used as the basis for the allocation of resources.

Control of the curriculum through procedures for evaluation and accountability has taken three main forms — the public examination, local authority demands both for statements of school curricula, and, more recently, for staff appraisal and the work of national agencies such as the Assessment of Performance Unit of the Department of Education and Science. There are of course dangers in this kind of generalization. And, since there is not the scope here to explore all these developments in full, we can only attempt to avoid these dangers by agreeing that they have not in all cases had the effect of controlling and directing the curriculum — the procedures of some local authorities, for example, have been permissive and enabling rather than *dirigiste* — and certainly they have not all been planned as forms of control, as we will see later when we look in slightly more detail at the work of the Assessment of Performance Unit (APU). What must be asserted, however, and explained, is that too often the forms of evaluation and appraisal adopted have in effect controlled and directed the curriculum, that, further, they have done so in ways inimical to that view of education as individual development we have recommended in earlier chapters and that, finally, they have done this, at least in part, because of certain assumptions they have made about knowledge and about values.

For the forms adopted for the evaluation of the curriculum as a basis both for teacher and school accountability and for the development of the curriculum, and, more recently, for staff appraisal for the same purposes have most often been highly simplistic in their conception. They have more often been summative than formative (Scriven 1967; Stenhouse 1975), concerned to measure achievement rather than to offer evidence for continuous development; they have been concerned with cost-effectiveness, and in general with the attainment of prespecified goals, rather than with questions of value, with assessing the efficiency of the means rather than the desirability of the ends (White 1971); they have been concerned with the acquisition of knowledge rather than the manner in which that knowledge has been acquired, with quantitative rather than qualitative judgements (Blenkin and Kelly 1981). They have thus led to forms of evaluation and accountability variously described as utilitarian, instrumental, hierarchical or bureaucratic (Elliott 1976; Sockett 1976; MacDonald 1975).

Again it must be stressed that, while this may not always have been the intention, it has too often been the effect. As Del Goddard has said in response to the Government White Paper *Teaching Quality* (DES 1983), 'the monitoring and external assessment of teachers undertaken in a hierarchical framework may have as its intention the improvement of teaching quality. But . . . the effect is often the opposite, and the assumption that it encourages a positive climate for improvement does not stand up to close theoretical or practical analysis' (1985, p.35). And again, 'The view contained in the White Paper of the profession and the task of teaching is derived from a school of thought that places the teacher in the role of a carrier of knowledge with transmission skills. Teachers are seen in the context of the subjects they teach, and knowledge and understanding of educational issues and pedagogy are relegated to a very poor second . . . It also reflects a continuing failure to recognize what constitutes a professional teacher' (ibid.). One might add that, as was suggested earlier, the concept of pedagogy adopted is a highly simplistic one, embracing little more than methodological know-how.

To set up procedures which attempt to evaluate the curriculum or to appraise teacher performance in terms of content or products or a blend of both, in terms of knowledge acquired by pupils or prespecified performance objectives attained, is to impose that model of curriculum planning and that view of education on the teachers who are the subjects of these procedures, whether this is intended or not. More serious, from the point of view of the theme of this book, is the corollary of this, that, by promoting that model and that view of education, these procedures are inhibiting, and even destroying, the view of education as a process of individual growth and development, with all the consequences of that which earlier chapters have attempted to point out. As we saw in Chapter 3 when discussing Dewey's views, the only criteria of evaluation for education as a developmental process are those which derive from the notions of growth and development themselves.

For procedures which emphasize content and product as what matters in schooling cannot accommodate the view of education as process. They cannot evaluate or assess the development which has occurred as a result of the educational experiences provided; they can only measure what can be reproduced either in propositional form or in performance. They cannot appraise the quality or the manner of pupils' learning, their individual response to what has been offered, the extent to which their learning satisfies those criteria of active learning which, as we saw in Chapter 4, developmental psychology insists are crucial to intellectual development in the full sense; they can only quantify the knowledge acquired, whether it is 'inert' or active. They cannot allow for that individual development we have also stressed as important; they can only measure every pupil against common standards, whether expressed as norms or criteria — a prime source of educational inequality. They thus evince, as was suggested earlier, a less sophisticated view of children's minds than certain shoe manufacturers profess to have of their feet. And lastly, they have the greatest difficulty in encompassing dimensions of development beyond the cognitive, other than by attempts to reduce them to some form of cognition in the manner we discussed in Chapter 8. They can only evaluate what they can quantify and measure, so that the affective dimension, even that which we have seen is inextricably interwoven with the cognitive, must always elude them.

It might perhaps be worth adding here that, although the main focus of our concern in this chapter is on the effects of the current procedures being recommended and adopted at the political level, we should not forget that the same kinds of effect can be seen emanating from sources within education, both 'academic' and professional. This after all is the main thrust of that general rationalist position this book has been concerned to challenge. It is also the result of the kind of 'scientific' research into educational practice which it was earlier suggested has been every bit as inhibiting of the practice of teachers because of serious limitations of scope and outlook in the research methodology, design and specifications adopted (Kelly 1981), because, in fact, it has adopted uncritically precisely the same assumptions that the politicians have made. It was claimed in Chapter 5, for example, that the uncritically accepted assumptions about knowledge, about education and about the curriculum which underlie research such as that undertaken by Neville Bennett's teams (1976, 1984) have precisely this same effect of pressing upon teachers a model of education which may not be theirs and, precisely because it makes no attempt to justify its stance on these issues, certainly has the effect of discouraging a proper extension of the debate to the models of knowledge, education and curriculum themselves.

The general problems of procedures of this kind, then, are several. First they fail to evaluate large areas of the school curriculum which many people would wish to argue are very important. Thus those aspects of schooling begin to lose ground and less attention comes to be given to the dimensions of children's development they promote. Alternatively, in order to hold their ground, the subjects or areas of the curriculum concerned attempt to establish themselves according to the terms of the evaluation procedures, to accept the rules of that game, and adopt the strategies which we saw in Chapter 4 have been effective in the establishment of other subjects in the curriculum, but which have, in doing so, rendered those subjects less valuable educationally to a majority of pupils. Thus art begins to give way to history of art, domestic science becomes 'food and nutritional studies', physical education shifts its focus away from outdoor pursuits towards the study of anatomy and physiology, moral education is defined more in terms of 'moral knowledge' than of moral development and Craft, Design and Technology has to continue to resist the pressures on it to become some form of technological training. They thus become, as was suggested in Chapter 4, far less valuable *educationally* than they might be, and in particular they lose most of the value they ought to have for a large proportion of the school population.

Secondly, these procedures invite teachers to take an instrumental view of their task and to work towards the objectives prespecified, if only implicitly, by the forms of evaluation. This means not only that they see what they are doing in terms of aims and objectives extrinsic to it, but also that these are aims and objectives set by others, by those responsible for the forms of evaluation and appraisal being employed.

Thirdly, teachers are encouraged to view the curriculum in terms of its cognitive content. Procedures of evaluation, appraisal and accountability which stress the acquisition of knowledge by measuring the quantity of knowledge acquired, and which value only the propositional knowledge pupils can display a mastery of, invite teachers to see their role in terms of the transmission of such knowledge and even the teaching of subjects. Thus they add to that encouragement to this view which already exists in the forms of training most teachers have been given, and which it is now overt government policy that all shall be given in the future, and those rationalist influences on the curriculum we have described elsewhere.

Lastly, because they promote in teachers these kinds of view of the curriculum and of their role, they discourage the development of alternative views of education such as that outlined in our earlier chapters. Several features of this must be noted. There is, first, the effect of this on those teachers already committed to a different view who are forced by these procedures into adopting modes of teaching they are uncomfortable with or even opposed to. Then there is the absence of any encouragement to other teachers to ask questions of a searching kind about their work and, in particular, about the subject-knowledge they are offering. For these procedures encourage teachers to ask only *how* they should teach their subjects when the most important question for teachers to face is *why* they should teach them. And, lastly, for this reason they are inhibiting of curriculum development, curriculum change, curriculum evolution. For all that will change as a result of these forms of evaluation will be the means, the methods adopted to attain the objectives or to transmit the knowledge; questions of ends are not raised because they do not figure as part of any debate, so that there is no scope for the desirability of those objectives or that knowledge ever to be questioned or even discussed. And without that kind of questioning and discussion there can be no proper development even of the objectives and the content themselves. This is an example, as we saw earlier, of one of the claims made by John Stuart Mill in support of freedom of thought; 'truth', whatever that is, can only emerge and can only be asserted with conviction, if it is constantly measured against alternative views.

It is often claimed that evaluation procedures are directed as much towards curriculum development, and methods of appraisal as much towards teacher development, as towards accountability. And, indeed, as we saw earlier, any concept of curriculum or teacher development requires that they should be. If they are to meet those requirements they need to be a good deal more sophisticated than many of those currently being advocated and, indeed, implemented.

We will turn later to a consideration of what these more sophisticated procedures might look like. First, however, it may help to demonstrate the validity of the claims just made if we look at the experience of the major national agency for the monitoring of the curriculum, the Assessment of Performance Unit (APU) of the Department of Education and Science. For the history of that Unit does seem to illustrate many of the points we are making here, not least that general, and very important point, that these are often the effects of monitoring procedures even if they are not the intention, and even when the intention to avoid them is clearly asserted at the outset.

The Assessment of Performance Unit

The Assessment of Performance Unit established by the Department of Education and Science is the most obvious, the most important and certainly the best-known attempt to establish mechanisms for the monitoring of standards in schools in the United Kingdom. The intention to create it was first announced in a Government White Paper, *Educational Disadvantage and the Educational Needs of Immigrants* (DES 1974) in 1974, and it came into being in the following year. Its terms of reference are 'to promote the development of methods of assessing and monitoring the achievement of children at school, and to seek to identify the incidence of underachievement'. The intention is also to make those findings which result from its investigations available to those responsible both for the work of the schools and for the allocation of resources. It was given four tasks:

To identify and appraise existing instruments and methods of assessment which may be relevant for these purposes [i.e. those purposes expressed in its terms of reference].

To sponsor the creation of new instruments and techniques of assessment, having due regard to statistical and sampling methods.

To promote the conduct of assessment in cooperation with local education authorities and teachers.

To identify significant differences of achievement related to the circumstances in which children learn, including the incidence of underachievement, and to make the findings available to those concerned with resource allocation within government departments, local education authorities and schools.

It can thus be seen that from the outset there existed in its brief the seeds of some of those problems we discussed earlier. The emphasis on achievement and underachievement suggests a view of education which may well not embrace the idea of growth and development. Concern with the allocation of resources also encourages the view that financial accountability might be of more concern than curriculum development. Indeed, the recently retired Administrative Head of the Unit, Jean Dawson, has stated quite explicitly, 'We are not a covert agency for curriculum development' (Dawson 1984, p.126).

However, against this, it must also be made clear that from the beginning it was stressed that the role of the Unit was to attempt to gain and make known a picture of education in the country as a whole, not to identify individual teachers, schools, local authorities or even individual pupils, but to provide a national picture against which individuals might measure themselves. It is also the prime task of the Unit to establish a system of monitoring which will facilitate the detection of trends in performance, whether standards are rising or falling. Thus, it was the intention from the outset to devise mechanisms which would indicate and evaluate what was actually occurring and to avoid any semblance of direction or control. Indeed, this is the thrust of Jean Dawson's comment quoted above.

This intention is reflected in the procedures which have been adopted by the Unit for the monitoring process. The policy has been one of light and random sampling; no one pupil, teacher or school has been exposed to any full battery of tests; and only one person has access to both the data and the knowledge of the individual sources of those data. Thus every effort has been made to achieve a genuine anonymity and to discourage teachers from 'teaching to the tests' and thus restricting the range and nature of the work undertaken in schools.

The same concern to avoid this kind of restriction is to be seen in the choice of areas to be monitored. The areas initially selected for monitoring were six — mathematics, language, science, social and personal development, aesthetics and physical development. It is the current intention to add to these design and technology. This choice may be seen as reflecting not only a concern to avoid restricting the range of work in schools, but also as an attempt to see the curriculum in terms of development rather than merely knowledge acquisition, and even to recognize the importance of forms of development beyond the cognitive. Indeed, the terminology used by the Unit itself to describe these areas is 'lines of development' rather than 'subjects' or 'curriculum areas' and it favours adjectival rather than substantive designations for them — mathematical, linguistic, scientific, social and personal, aesthetic and physical — thus reflecting, at least in part, the 'eight adjectives' approach of *Curriculum 11-16* (DES 1977).

It is interesting, however, even if one concedes that the enterprise began with these very best of intentions, to consider the realities of its ten years of operational existence.

First, it is of some significance that it has made much more rapid headway in the more overtly cognitive areas of the curriculum than elsewhere. Indeed, in some other areas it has made no headway at all and has conceded defeat. In the case of both mathematics and language, where admittedly there was earlier work on testing to be built on, rapid progress has been made towards developing a programme of monitoring and implementing that programme. The first survey of mathematical abilities was conducted in 1978 and of linguistic abilities in 1979. On the other hand, 'personal and social development, a delicate and politically sensitive area, has fallen by the wayside' (Dawson 1984, p.127), although a discussion paper has been published and a major literature survey has been made available. Furthermore, 'having taken the advice of the Consultative Committee, the Secretary of State has decided that the Unit should not engage in monitoring children's physical development' (ibid.). Also, 'No decision has yet been taken on the report of the aesthetics group' (ibid.), but we noted in Chapter 8 that a major strategy adopted by that group to render aesthetic development accessible to testing mechanisms was to attempt to reduce much of it to some form of cognition. Development in the scientific area has been slower but in some ways more interesting and we will return to that in a moment.

First, we must attempt to discover what lessons there are to be learnt from this experience. To begin with we should note the dangers we discussed earlier that teachers are likely to 'teach to the tests' and that, even if they do not go to that extreme, they are likely to concentrate in planning their curricula on those areas which continue to be subject to monitoring to the detriment of those which do not. In short, within the areas which are tested there is a strong temptation to frame syllabuses in accordance with the major concerns of the test mechanisms — as happens under the influences of the public examinations — and in the overall planning of the curriculum there will be a comparable temptation to give undue emphasis to the areas by reference to which performance is evaluated.

Such evidence as there is of this happening is admittedly at present rather thin and largely anecdotal. This may be due to the light sampling techniques which the Unit has deliberately adopted. If so, its initial claims may be justified. This is a question, however, which is urgently in need of exploration and research. It might of course be argued that the work of the Unit is unlikely to have anything like the impact on the Secondary curriculum of the public examination system (Gipps 1984). However, to say that is to ignore the fact that it may well reinforce the effects of the public examination system in encouraging emphases on those subjects which are examined and a corresponding devaluing of those which are not — i.e. those very areas which the APU has either already withdrawn from or has failed to make any progress in — aesthetic, physical and social and personal development. Nor should its potential impact on the Primary school be ignored. And we must also note the dangers of encouraging there a view of the curriculum in terms of its content, of assessing the quantity of knowledge transmitted rather than the quality of the learning which has taken place, and of promoting the maintenance of existing subject boundaries, in spite of what we saw in Chapter 4 are the very slender forms of justification for these. This can lead in turn to the adoption by teachers of a simplistic view of their role, seeing it as it seems to be defined by the monitoring procedures rather than through the exercise of their own professional judgement.

This, then, raises questions about the monitoring instruments themselves and suggests another lesson which might be learnt from the work of this Unit. For it is clear that whether monitoring has this kind of effect on the curriculum or not will be decided entirely by the instruments adopted to carry out the monitoring process. This brings us to a brief consideration of the area of the curriculum or 'line of development' we have not yet examined — the scientific area.

There is no doubt that in all areas an attempt has been made to develop sophisticated instruments nor that there has been some success in doing this. It is perhaps the science team, however, which has come closest to achieving forms of monitoring which can avoid the worst of the problems we have been attempting to identify. For a deliberate attempt has been made by this team not only to analyse the component parts of the development of scientific thinking and to develop instruments for testing these, but also to devise methods of testing the totality of scientific development and thus, by inference, the quality of pupils' learning in this field. In the terminology we have used throughout this book, this can be seen as an attempt to evaluate scientific development or learning as a process rather than as a product or as the acquisition of knowledge-content. It thus represents an important step away from those features of evaluation, appraisal and accountability which we saw have an inhibiting effect on this approach to education towards the development of forms of monitoring which may positively promote it and which certainly offer some hope of evaluating it.

For the science group, centred at the University of Leeds and at Chelsea College, London, attempted to develop a 'holistic' form of monitoring which would embrace not only the acquisition of scientific concepts but also the ability to apply and to use them, to solve problems, to perform investigations — even in contexts which might not be regarded as obviously 'scientific'. It thus has attempted also to get beyond the confines of traditional definitions of science. For example, pupils, as part of the testing procedure, have been asked to make decisions concerning such things as the selection of the most suitable clothing material for mountaineering expeditions and thus to demonstrate their scientific understanding, their ability to think 'scientifically' rather than merely to reveal the extent of their scientific 'knowledge'. Thus one major planned focus for monitoring in this area has been the process of scientific development, and we have a first step towards the establishment of evaluation procedures which may promote rather than inhibit that view of education and that approach to curriculum planning. Indeed, there is already some evidence that where teachers have chosen to teach to these tests the quality of their work has been raised. Thus teaching to the tests can be a two-edged consequence of this kind of monitoring. Its effects need not be detrimental. Further, there is evidence that some of what has emerged from the testing has been used to some effect diagnostically and has led to real improvements in the quality of teaching.

Inadequacies still exist, however, inadequacies of the kind which have been highlighted throughout. It has been claimed (Brown 1980) that it is still the case that 'the science skills which are definable and the outcomes which are precisely measurable will . . . be tested well in the national monitoring', but that 'only a limited attempt is being made to test the less easily definable skills like creative thinking and imaginative reasoning and their less reliably measurable outcomes'. Maurice Holt (1981, p.80), in considering these comments and in attempting himself to evaluate the work of the APU in general, has gone on to claim that 'the tester's search for objective certainty is a quest for an unattainable goal' and that the work of the Unit represents 'attempts to reduce a complex and ultimately impenetrable process to measurable outcomes' (ibid.), attempts which 'inevitably . . . present a distorted view of what they claim to measure' (ibid).

This is precisely what is being emphasized here as a major danger of this kind of procedure. What is also being suggested here, however, is that this kind of danger might be avoided if the focus were switched from outcomes to procedures and the search were not for objective certainty but for something far less precise, something rooted not in the rationalist's view of knowledge and standards but in the rather less firm soil of empiricism. The APU science team may not have achieved this shift, but its attempts to find testing mechanisms and devices of a less restricting form may have got the process started.

The APU is about to turn its attention to the area of design and technology, through the work of a team which will be centred at Goldsmiths' College, London, and it is hoped that developments in that field will continue the movement in this direction. And there is good reason to hope for this. For, as we have noted several times, the development of that area of the curriculum in recent times, more than any other area of the Secondary school curriculum, has been predicated on a concern for what it can contribute to the processes of educational development. It has steadfastly resisted invitations to plan and evaluate its work in terms of its products, and it has already, through the public examination boards, developed some techniques for assessing the quality of pupils' thinking and learning rather than merely the content or the products of that thinking. There is thus a base from which it is not unreasonable to hope that instruments might be developed, whose scope will extend well beyond the confines of design and technology, and which will enable us to plan and evaluate our curricula in terms of the growth and development of their recipients rather than the transmission of what currently counts as valuable knowledge, and thus to begin our curriculum planning from considerations of the pupil rather than of its knowledge-content.

This leads us finally to a consideration of what might be the major features of forms of evaluation, appraisal and accountability which might match such a view of curriculum.

Towards a more sophisticated and enabling model

We should begin by noting that more sophisticated models do exist and have been around for some time. Forms of evaluation have been devised and implemented specifically in order to allow for this kind of approach to the curriculum and to permit its continued development — forms which have deliberately avoided directing the course of such development by offering the planner data for his/her own planning rather than predetermining goals. These have also been offered for use in procedures for accountability.

A major step forward in the development of these more sophisticated forms and techniques of evaluation came with the Humanities Curriculum Project (HCP) in the late 1960s (Stenhouse 1975). For a central feature of that project was its deliberate avoidance of the use of prespecified objectives, so that it created a curriculum project which, as its evaluator, Barry MacDonald, said, provided 'no ready-made niche for the evaluator' (MacDonald 1973, p.82). The details of this project and its evaluation have been well described and analysed elsewhere, notably in the work of the project director, Lawrence Stenhouse, himself (1975, 1980) and Barry MacDonald (op.cit). What we must note here, however, is that an alternative approach to evaluation was found, one that did not depend on the prespecification of curriculum objectives or of subject-content and thus did not determine in advance what the curriculum was to achieve. Barry MacDonald called this approach 'holistic' and said of it, 'In view of the potential significance of so many aspects of the project, a complete description of its experience was needed initially, as was awareness of a full range of relevant phenomena' (op.cit., p.83). Selection within and between these data could only be made at a later stage when the criteria of such selection began to emerge from the continuing experience of implementation and evaluation. 'Evaluation design, strategies and methods would evolve in response to the project's impact on the educational system and the types of evaluation problems which that impact would throw up' (ibid.).

The central concern, then, was not to determine in advance what the forms of evaluation would be, and thus, as we have seen, to allow those forms to direct and control the curriculum itself. It was to describe what was there to be seen and to let the evaluation criteria evolve with the curriculum itself. Similar approaches have been variously described by others as 'illuminative' (Parlett and Hamilton 1975), concerned with 'description and interpretation rather than measurement and prediction' (op.cit., p.88), as 'portrayal' (Stake 1972), concerned to portray the programme as a whole and reveal its 'total substance', as 'responsive' (Hamilton 1976), a form of evaluation which 'responds to the wide range of questions asked about an innovation and is not trapped inside the intentions of the programme-builders' (op.cit., p.39).

More sophisticated forms of curriculum evaluation do exist, therefore, both in theory and in practice. Their main concern is not with decision-making but with providing information for decision-makers. They see curriculum evaluation as part of curriculum development and thus as a form of curriculum research. They have also led, although here perhaps more in theory than in practice, to forms of accountability which are democratic, intrinsic and professional rather than bureaucratic, instrumental and hierarchical (MacDonald 1975; Elliott 1976; Sockett 1976). If we are to see what a more sophisticated and enabling model of evaluation, appraisal and accountability might look like, therefore, we may best do that by picking out some central features of these models.

The first characteristic of these forms of evaluation is that they begin from a recognition that there are value positions implicit in every curriculum specification, that these are problematic and that every attempt must be made to avoid their reification or ossification. They thus reflect a move away from a rationalist perspective towards one which acknowledges the tentative nature of knowledge, the resultant lack of any objective basis for judgements of value and the need to permit continued debate and consequent modification of curriculum provision. They are specifically designed to enable continuous evolution and development of the curriculum, precisely because they do not start from any preconceived notion of what it must be for all time.

They encourage, therefore, curriculum planning which begins by specifying its implicit value positions and acknowledges these to be themselves a part of what is to be evaluated, rather than by prestating content to be transmitted or behavioural objectives to be attained, and thus leaving questions of the validity of that content or those objectives out of the evaluation process or specification, and consequently abandoning them to some largely random form of determination.

Further, they attempt to allow for the fact not only that the worthwhileness of knowledge and the adoption of the value positions education requires are themselves part of the debate, but also that the organization of knowledge into subjects or disciplines or any other kinds of grouping is, if not arbitrary, at least a function of factors other than those claimed by the rationalist to be integral to or implicit in the knowledge or the subjects themselves. Subjects have no existence in their own right, as rationalism would, at least in some cases, have it; they are themselves open to the same processes of development and evolution as knowledge itself; so that our curriculum evaluation, as well as our curriculum planning, must allow for this. It is not only the case, then, that our assessment must be criterion-referenced rather than norm-referenced; it is also the case that the criteria we use for such referencing must be different. They must be procedural rather than terminal; they must allow for the notion of education as development and not merely as knowledge or skills acquisition.

These procedures have been designed, therefore, to promote that very view of education and approach to curriculum planning this book has been advocating and to replace those procedures which would push education down the rationalist road.

In order to do this, they have further had to stress one key element in the evaluation process — the involvement of the teachers themselves. For it will be self-evident that, if evaluation, appraisal and accountability procedures are imposed on teachers from outside, if they are created and operated by others, the teachers must be strongly tempted to be constantly looking over their shoulders to the criteria of evaluation being used, so that these will quickly become their criteria for planning and thus the evaluation tail will wag the curriculum dog. If, on the other hand, the evaluation procedures are concerned to describe, to illuminate, to portray what is going on in order to promote its continuing development, it must be recognized that that continuing development is largely in the hands of the teachers themselves and the exercise of their professional judgement, and thus will only happen if the teachers are themselves involved in the process of evaluation as well as in that of planning and implementation. We noted earlier the criticisms offered by Del Goddard of the 'external assessment of teachers undertaken in a hierarchical framework' (1984, p.35). He goes on to claim that that approach 'also reflects a continuing failure to recognise what constitutes a professional teacher' (ibid.). The continued development of education and the continued development of its recipients requires that the teachers themselves be involved in all aspects of its planning and its evaluation.

The form of this involvement of teachers is a complex issue and not one into which it is the intention to venture very far here. Some would advocate little more than the taking of teachers into the confidence of the evaluators and the inclusion of them in the evaluation team. Little as this is, it would represent a big step forward for some of the procedures currently advocated and used for the evaluation of schools and the appraisal of teachers, and, indeed, the procedures still being used — or, worse, currently being reinvented — by many local authorities, advisers and HMI. A major inspection of a school by HMI, followed by an oral report to its governors and, some time later, a written report to governors, parents, staff and the general public (the currently accepted procedure), represents anything but a dialogue with the teachers concerned. And if one adds to that the follow-up demands for information as to what has been done in response to that report, one can see how little involvement of teachers there is in current practices, and, further, how totally irrelevant is thought to be any views they might have about their own curricula. Involvement even at this minimal level, then, would represent progress.

There are those, however, who claim that much more than this is needed if genuine development is to result from procedures for evaluation, that teachers should be permitted, and also helped, to conduct their own evaluations. This, it is argued, they do anyway; it is an important part of their day-to-day planning. They should be provided, both by their initial courses of preparation for teaching and by subsequent in-service courses, with the skills and techniques to conduct full and proper evaluation of their work both as individuals and as members of the staffs of schools. Thus we have notions of school-based evaluation as a support to school-based curriculum development, of self-assessment or self-appraisal by teachers and even of the teacher as researcher (Stenhouse 1975).

Only by these kinds of procedure, it is argued, will the teacher be free to get on with his/her professional task, the education — in the full sense — of the pupils. This is a task which requires pedagogic skills which go far beyond mere methodology and which must include professional skills of self-assessment. Nor are these evaluation procedures which rule out the possiblity of teacher accountability. Rather they offer a form of accountability which is likely to be positive and productive in educational terms. For there ought not to be a conflict between evaluation for curriculum development and evaluation for accountability. There can be no point to accountability unless that point is to raise standards and improve the quality of performance, and that is what curriculum development, and its corollary, teacher development, mean. The concern must therefore be to avoid forms of evaluation and accountability which are not carefully designed to promote curriculum development, since these must in every sense be inhibiting, counter-productive and ultimately self-defeating. We must work to create procedures which will support teachers in their professional task of offering the best possible educational value to all their pupils. And pre-eminent among the essential ingredients of such procedures must be a central role for the teachers themselves. To quote Maurice Holt (1981, p.81) again, 'if education is to be improved . . . then the way to do it is not by vain attempts to measure what happens but by helping teachers to define and solve curriculum problems.'

If this is so, then the efforts and resources currently being devoted to assessing and appraising teacher performance might be better directed towards raising the standards of teacher professionalism and, in particular, towards assisting teachers to develop not only the skills but also the attitudes of mind necessary to engage as individuals in self-appraisal and as a profession in forms of peer-group appraisal. At the national level the establishment of a Teachers' Council is long overdue and would be an important step in the right direction. The establishment of such a council in itself, however, would do little to resolve the problems we have been identifying in this chapter; indeed it might add to them by providing another controlling body to which teachers might be constantly looking over their shoulders. It can only work if it is associated with a general move at all other levels to encourage self- and peer-appraisal, the acceptance of this as the focus of accountability procedures and the establishment of appropriate forms of education and support for the teachers themselves in implementing these procedures.

Such developments must also be associated with a complete rethinking of many aspects of education of the kind this book has been concerned to advocate. In particular, it must be associated with some rigorous questioning of the validity of that rationalist perspective which has for too long dominated educational thinking and planning in the United Kingdom. Unless we are prepared to question that, there is no point in continuing to develop new forms of evaluation, appraisal and accountability. For, within the rationalist view of education, the old simplistic forms are more than adequate. The corollary of that, however, is that the adoption of those forms will confine us to such a rationalist view. And that is the emphatic message which emerges from any kind of analysis of current political intervention in curriculum planning and development.

Alternative forms of evaluation and accountability, of a kind which can match the view of curriculum we have been advocating, are available then. They can be used and developed if such a solution is sought or desired. The important question in the current political climate, however, is not whether they are possible, but whether they are felt to be desirable, or rather not whether they are in themselves desirable but whether the forms of curriculum they are designed to facilitate and support are acceptable. One has reluctantly to surmise that they are not, that it is not ignorance so much as fear that prompts many of the current approaches to evaluation, appraisal and accountability, not educational desirability but a, perhaps misplaced, sense of political expediency.

This brings us back to one of our continuing themes — the conflict between the teaching profession and its political masters. It will perhaps be clear from the foregoing that it is only through the increased professionalism and professionalization of teachers that the forms of education which have been advocated in this book can have any chance of materializing. The kind of education which has been envisaged here, consisting as it does centrally of the development of each pupil as an individual, is not something that can be achieved by remote control, by central fiat, by the establishment of a common core curriculum or (and perhaps even less) by the more subtle means of adopting *dirigiste* procedures for evaluation, appraisal and accountability. The attainment of this kind of education must rest, to a very large extent if not totally, in the hands of the teachers. Education, as we have defined it here, can only emerge from the right kind of interaction between teacher and taught, and that is not something which can be dictated from the outside. The message, then, must be that education requires less external control rather than more, that teachers need more freedom of action not less. And that lesson must be applied not only to direct forms of external control but also, and especially, to those more insidious forms we have been concerned to identify and discuss in this chapter.

All current signs, however, point in the opposite direction. It is clear that the quality of teachers will be crucial to the development of education along these lines; yet current official definitions of teaching quality (DES 1983) and directives concerning the content of courses of initial teacher education emphasize knowledge assimilated and skills acquired for the transmission of that knowledge as the prime indicators of such quality, seeing the teacher, as we earlier saw Del Goddard putting it, 'in the role of a carrier of knowledge with transmission skills' (1985, p.35). If personal qualities are extolled, they are valued only or largely as devices helpful in the process of such transmission. This view is reflected most obviously in the move towards increasing the proportion of teachers whose preparation has consisted of three years of the study of a subject or subjects and only one year of teacher education, and in the current requirement that all teachers following four-year concurrent courses whether preparing to work with Nursery-age children or with VIth formers, must spend at least two of those years studying subject-content. The transmission model of education is apparent and behind it either a tacit rationalism or, worse, a confusion of the educational with the academic and that imposition of the values of the dominant power-group in society we have referred to so often.

That similar values and assumptions underlie much of the current move towards increased accountability and teacher appraisal can be seen from what has already been said in this chapter. In spite of all the trends within education and within both the theory and the practice of curriculum development towards the need for increased teacher-involvement, for self-evaluation and so on, it is plain that only lip-service is paid to this in any official pronouncements on curriculum.

It is for this reason that it was suggested in Chapter 4, when we previously touched on the issue of the struggle for control of the curriculum between teachers and their political masters, that it is highly unlikely that we will see in the immediate future the establishment of anything like a General Teaching Council — certainly not as a body with real responsibility for or powers of curriculum development. For the establishment of such a body, for any purpose other than the disciplining of teachers, would be to swing the balance of curricular control away from the politicians and the administrators, and their record in recent years makes it plain that this is something they will resist to the death.

One cannot be optimistic, then, but one can attempt — as this book has done, and especially this chapter — to draw attention to some of the realities of current trends in the control of the curriculum and current constraints on curriculum development in schools. In particular, one can reveal their rationalist assumptions and draw attention to the weaknesses of this as a base from which to engage in any kind of planning that is truly educational.

Summary and conclusions

This chapter set out to demonstrate that those rationalist assumptions about curriculum which earlier chapters have identified are being reinforced, explicitly and implicitly, by many aspects of the current, politically motivated, pressures for evaluation, appraisal and accountability in education. The further implication of that is that those problems which we have identified as having their source in these rationalist assumptions are also being thus aggravated. It was noted that the emphasis on knowledge-content, on subjects and on products as the prime considerations in planning the curriculum was also reflected in the procedures devised for its evaluation, and that this was detrimental and indeed inimical to the establishment of any notion of education as growth or development. It was further stressed that the same emphasis on the cognitive, on that which can be most readily quantified and measured, is also inhibiting to the growth of a view of education and of the curriculum which transcends the cognitive and embraces aspects of human development in the affective domain.

It was suggested that these are the inevitable effects of procedures which are predicated on this kind of view, even when, as the example of the work of the Assessment of Performance Unit illustrated, every effort is made to avoid such consequences. What is needed, it was argued, is a set of procedures for evaluation, appraisal and accountability which is based on different, non-rationalist, assumptions, which accepts a looser, more tentative and more open approach both to evaluation and to the curriculum itself and which, as a result, will permit the continuing development of the curriculum and of an approach to it which emphasizes its concern with the development of the individual rather than the transmission of knowledge or the attainment of predetermined objectives.

It was finally claimed that such procedures must evince two major features. The first of these is a full involvement of teachers themselves in the evaluation process. The second is the adoption of a non-rationalist epistemology, the rejection of those confident assumptions about the nature of knowledge and the validity of value positions which rationalism encourages and the recognition that the status of both knowledge and values is highly problematic and must itself be part of the curriculum debate and thus of the evaluation and accountability procedures.

It is this that brings us back to our central concern and which reveals the relevance of the issue of evaluation and accountability to that concern. For, like all the other issues we have explored in Part Two, it raises important questions about the status of knowledge and of values, illustrates for us the results of accepting the rationalist theory of that status and reveals again how far the adoption or the assumption of that theory puts at risk some of those features our earlier chapters have suggested are important aspects of any form of education worthy of the name.

It has also proved, as we suggested it might, an issue which has drawn together most of the points those earlier chapters have made. For the features they suggested might be seen as important in education and which they further suggested a rationalist perspective puts at risk were those very things which this chapter has revealed the more simplistic forms of evaluation and accountability cannot cope with and thus also put at risk. The ideas of education as a series of processes of development, of such development as individual development, of such individual development as essential to the attainment of educational equality and of such development as embracing domains beyond that of the cognitive, were all of them aspects of education which earlier chapters identified not only as important but also as incapable of inclusion in any consistent rationalist theory either of knowledge or of education. They are also aspects of education which this chapter has revealed as under threat from the more simplistic procedures for evaluation, appraisal and accountability which are themselves fundamentally rationalist in their central assumptions, and from the central features of the current political climate in the United Kingdom.

The chapter has also revealed that more sophisticated procedures are available and can be developed further. A central feature of these, however, and a prime necessity for their further development is a rethinking of the epistemological basis of curriculum planning. For, like those other features of education we have been concerned to identify and advocate, they necessitate the kind of tentative view of knowledge and of values which rationalism by definition cannot adopt, but which we have seen is fundamental to an empiricist/pragmatist epistemology. The realities of those current procedures which we have attempted to explore in this chapter have thus reinforced the more theoretical discussions of earlier chapters in urging on us the conclusion that rationalism has had its day, has had too long a run, and that its rejection by professional philosophers must now be followed by its rejection by educationists. Whether one can also look forward to its rejection by those who hold the reins of political power is another, and very different, question.

POSTSCRIPT

It is always a good thing when on the completion of a book one has to go back and rewrite one's Introduction. For it is evidence that one's own thinking has evolved in the process of writing, and further evidence that prespecified objectives are limiting in any aspect of intellectual endeavour.

The book began as an attempt to explore the major perspectives on knowledge and their implications for educational planning, and, in particular, to draw attention to the fact that there is more than one perspective which can quite rationally and logically be adopted and that to fail to recognize this represents a serious intellectual and professional inadequacy. There was also, it must be admitted, a personal leaning towards that empiricist/pragmatist perspective which is the one which is usually ignored or put down, and which is the base of that form of education I have always personally favoured. Writing this book, however, has led me to a total conviction that the other perspective is philosophically unsound, and even inconsistent, and that it is educationally unattractive and inhibiting, and to the view that those 'philosophers of education' who have thrust it upon us, or at least reaffirmed it as the base for curriculum planning, have done education a great disservice. In doing so, they have offered a theoretical perspective on education which is based on an inadequate understanding both of philosophy and of education. 'Philosophy of education', in short, has for the most part been neither good philosophy nor good education.

This also reveals the danger of allowing any one 'discipline' to determine the substance of educational practice, of adopting that simplistic view to which we have referred earlier on several occasions that the philosopher can determine our educational ends, while proponents of the other disciplines help us with the means. Enough has perhaps been said in this book to demonstrate that the two are inextricably interwoven and that educational planning must take account of what all kinds of study can offer at every level. It has suggested in fact that the study of education is *sui generis* and that it is only when we accept that and all it entails that we will provide ourselves with a proper basis for educational planning.

Now, after years of misleading theory, we are into the age of political misdirection. Both must be resisted and for the same reasons. For both lead us away from a concern with the pupil towards undue attention to the knowledge-content of schooling or its end-products, to demands felt to be implicit in the knowledge itself or the needs of society. Both of these may be legitimate concerns of schooling, but, if education is not to be merely equated with schooling, it must go beyond these concerns and direct itself to more sophisticated kinds of change which occur in the individual as a result of exposure to educational experiences. This is the force of Mark Twain's famous dictum, 'Don't let your son's schooling interfere with his education'. It has been the contention of this book that that is a dictum worthy of detailed analysis and, further, that that analysis must begin from a questioning of the rationalist base of much that currently passes for education.

BIBLIOGRAPHY

Archambault, R.D. (ed.) (1965) *Philosophical Analysis and Education*. London: Routledge.

Arnold, Matthew *Culture and Anarchy*.

Ayer, A.J. (1936) *Language, Truth and Logic*. London: Gollancz.

Bantock, G.H. (1968) *Culture, Industrialisation and Education*. London: Routledge.

Benedict, R. (1946) *Patterns of Culture*. Harmondsworth: Penguin.

Benjamin, H. (1939) The saber-tooth curriculum, 7-15 in Hooper (ed.) (1971).

Bennett, S.N., (1976) *Teaching Styles and Pupil Progress*. London: Open Books.

Bennett, S.N., Desforges, C., Cockburn, A. and Wilkinson, B. (1984) *The Quality of Pupil Learning Experiences*. London: Lawrence Erlbaum Associates.

Berkely, Bishop George, *Three Dialogues between Hylas and Philonous*.

Bernstein, B.B. (1967), Open Schools, Open Society? *New Society* September 14th.

Blenkin, G.M. and Kelly, A.V. (1981) *The Primary Curriculum*. London: Harper and Row.

Blenkin, G.M. and Kelly, A.V. (eds.) (1983) *The Primary Curriculum in Action*. London: Harper and Row.

Bloom, B.S. et al. (1956) *Taxonomy of Educational Objectives 1: Cognitive Domain*. London: Longmans.

Blum, A.F. (1971), The corpus of knowledge as a normative order: intellectual critique of the social order of knowledge and commonsense features of bodies of knowledge, 117-132 in Young (ed.) (1971).

Blyth, W.A.L. (1965) *English Primary Education: A Sociological Description, Vol. 2 Background*. London: Routledge.

Bowles, S. and Gintis, H. (eds.) (1976) *Schooling in Capitalist America*. London: Routledge.

Broad, C.D. (1930) *Five Types of Ethical Theory*. London: Routledge.

Brookfield, S. (1982) Evaluation Models and Adult Education, 95-100 in *Studies in Adult Education* 14.

Brown, R. (1980) A visit to the APU, 78-81 in *Journal of Curriculum Studies*, 12,1.

Bruner, J. et al. (1968) *Towards a Theory of Instruction*. New York: Norton.

Childs, J.L. (1956) *American Pragmatism and Education*. New York: Holt.

Coard, B. (1971) *How the West Indian Child is Made ESN in the British School System*. London: New Beacon.

Cox, C.B. and Dyson, A.E. (eds.) (1969a) *Fight for Education: A Black Paper*. Manchester: Critical Quarterly Society.

Cox, C.B. and Dyson, A.E. (eds) (1969b) *Black Paper Two: The Crisis in Education*. Manchester: Critical Quarterly Society.

Dawson, J. (1984) The work of the Assessment of Performance Unit, 124-132 in Skilbeck (ed.) (1984).

Dearden, R.F. (1967) Instruction and learning by discovery, 135-155 in Peters (ed.) (1967b).

Dearden, R.F. (1968) *The Philosophy of Primary Education*. London: Routledge.

Dearden, R.F. (1976) *Problems in Primary Education*. London: Routledge.

Deem, R. (ed.) (1980) *Schooling for Women's Work*. London: Routledge.

Descartes, René, *A Discourse on Method*.

Dewey, John (1902) *The Child and the Curriculum*.

Dewey, John (1915) *The School and Society*.

Dewey, John (1916) *Democracy and Education*.

Dewey, John (1938a) *Logic, the Theory of Inquiry*.

Dewey, John (1938b) *Experience and Education*.

Dewey, John (1948-new edition) *Reconstruction in Philosophy*.

Dhondy, F. (1978) Teaching young blacks, 80-85 in *Race Today*, May/June, also 257-269 in James and Jeffcoate (eds.) (1981).

Donaldson, M. (1978) *Children's Minds*. Glasgow: Fontana, William Collins.

Downey, M.E. and Kelly, A.V. (1978) *Moral Education: Theory and Practice*. London: Harper and Row.

Edwards, G. (1983) Processes in the Secondary school: MACOS and beyond, 279-308 in Blenkin and Kelly (eds.) (1983)

Egan, K. (1983) Children's path to reality from fantasy: contrary thoughts about curriculum foundations, 357-371 in *Journal of Curriculum Studies*, 15,4.

Eisner, E. (1979) The contribution of painting to children's cognitive development, 109-116 in *Journal of Curriculum Studies*, 11,2.

Eisner, E. (1982) *Cognition and the Curriculum*. New York: Longman.

Elliott, J. (1976) Preparing teachers for classroom accountability, 49-71 in *Education for Teaching*, 100.

Esland, G.M. (1971) Teaching and learning as the organisation of knowledge, 70-115 in Young (ed.) (1971).

Feinberg, W. (1975) *Reason and Rhetoric: the intellectual foundations of 20th century liberal educational policy*. New York, Wiley.

Freire, P. (1972) *Pedagogy of the Oppressed*. Harmondsworth, Penguin.

Friedlander, B. (1965) A psychologist's second thoughts on concepts, curiosity and discovery in teaching and learning. *Harvard Educational Review*, 35,1.

Frith, D. (1983) Why Croydon has got it wrong, *Times Educational Supplement*, December 23rd.

Fuller, M. (1980), Black girls in a London comprehensive, 52-65 in Deem (ed.) (1980), also 270-287 in James and Jeffcoate (eds.) (1981).

Gallie, W.B. (1952) *Peirce and Pragmatism*. Harmondsworth: Penguin.

Galton, M., Simon, B. and Croll, P. (1980) *Inside the Primary Classroom*. London: Routledge.

Galton, M. and Simon, B. (eds.) (1980) *Progress and Performance in the Primary Classroom*. London: Routledge.

Gipps, C. (1984) An evaluation of the Assessment of Performance Unit, 142-148 in Skilbeck (ed.) (1984).

Gladwin, T. (1964) Culture and logical process, 108-120 in Keddie (ed.) (1973).

Goddard, D. (1985) Assessing teachers: A critical response to the Government's proposals, 35-38 in *The Journal of Evaluation in Education* 8.

Goodson, I.F. (1981) Becoming an academic subject: patterns of explanation and evolution, 163-180 in *British Journal of Sociology of Education*, 2,2.

Goodson, I.F. (1983) *School Subjects and Curriculum Change*. Beckenham: Croom Helm.

Goodson, I.F. (1985a) Subjects for study, 343-367 in Goodson (ed.) (1985b).

Goodson, I.F. (ed.) (1985b) *Social Histories of the Secondary Curriculum: Subjects for Study*. London and Philadelphia: Falmer.

Goodson, I.F. and Ball, S.J. (eds.) (1984) *Defining the Curriculum: Histories and Ethnographies*. London and Philadelphia: Falmer.

Gordon, P. and Lawton, D. (1978) *Curriculum Change in the Nineteenth and Twentieth Centuries*. London: Hodder and Stoughton.

Gordon, P. and White, J. (1979) *Educational Philosopher.* London: Routledge.

Gulbenkian Foundation (1982) *The Arts in Schools.* London: Calouste Gulbenkian Foundation.

Hamilton, D. (1976) *Curriculum Evaluation.* London: Open Books.

Harris, K. (1979) *Education and Knowledge: The Structured Misrepresentation of Reality.* London: Routledge.

Hemming, J. (1980) *The Betrayal of Youth.* London, Boston: Marion Boyars.

Hesse, Herman *The Glass Bead Game.*

Hesse, Herman *The Prodigy.*

Hirst, P.H. (1965) Liberal education and the nature of knowledge, 113-138 in Archambault (ed.) (1965), also 87-111 in Peters (ed.) (1973b).

Hirst, P.H. (1969) The logic of the curriculum, 142-158 in *Journal of Curriculum Studies,* 1,2 also 232-250 in Hooper (ed.) (1971).

Hirst, P.H. (1974) *Knowledge and the Curriculum.* London: Routledge.

Hirst, P.H. and Peters, R.S. (1970) *The Logic of Education.* London: Routledge.

Hobhouse, L.T. (1918) *The Metaphysical Theory of the State.* London: Allen and Unwin.

Hoggart, R. (1957) *The Uses of Literacy.* Harmondsworth: Penguin.

Hoggart, R. (1978) The uncertain criteria of deprivation, 171-193 in King (ed.) (1978), also 31-44 in Kelly (ed.) (1980b).

Holt, M. (1981) *Evaluating the Evaluators.* London: Hodder and Stoughton.

Hooper, R. (ed.) (1971) *The Curriculum: Context, Design and Development.* Edinburgh: Oliver and Boyd.

Hoyle, E. (1969a) How does the curriculum change? 1 A proposal for enquiries, 132-141 in *Journal of Curriculum Studies,* 1.

Hoyle, E (1969b), How does the curriculum change? 2 Systems and strategies, 230-239 in *Journal of Curriculum Studies,* 1,2

Hume, David *A Treatise on Human Nature.*

Illich, I. (1971) *Deschooling Society.* London: Calder.

Jackson, B. and Marsden, D. (1962) *Education and the Working Class.* London: Routledge.

James, C.M. (1968) *Young Lives at Stake.* London: Collins.

James, William (1902) *The Varieties of Religious Experience.* London: Longmans.

James, A. and Jeffcoate, R. (eds.) (1981) *The School in the Multicultural Society.* London: Harper and Row.

Jones, R.M. (1972) *Fantasy and Feeling in Education.* Harmondsworth: Penguin.

Kant, Immanuel *Critique of Pure Reason.*

Kant, Immanuel *Groundwork of the Metaphysics of Morals.*

Keddie, N. (1971) Classroom Knowledge, 131-160 in Young (ed.) (1971).

Keddie, N. (ed.) (1973), *Tinker Tailor... The Myth of Cultural Deprivation.* Harmondsworth: Pengiun.

Kellmer-Pringle, M.L. and Edwards, J.B. (1964) Some moral concepts and judgements of junior school children. *Journal of Social and Clinical Psychology.*

Kelly, A.V. (1980a) Ideological constraints on curriculum planning, 7-30 in Kelly (ed.) (1980b).

Kelly, A.V. (ed.) (1980b) *Curriculum Context.* London: Harper and Row.

Kelly, A.V. (1981), Research and the Primary Curriculum, 215-225 in *Journal of Curriculum Studies,* 13, 3.

Kelly, A.V. (1982) *The Curriculum: Theory and Practice.* London: Harper and Row.

Kelly, A.V. (1985) Primary Practice − a review article. A view from Higher Education, 22-23 in *The New Era* 66,1

King, E.J. (ed.) (1978) *Education for Uncertainty.* London: Sage.

Krathwohl, D.R. et al. (1964) *Taxonomy of Educational Objectives II. Affective Domain.* London: Longmans.

Labov, W. (1969), The logic of non-standard English, 1-31 in *Georgetown Monograph on Language and Linguistics* Vol. 22, also 21-66 in Keddie (ed.) (1973).

Labov, W. (1972) *Language in the Inner City: Studies in the Black English Vernacular.* Philadelphia: University of Pennsylvania Press (also Oxford: Blackwell).

Lawton, D. (1973) *Social Change, Educational Theory and Curriculum Planning.* London: University of London.

Lawton, D. (1975) *Class, Culture and the Curriculum.* London: Routledge.

Lawton, D. (1980) *The Politics of the School Curriculum.* London: Routledge.

Locke, John *An Essay Concerning Human Understanding.*

MacDonald, B. (1973) Humanities Curriculum Project, 80-90 in Schools Council (1973).

MacDonald, B. (1975) Evaluation and the control of education, 125-136 in Tawney (ed.) (1975).

Mead, M. (1928) *Coming of Age in Samoa*, Harmondsworth: Penguin.

Michaels, L. and Rich, C. (eds.) (1980) *The State of the Language*. University of California.

Mill, John Stuart *On Liberty*.

Mill, John Stuart *Utilitarianism*.

Miller, J. (1980) How do you spell Gujerati, sir?, 140-151 in Michaels and Rich (eds.) (1980), also 104-115 in James and Jeffcoate (eds.) (1981).

Nathanson, P. (1951) *John Dewey. The reconstruction of the democratic life*. Twentieth Century Library.

Newbold, M. and Rubens, M. (1983) *Some Functions of Art in the Primary School*. London: Inner London Education Authority.

Nicholas, E.J. (1983) *Issues in Education: a comparative analysis*. London: Harper and Row.

Nunn, T.P. (1920) *Education: Its Data and First Principles*. London: Arnold.

O'Connor, D.J. (1957) *An Introduction to the Philosophy of Education*. London: Routledge.

Papert, S. (1980) *Mindstorms: Children, Computers and Powerful Ideas*. Brighton: Harvester.

Parlett, M. and Hamilton, D. (1975) Evaluation as illumination, 84-101 in Tawney (ed.) (1975).

Peirce, Charles Sanders (1931-5) *Collected Papers of Charles Sanders Peirce*, Vols I-VI. Harvard: Harvard University.

Peters, R.S. (1965) Education as initiation, 87-111 in Archambault (ed.) (1965).

Peters, R.S. (1966) *Ethics and Education*. London: Allen and Unwin.

Peters, R.S. (1967a) What is an educational process?, 1-23 in Peters (ed.) (1967b).

Peters, R.S. (ed.) (1967b) *The Concept of Education*. London: Routledge.

Peters, R.S. (1969a) A recognisable philosophy of education: a constructive criticism, 1-20 in Peters (ed.) (1969b).

Peters, R.S. (1969b) *Perspectives on Plowden*. London: Routledge.

Peters, R.S. (1973a) *Reason and Compassion*. London: Routledge.

Peters, R.S. (ed.) (1973b) *The Philosophy of Education*. Oxford: Oxford University.

Petter, G.S.V. (1970) Coherent secondary education, 38-43 in *Trends in Education*.

Phenix, P.H. (1964) *Realms of Meaning*. New York: McGraw-Hill.

Piaget, J. and Inhelder, B. (1971) *Mental Imagery in the Child*. London: Routledge.

Plato, *The Republic.*

Popper, K. (1945) *The Open Society and Its Enemies.* London: Routledge.

Powell, E. (1985) A Modern Barbarism *Times Educational Supplement,* January 4th.

Pring, R. (1973) Objectives and innovation: the irrelevance of theory, 46-54 in *London Educational Review,* 2.

Reid, W.A. (1978) *Thinking about the Curriculum.* London: Routledge.

Richards, R. (1983) Learning through science, 96-114 in Blenkin and Kelly (eds.) (1983).

Rogers, C. (1969), *Freedom to Learn; a view of what education might become.* Columbus: Merrill.

Rousseau, Jean-Jacques *Emile.*

Rousseau, Jean-Jacques *The Social Contract.*

Russell, B. (1939) *A History of Western Philosophy.* London: Allen and Unwin.

Ryle, G. (1949) *The Concept of Mind.* London: Hutchinson.

Sartre, Jean-Paul (1948) *Existentialism and Humanism.* London: Hutchinson.

Sartre, Jean-Paul (1957) *Being and Nothingness.* London: Methuen.

Scheffler, I. (1967) Philosophical models of teaching, 120-134 in Peters (ed.) (1967b).

Schools Council (1967) *Society and the Young School Leaver,* Working Paper 11. London: HMSO.

Schools Council (1970) *The Humanities Project: An Introduction.* London: Heinemann.

Schools Council (1973) *Evaluation in Curriculum Development: Twelve Case Studies.* Schools Council Research Studies. London: Macmillan.

Schools Council (1975a) *The Whole Curriculum 13-16,* Working Paper 53. London: Evans/Methuen

Schools Council (1975b) *The Curriculum in the Middle Years,* Working Paper 55. London: Evans/Methuen

Schools Council (1981) *The Practical Curriculum,* Working Paper 70. London: Methuen.

Schools Council (1983) *Primary Practice,* Working Paper 75. London: Methuen.

Scriven, M. (1967) The methodology of evaluation, 39-89 in Stake (ed.) (1967).

Shipman, M. (1971), Curriculum for inequality? 101-106 in Hooper (ed.) (1971).

Skilbeck, M. (ed.) (1984) *Evaluating the Curriculum in the Eighties.* London: Hodder and Stoughton.

Smart, N. (1968) *Secular Education and the Logic of Religion*. London: Faber.

Smith, B.O., Stanley, W.O. and Shores, J.H. (1971) Cultural roots of the curriculum, 16-19 in Hooper (ed.) (1971).

Snow, C.P. (1959) *The Two Cultures*, London: Cambridge University Press.

Snow, C.P. (1969) *The Two Cultures* and *A Second Look:* an expanded version, *The Two Cultures and the Scientific Revolution*. London: Cambridge University Press.

Sockett, H. (1976) Teacher accountability, 34-57 in *Proceedings of the Philosophy of Education Society*.

Spinoza, Baruch *Ethics*.

Stake, R.E. (ed.) (1967) *Perspectives of Curriculum Evaluation*. American Educational Research Association, Monograph Series on Curriculum Evaluation. Chicago: Rand McNally.

Stake, R.E. (1972) *Analysis and portrayal*. Paper originally written for American Educational Research Association Annual Meeting presentation in 1972. Republished as 'Responsive evaluation' in *New Trends in Education* No. 35 (1975), Göteborg: Institute of Education.

Stenhouse, L. (1970) Some limitations on the use of objectives in curriculum research and planning, 73-83 in *Paedagogica Europea*.

Stenhouse, L. (1975) *An Introduction to Curriculum Research and Development*. London: Heinemann.

Stenhouse, L. (ed.) (1980) *Curriculum Research and Development in Action*. London: Heinemann.

Stewart, W.A.C. and McCann, W.P. (1967/8) *The Educational Innovators* Vols. 1 and 2. London: Macmillan.

Tawney, D. (ed.) (1975) *Curriculum Evaluation Today: Trends and Implications*. Schools Council Research Studies. London: Macmillan.

Thompson, E.P. (1963) *The Making of the English Working Class*. London: Gollancz.

Thompson, K.B. (1972) *Education and Philosophy*. Oxford: Blackwell.

Walsh, W.H. (1969) *Hegelian Ethics*. London: Macmillan.

Warnock, M. (1977) *Schools of Thought*. London: Faber.

Wellington, J.J. (1981) Determining a core curriculum: the limitations of transcendental deductions, 17-24 in *Journal of Curriculum Studies*, 13,1.

West, E.G. (1965) Liberty and education: John Stuart Mill's dilemma, 129-142 in *Philosophy*, XL.

White, J.P. (1968) Education in obedience. *New Society*, 2 May.

White, J.P. (1971) The concept of curriculum evaluation, 101-112 in *Journal of Curriculum Studies*, 3,2.

White, J.P. (1973) *Towards a Compulsory Curriculum*. London: Routledge.

Whitehead, A.N. (1932) *The Aims of Education*. London: Williams and Norgate.

Williams, R. (1958) *Culture and Society 1780-1950*. London: Chatto and Windus (also Penguin Books 1961 and 1963).

Williams, R. (1961) *The Long Revolution*. London: Chatto and Windus.

Wilson, J. (1971) *Education in Religion and the Emotions*. London: Heinemann.

Wilson, J., Williams, N. and Sugarman, B. (1967) *Introduction to Moral Education*. Harmondsworth: Penguin.

Wilson, P.S. (1971) *Interest and Discipline in Education*. London: Routledge and Kegan Paul.

Woods, R.G. and Barrow, R.St.C. (1975) *An Introduction to Philosophy of Education*. London: Methuen.

Young, M.F.D. (ed.) (1971) *Knowledge and Control*. London: Collier-Macmillan.

Government reports and other official publications referred to in the text

Assessment of Performance Unit (1983) *Aesthetic Development*. London: HMSO.

Board of Education (1926) *The Education of the Adolescent* (The Hadow Report on Secondary education). London: HMSO.

Board of Education (1931) *Primary Education* (The Hadow Report on Primary education). London: HMSO.

Central Advisory Council for Education (1959) *15 to 18* (The Crowther Report). London: HMSO.

Central Advisory Council for Education (1963) *Half Our Future* (The Newsom Report). London: HMSO.

Central Advisory Council for Education (1967) *Children and Their Primary Schools* (The Plowden Report), London: HMSO.

Department of Education and Science (1972) *Educational Disadvantage and the Educational Needs of Immigrants*. London: HMSO.

Department of Education and Science (1977a) *Curriculum 11-16*, London: HMSO.

Department of Education and Science (1977b) *Education in Schools: A consultative document*. London: HMSO.

Department of Education and Science (1978) *Primary Education in England: A Survey by HM Inspectors of Schools.* London: HMSO.

Department of Education and Science (1979) *Aspects of Secondary Education in England: A Survey by HM Inspector of Schools.* London: HMSO.

Department of Education and Science (1980) *A Framework for the School Curriculum.* London: HMSO.

Department of Education and Science (1981) *The School Curriculum.* London: HMSO.

Department of Education and Science (1983) *Teaching Quality.* London: HMSO.

Department of Education and Science (1984a) *English from 5-16. Curriculum Matters 1,* London: HMSO.

Department of Education and Science (1984b) *Curriculum 11-16: towards a statement of entitlement.* London: HMSO.

Department of Education and Science (1985a), *The Curriculum from 5 to 16. Curriculum Matters 2,* London: HMSO.

Department of Education and Science (1985b) *Education for All: The Report of the Committee of Inquiry into the Education of Children from Ethnic Minority Groups* (The Swann Report), Cmnd 9453. London: HMSO.

Inner London Education Authority (1985) *Improving Primary Schools. Report of the Committee on Primary Education* (The 'Thomas' Report). London: ILEA.

INDEX OF NAMES

INDEX OF SUBJECTS

'Preparatory' influences on the Primary
  curriculum, 104, 110
Preschool education, 168
Primary,
  education, 45, 54, 86, 103ff
  schools, 33, 58, 103ff, 210, 213, 224
Problem-solving, 50, 51, 53, 54
Process, curriculum/education as, xviii, xix,
  xx, xxi, 5, 6, 7, 54, 55, 61, 63, 70, 75, 89,
  93, 94, 95, 96, 97, 103, 106, 110, 111,
  112, 113, 117, 118, 120, 122, 123, 124,
  126, 127, 130, 133, 150-1, 153, 166,
  176ff, 181, 183, 192, 207, 213, 215, 218,
  225, 226
  see also 'Development, education as' and
  'Growth, education as'
Product, curriculum/education as, 5, 55, 67,
  102, 103, 106, 114, 117, 124ff, 192, 213,
  214, 215, 218, 225, 226, 234, 238
  see also 'Objectives'
Productivity, economic, 63, 67, 68, 74, 117,
  123, 130, 214
  see also 'Industrial efficiency'
Professionalism of teachers, 231, 232
Professional teacher, 218, 229
Professionalization of teachers, 88, 232
'Progressive' theories of education, xv, xix,
  105, 107, 108, 109, 110, 111, 112, 113
  see also 'Child-centred theories' and
  'Process, curriculum/education as'
Psychology, xiii, 46, 50
  behaviourist, 91, 93, 94, 108, 116, 119,
  125, 151, 156, 193
  developmental, xviii, xx, xxi, 64, 90, 91ff,
  97, 108ff, 111, 112, 152, 186, 198, 213,
  218
  Gestalt, 25
Psychopath, 203-4
Publications, official, 117, 122, 124, 212,
  213-4, 233
'Public educators', 161, 164, 166
Public schools, 136, 138
Punishment, 202

Quadrivium, 134, 136

Race, 81, 88
Rationalism, xv-xvi, xvii, xviii, xx, xxi, 3, 6-7,
  8ff, 16, 19, 20, 23ff, 38, 47, 51, 53, 67,
  68, 69, 70, 71, 73, 74, 75, 76, 77, 78, 79,
  83, 85, 86, 90, 91, 92, 95, 97, 101, 102,
  103, 104, 106-7, 108, 113, 114, 115, 116,
  117, 118, 119, 121, 122, 123, 124, 125,

126, 127, 128, 129, 130, 132, 133, 134,
  135, 136, 139, 140, 141, 142, 144, 148,
  149, 151, 152, 153, 159, 163, 164, 165,
  166, 167, 168, 169, 170, 172, 174, 175,
  176, 177, 178, 179, 180, 181, 184, 185,
  186, 187, 187ff, 194, 196, 197, 198, 199,
  200, 201, 201-2, 204, 207, 208, 210, 212,
  213, 214, 215, 216, 219, 220, 226, 228,
  229, 231, 233, 233-4, 234-5, 238
Reading, 110
Reduction to the cognitive, 186, 188, 191ff,
  194, 194-5, 199, 204, 205, 206, 208, 218,
  223
Reification,
  of knowledge, 79, 94, 127, 200
  of values, 228
Relativism, 135, 167, 174, 175, 180
Relevance, 138, 214
Religion, 4
Religious Education, 198, 201
Repression, 11, 202ff, 208
Research, educational, xiv-xv, xxi, 91, 116,
  127
  see also 'Scientific study of education'
Resources, allocation of, 213, 216, 221, 222
Respect for persons, 28, 30
Revelation, 11-2, 35, 53
Rhetoric, 136
'Right rule', 200, 204
Role, teacher's 122

Salaries, Teachers', 87
School Certificate, 136, 137
Science, 4, 5, 10, 13, 16, 17, 22, 25, 29, 31,
  40, 41, 47, 48, 49, 49-50, 51, 52, 57, 58,
  61, 62, 71, 72, 73, 106, 118, 129, 130,
  131, 139, 140, 141, 142, 174, 195, 197,
  199, 212, 223, 224ff
'Scientific' study of education, xiii, xvi, 91,
  115, 139, 219, 224, 226
Secondary,
  education, 83, 110, 141, 144, 147, 162,
  212
  schools, 104, 123, 137, 138, 144, 148,
  211
Self-image, 202
Self-interest, 18
Sense data, 12
Senses, 8, 9, 9-10, 11, 12, 13, 14, 15, 16, 20,
  22, 24, 77, 106
Sixth Forms, 138, 142, 143, 146, 233
Skills, 63, 65, 70, 155, 156, 212, 225, 229,
  230, 231, 232